FAITH AND THE VITALITIES OF HISTORY

Makers of Modern Theology
Edited by Jaroslav Pelikan

PUBLISHED:

Peter C. Hodgson
THE FORMATION OF HISTORICAL THEOLOGY
A Study of Ferdinand Christian Baur

Philip Hefner
FAITH AND THE VITALITIES OF HISTORY
A Theological Study Based on the Work of Albrecht Ritschl

FORTHCOMING:

Paul Sponheim
KIERKEGAARD

Gerhard Spiegler
SCHLEIERMACHER

G. Wayne Glick
HARNACK

Albrecht Ritschl

*A Theological Study Based on
the Work of Albrecht Ritschl*

FAITH AND THE
VITALITIES OF
HISTORY

PHILIP HEFNER

HARPER & ROW, PUBLISHERS
NEW YORK

Grateful acknowledgment is made to the following for permission to reprint certain materials:

CHURCH HISTORY for extracts from "Baur Versus Ritschl on Early Christianity," XXXI, 3, 259-278; and for extracts from "The Role of Church History in the Theology of Albrecht Ritschl," XXXIII, 3, 338-355.

FORTRESS PRESS, Philadelphia, for extracts from Word and Faith by Gerhard Ebeling, copyright 1963 by SCM Press Ltd.

HARCOURT, BRACE & WORLD, PUBLISHERS, New York, for extracts from "Tradition and the Individual Talent," from Selected Essays by T. S. Eliot, copyright 1951 by T. S. Eliot.

HARPER & ROW, PUBLISHERS, New York, for extracts from Current Issues in New Testament Interpretation edited by William Klassen and Graydon F. Snyder, copyright 1962 by William Klassen and Graydon F. Snyder: for extracts from The New Hermeneutic edited by James M. Robinson and John B. Cobb, Jr., copyright 1964 by James M. Robinson; for extracts from Treasure in Earthen Vessels by James M. Gustafson, copyright 1961 by James M. Gustafson.

HERDER AND HERDER, PUBLISHERS, New York, for extracts from Mary, Mother of the Lord by Karl Rahner, copyright 1963 by Herder KG.

THE LUTHERAN QUARTERLY for extracts from "Albrecht Ritschl and His Current Critics," XIII, 2, 103-112.

CHARLES SCRIBNER'S SONS, PUBLISHERS, New York, for extracts from The Rationality of Faith by Carl Michalson, copyright 1963 by the University of Virginia.

FIRST EDITION

LIBRARY OF CONGRESS CATALOG CARD NUMBER: 66-15038

C-Q

To my parents

ELIZABETH MITTELSTADT HEFNER

THEODORE GODFRED HEFNER

Look to the rock from which you were hewn,
and to the quarry from which you were digged.

Contents

Editor's Preface

The vagaries of theological fashion have a curious way of burying and then of recovering their own ancestors. Thus when Adolf Harnack (himself a "Maker of Modern Theology") had completed the first volume of his monumental History of *Dogma,* he wrote to Albrecht Ritschl, under the date of December 19, 1885: "My theological work took its start from the study of your *The Rise of the Old Catholic Church* seventeen years ago, and since that time there has scarcely been a quarter of a year in which I have not continued to learn from you." Few theologians during the past two generations would be able to pay Ritschl such a generous compliment; few enough in the past generation would be able to say as much even about Harnack. Yet none would dispute that in the century between the death of Schleiermacher in 1834 and the death of Harnack in 1930 the most imposing figure in Continental Protestant theology was Albrecht Ritschl.

H. R. Mackintosh sought to explain this anomaly in his epigram of the 1930s: "Ritschl at the moment belongs, like Tennyson, to the 'middle distance,' too far for gratitude, too near for reverence. He is behind a passing cloud today." Now, more than thirty years later, there is some indication that the cloud is ready to begin passing from over Ritschl, if not from over Tennyson. For Ritschl to be rediscovered and his role in the making of modern theology to be reassessed, it is necessary to look not only at the constructive proposals he made for the theological interpretation of the Christian message, but at the foundation of those proposals in his own interpretation of Christian history. Strangely enough, despite the massive preponderance of historical works in Ritschl's literary output, historians of the development of modern theology have given scant attention to these works and have preferred to base their summaries of Ritschl's thought on a fraction of his bibliography.

Philip Hefner's study of Ritschl is an effort to redress the balance. Considering Ritschl a theologian who had his foundation in history, Mr. Hefner assesses both the strengths and the weaknesses of the Ritschlian theology on the basis of the role played by historical considerations in the formulation of its theological conclusions. This does not mean that this volume is concerned principally with a chapter in the evolution of Christian historiography. Although Ritschl did devote a large part of his life and works to historical study, he did not see himself as a historical scholar in quite the same sense that both his sometime mentor, Ferdinand Christian Baur, and his most famous disciple, Adolf Harnack, did. Even Ritschl's *History of Pietism* (a work so dominant in church history that practically every article or dissertation on any problem in the history of Pietism must endeavor somehow to disengage itself from Ritschl) was intended to make a constructive theological point and not merely a historical one: that Pietism as it developed was a foreign body in Protestant devotion and theology and that its valid emphases needed to be put into a living connection with the faith and teaching of the Reformation.

Since Ritschl's concern, even in his historical work, was finally with theological reconstruction, it is quite fitting that this volume does not content itself with a purely historical exposition of the thought of Ritschl and its importance for its own time. Instead, the author has taken upon himself the more courageous, but also more hazardous, enterprise of formulating a constructive statement about "the vitalities of history," with implications for the methodology and the stance of any Christian theology. He goes on to clarify this statement by indicating its affinities with, and its divergences from, some of the principal theological options under discussion today. He also relates the theological enterprise as he understands it to other currents of contemporary thought that seem to be relevant to its tasks.

All in all, Mr. Hefner's *Leistung* is a *Wagnis:* his achievement is an act of daring. And this is as Ritschl would have wanted it to be, much as he would have protested against some of the conclusions to which the *Wagnis* leads. It is certainly one criterion of the greatness of any theologian that he continues to stimulate those who come after him, including those whose theological position contrasts most sharply with his own. Not only from his faithful pupils and epigons, but also from his later challengers can his importance be determined. Measured by this criterion, Ritschl is far more important than the present evaluations of his theology would suggest. For even those who have arisen to protest against his teaching owe him more than either they or even he would often be willing to admit. Both by its analysis and by its alternative proposals, this volume shows what it is that makes Albrecht Ritschl a "Maker of Modern Theology."

JAROSLAV PELIKAN
Yale University

Author's Preface

"I am indebted . . . to far more people, writers and living persons, than I can name. I have borrowed and stolen, have sucked the blood of thought, from so many that I no longer know whom to thank for what."[1] These words, from the pen of a distinguished teacher under whom I was fortunate enough to study, hold particular relevance for a study whose chief theme is the theologian's dependence upon the persons and the epochs that have gone before him.

Many persons, teachers, colleagues, and students have helped me to shape the thought expressed in this book; I can mention only a few of them here. At the University of Chicago, where the first three chapters of this study were first conceived, Professor Jaroslav Pelikan (now of Yale University) provided guidance, criticism, and encouragement. Professor Joseph Sittler has served in many different ways to influence and correct the manuscript. To two colleagues, O. J. Jorgenson and Robert L. Wilken, I owe thanks for reading the manuscript meticulously. All of these men have set standards for the book which I have not been able to meet, and for that I alone must take responsibility.

The president of my seminary, Dr. Donald R. Heiges, assisted this work materially by lightening certain responsibilities which otherwise would have delayed its appearance. For this "administrative favor," I am grateful. In addition, gratitude must be expressed to Mrs. Mary Miller, who has typed the manuscript at several stages of its development.

Finally, I record here my debt to my wife, who has supported this work in so many ways, since its very beginning.

P. J. H.

The Epiphany of Our Lord, 1965
Gettysburg, Pennsylvania

[1] Henry Grady Davis, *Design for Preaching* (Philadelphia: Muhlenberg Press, 1958), p. vii.

FAITH AND THE
VITALITIES OF
HISTORY

Introduction

THE TERM "HISTORY" appears in the title of this book, and it dominates every page that follows, even as the book appears as one volume in a series whose title "Makers of Modern Theology" suggests a historiographical intention. It would be a mistake, however, for the reader to suppose that this is a historian's study, just as it would be unfortunate if the reader were to conclude that since Albrecht Ritschl occupies the center of attention here, the book is a definitive biographical work on the man. Contrary to these expectations, this study is an essay in theological methodology, which takes its cue from Albrecht Ritschl. In no sense has the study of Ritschl been an end in itself. Rather, having begun with Ritschl, we use him as a guide to certain contemporary problems, arguing in turn that since he can be provocative guide, he deserves to be included in the pantheon of "Makers of Modern Theology."

How should one approach a "Maker of Modern Theology?" How should one demonstrate that he belongs in such an august club? Most obviously, one could write a definitive critical biographical work, and then trace the fate which later decades have dealt the man's chief concerns and contributions. This approach would provide an up-to-date interpretation of the man, with a handy guide to the influence and present state of his major ideas. Someone, preferably a historian of contemporary theology, should do such a book on Ritschl in order to counter the almost malicious treatment he has been accorded in recent critical literature.[1] Such a study would demonstrate that Ritschl's persisting influence has indeed helped to make modern theology what it is. A second method might describe the current theological scene, isolating the chief issues

[1] See Philip Hefner, "Albrecht Ritschl and His Current Critics," *The Lutheran Quarterly*, (2) 13:108–109, 1961.

that concern theologians today, and then indicate how relevant Ritschl's thought is to these issues. Were this done, we would be able to evaluate the distinct contribution that Ritschl made to the dialogue that theologians find themselves engaged in today.

The present study follows a plan different from either approach. I have tried to take Ritschl as he stands, illumining the mainspring of his theological methodology in its own integrity, with special care to uncover his own intentions in his work. Then, having thrown light on this methodology and its intentions, I have launched into a broad discussion of the issues that Ritschl's work inevitably raises—namely, the interweavings of life and history —indicating the larger ramifications attached to them and outlining what must be taken into consideration if these issues are to be dealt with adequately. My assumption is that we understand a man better when we understand the whole range of problems that are pertinent to his work. With this whole range of pertinent problems in mind, we can better comprehend the significance of the path Ritschl took in his work, and we can more responsibly evaluate his theological methodology. This is true even if the whole range of pertinent problems was not visible to Ritschl himself. Finally, I have picked up current theological discussions (in the work of Gerhard Ebeling and James M. Robinson) with the precise intention of illustrating how the issues raised by Ritschl's methodology fare today and how they should influence contemporary methodology.

The first phase of this study—the analysis of Ritschl's own methodology—is straightforward, requiring little explanation. The second and third phases—discussion of the larger ramifications attaching to the issues Ritschl raised, together with illustrations drawn from current theological work—may seem less straightforward. The second phase, in Chapter 4, uses the discussion of Ritschl's larger significance as a point of departure from which to set forth a theological program of my own, which seeks to resolve certain current problems. This program intends to resolve the issues that grow inevitably out of Ritschl's methodology, and in the very process of resolution to imply a larger critique of Ritschl's work. In the third phase, a study of Ebeling and Robinson serves as counterpoint against which Ritschl's methodology is clarified and my own program is argued. Ebeling and Robinson seem appropriate for two reasons: both stand as major figures, in postwar Protestant theology, whose concepts any theological discussion today must reckon with; and both seem also to have argued their cases in a way methodologically similar enough to Ritschl to be instructive in illumining how his presuppositions fare in the theological discussions of our day.

As a result of this kind of comprehensive attention—description of the man himself, analysis of the broader significance of the issues he raises, and discussion of contemporary methodologies—I have concluded that Ritschl deserves a place among the "Makers of Modern Theology" by virtue of the fact that three-quarters of a century after his death we can still use his ideas as a starting-point for probing the problems of theological methodology in a profound way.

As a consequence of my methodology, however, this study is marked by a tension, if not a dichotomy, that I consider not only unavoidable but even necessary for the methodology of Christian theology. The tension resides in my refusal to juxtapose history (in this case, a historical figure and his thought) and theological thinking about contemporary problems in favor of an attempt to fuse history and contemporary thinking into a single and unified methodology. The first half of this essay, therefore, argues an unabashed theological interpretation of Ritschl, while the second half takes up the materials of that interpretation in order to make a point about what contemporary theology should be attempting. The entire book, then, expresses a concern about how theology should be structured: If it is true that a historian cannot but approach Christian history theologically, it is perhaps even more true that Christian theology must in some sense be shaped by historical factors.

The most profound understanding of Christian theology may indeed regard as primary its activity in bringing the history of the Christian tradition up-to-date, thereby giving contemporary intellectual force to a faith that is informed and undergirded by a community whose history extends for centuries. Therefore, I do not claim that the position outlined in Chapter 4 is Ritschlian (in fact, I would go to some length to deny it!); nor do I deny that the analysis in Chapters 1 through 3 represents some of my own contemporary concerns read into Ritschl. I have put a question to Ritschl, and I have discovered that as he answered he laid bare the heart of his own methodological concerns. As I have listened to Ritschl, turning both his answers and my own predilections to a genuinely contemporary problem in Christian theology, I have discovered that involvement with history is a gateway to true objectivity.[2] This concern for objectivity within relativity motivates the argumentation of Chapter 4, where Ritschl's methodology is measured against a contemorary program for theological methodology. I should also like to hope that this involvement has pointed a way

---

[2] Here, I find myself in agreement with Rudolf Bultmann: see his *Jesus and the Word* (New York: Scribner, 1958), "Introduction"; also his *Essays Philosophical and Theological* (New York: Macmillan, 1955), Chap. 12.

to overcoming relativism in history. By approaching a historical figure, Ritschl, with the concerns of my own generation, and fusing both in a constructive statement of methodology, I hope to have shown that both Ritschl and my own age can overcome relativism by pointing beyond themselves to concerns that have perennially confronted theology. I hope, too, that this study demonstrates that one understands a man's significance not only by setting him against the background of his own time (which I have not done in this book), but also by arguing through his concerns in the context of a later, more contemporary setting.

This essay offers a contribution in two areas—a new interpretation of Ritschl, and a constructive suggestion for theological methodology. Both contributions may seem strange. I have had to use uncommon terms to interpret Ritschl, because my studies of the man have led me to an understanding that departs drastically from the usual image of him found in the textbooks. Readers who have grown accustomed to the stereotype of "Ritschlian theology" may feel ill at ease with my Ritschl. Similarly, I have been forced to use strange terms to describe my own methodological program for theology, inasmuch as my elders and peers have not always furnished me with a ready-made vocabulary for what I want to say. Because this study does fall so neatly into two parts, it may be helpful to survey the problems that underlie each.

It has been apparent for some years that the final critical word has not been said about Albrecht Ritschl and his work.[3] The critical scholarly attention paid him in the generation since 1930 has been exceedingly sparse,[4] and it has for all practical purposes only partially illumined certain aspects of his thought—the ethical, philosophical, and philosophical-theological presuppositions and doctrinal elaborations (or the lack of them!). Evaluations have proceeded from various persuasions on the basis of this analysis, ranging from the admiration of Albert Temple Swing[5] to the ruthless and even condescending comments of Karl Barth.[6] By and large, however, Ritschl has been nearly forgotten—recalled at moments only to be showered with criticism.[7]

There are certain obvious questions to be raised about the range and adequacy of the critical scholarly analyses of Ritschl's work

[3] See *infra*, pp. 108 ff. for a detailed discussion of the comments of Professors Hugh Ross Mackintosh and Jaroslav Pelikan, who have called for a reassessment of Ritschl.

[4] For a discussion of this scholarly attention, see *infra*, pp. 000–000.

[5] Albert Temple Swing, *The Theology of Albrecht Ritschl* (London and Bombay: Longmans, 1901).

[6] Karl Barth, *Die Protestantische Theologie im. 19. Jahrhundert* (Zuerich: Evangelischer Verlag AG. Zollikon, 1952).

[7] See Hefner, *Lutheran Quarterly*.

and the overwhelmingly negative evaluations that have been drawn from the analyses. In regard to the critical analyses, the question arises as to why ethical and philosophical considerations should dominate the secondary literature when so much of Ritschl's own work (at least two-thirds, by a conservative estimate)[8] is primarily historical in character. Even more important is the question (which the secondary literature has not even touched upon): What is the significance of the quantitatively more important historical work for the more influential theological work? Or, to put it in different terms: Ritschl himself devoted most of his years and output to the investigation of and grappling with the material of the Christian tradition, but one finds scarcely a mention of this devotion in the extant secondary literature, not to mention the total omission of any attention paid to the interrelation between his concern for the tradition and his more explicit constructive theological work.[9] It would appear, then, that any contemporary analysis of Ritschl must come to terms with this strange discrepancy between the object of Ritschl's own concern and the concerns set forth by the critical analyses of his work. From this point of view, the present state of Ritschl scholarship is unsatisfactory on grounds of *instrinsic* considerations, to be found in the published output of Ritschl himself.

A question is also to be raised concerning the extremely negative evaluations of Ritschl which are so prevalent today. This question is raised on grounds of *extrinsic* considerations: Can a man who inspired and even dominated so many of the greatest minds of nineteenth-century Protestant though be so completely perverse a theological resource as the contemporary opinion would assert? A list of those men who were drawn to Ritschl in his own day and afterwards reads like an abridged Who's Who of Protestant Theology: Adolph von Harnack, Wilhelm Herrmann, Ernst Troeltsch, Bishop Nathan Soederblom, Ferdinand Kattenbusch—to name a few. The point is not that all of these figures were Ritschlians (although an impressive number were), but that these seminal minds of post-Ritschlian theology and church-life found in Albrecht Ritschl a man of startlingly different proportions from the man portrayed in the theological textbooks and journals today. This fact,

---

[8] See *infra*, p. 91.

[9] Broadly speaking, the following works are historical in nature: *Die Entstehung der altkatholischen Kirche; Die christliche Lehre von der Rechtfertigung und Versoehnung*, Vols. I and II; most of Ritschl's collected essays; *Geschichte des Pietismus*, 3 vols. The constructive works, all of which are historically oriented, might include: *Die christliche Lehre von der Rechtfertigung*, Vol. III; *Theologie und Metaphysik*. The only constructive works which are free from extensive historical excursuses are the shorter ones: *Die christliche Vollkommenheit* and *Unterricht in der christlichen Religion*.

too, looms so importantly before the contemporary Ritschl scholar that he cannot avoid it.

These questions, raised on the basis of intrinsic and extrinsic evidence, form the framework for any contemporary study of Albrecht Ritschl. Such a study is plainly of little value if it proceeds as it there were nothing new to say about Ritschl (thereby accepting the present state of Ritschl scholarship) or if it fails to offer a solution to the strange discrepancy between what critical scholarship has said about Ritschl and the structure and sequence of the man's own work.

This study attempts to interpret Ritschl within the context of this *Fragestellung*. The larger part of its argumentation is a demonstration of the thesis that the secondary literature has overlooked the significance of the larger part of the Ritschlian corpus —the historical writings; this literature thereby seriously disqualifies the adequacy of its own conclusions in presenting less than a full understanding of Ritschl and his work. The thesis of this essay is that in approaching Ritschl's work one's principle of interpretation must acknowledge that Ritschl's constructive theological achievement is inseparable from his historical judgments and commitments, respectively, concerning the Bible, early Christianity, Catholicism, the Reformation, Lutheranism, and Pietism. The argument suggests that it is the historical factors in Ritschl's thought rather than the psychological, philosophical, or philosophical-theological factors that are really the system-shaping factors in his theological achievement. Proceeding along these lines, a comprehensive scheme for interpreting Ritschl's work emerges: The career of his theological work took the shape it did because he understood history as he did. He was committed to this understanding, and he accepted the responsibility for the theological activity which commitment to such an understanding of history entailed. This activity consists almost wholly of documentation (including historical investigation and biblical exegesis), defense, and proclamation (or even propagandizing) of a certain historical continuity and its heritage. His understanding of history demanded that this documentation be undertaken; this documentation led naturally to the polemic against hostile groups; documentation and defense immediately revealed the lines which systematic elaboration would have to take if his understanding of history were to remain a live option in his own day. Underlying this interpretive scheme was the concern for historical continuity. This is the key to understanding Ritschl's work—so goes the argument; indeed, his theological achievement owes its shape to his preoccupation with a certain historical continuity. The precise character of this preoccupation will be elucidated below.

I have not engaged in a running dialogue with the secondary sources on Ritschl because the literature is silent on the themes that occupy the center of this study. The thesis concerning Ritschl's work that unfolds here is meticulously documented, and it is brought very briefly into relation with the totality of his work. The reader must judge its cogency for himself; the expert must decide whether its weight is enough to counterbalance the mass of scholarly literature that has chosen to deal with other aspects of the Ritschlian corpus.

The theologian who stands at the center of this dissertation certainly has been relegated to a historical limbo by contemporary theological discussion; but the problem of the significance of history for Christian theology has called forth an enormous amount of discussion in the past few decades, and its peak seems nowhere in sight. Despite the prolonged and vigorous discussion, there is by no means widespread agreement as to what the term "history" means or precisely what the "problem" is which it poses for the theologian, not to mention agreement on the resolution of that problem. Although they cannot be discussed in detail here, three alternative approaches to history can be enumerated.

(1) the approach of the *Heilsgeschichte* school, which was dominated by J. C. K. von Hofmann (professor at Erlangen, died 1877), lifts up certain biblical and cosmic events—for example, the creation, the eschaton—in which revelation occurs so as to make them the measure of all prior or subsequent history. These events are so dignified as to render negligible the significance and effect of contigency and development within the historical continuum.[10] (2) The existentialist aproach, represented by the contemporary German theologians, including Rudolf Bultmann,[11] Friedrich Gogarten,[12] and Gerhard Ebeling.[13] This school of thought has followed up Ernst Troeltsch's analysis of the relativism of history (*der Historismus*),[14] which leads man directly to the exis-

[10] See, for example, von Hofmann's understanding of Scripture, in *Biblische Hermeneutik* (Noerdlingen: C. H. Beck, 1880), Chap. IV. See also Karl Steck, *Die Idee der Heilsgeschichte*, in *Theologische Studien*, 56, 1959. Erich Fuelling, *Geschichtlichkeit und Christentum in der Theologie der Gegenwart* in *Studien der Luther-Akademie*, 6, 1958; also his *Geschichte als Offenbarung* in *Studien der Luther-Akademie*, N.F., 4, 1956.

[11] Rudolf Bultmann, *The Presence of Eternity: History and Eschatology* (New York: Harper & Row, 1957).

[12] Friedrich Gogarten, "Zur Frage nach dem Ursprung des geschichtlichen Denkens, Eine Antwort an Wilhelm Kamlah," in *Evangelische Theologie*, 14: 226–238, 1954.

[13] Gerhard Ebeling, *Word and Faith* (Philadelphia: Fortress Press, 1960), Chaps. 1, 10, and 14.

[14] Ernst Troeltsch, *Christian Thought: Its History and Application*, trans. F. von Huegel (Cleveland: Meridian Books, 1957), pp. 67–146.

tential moment of decision. This decision, insofar as it leads man to authentic existence, affords him the possibility of overcoming the meaninglessness which historicism carries with it, while at the same time taking into account the uniqueness of each relative moment in history. This school has its recent roots, of course, in the work of Martin Heidegger.[15] (3) The metaphysical approach, as articulated by members of the "process" school of philosophical theology stemming from S. C. Alexander[16] and Alfred North White-head.[17] This group gives attention to the metaphysical structure which inevitably sustains the movement and relativity of history, as well as the existential moment of decision. This larger meta-physical structure reveals the comprehensive scheme from which history derives its meaning and from which the relative moments derive their ultimate worth.

These three broad approaches do not exhaust the alternative ways in which theologians are dealing with history. But they do suggest the variety of perspectives and the confusion of meanings ascribed to the term "history" and the "problem" that it poses for theology. This range of perspectives suggests that the most press-ing task facing the student who is interested in this problem is a definition of terms.

This study approaches the problem of history in different terms from the three alternatives mentioned above. Its argumentation recognizes that the discussion to date has laid down the framework for any future handling of the problem. The discussion to date suggests that the problem of relativism and the demands of human existence cannot be overlooked in any attempt to deal with history in theology, but it insists that the Christian concern for transcend-ent meaning in history must not be sacrificed to modern scepticism or cynicism. And, although the metaphysicians have by no means argued their case in a completely persuasive manner, the student who chooses to deal with this problem cannot overlook their sug-gestions. In Chapter 4 this study sketches an understanding of his-tory which attempts to take all of these factors into account.[18] But, proceeding from a careful definition of terms, this study sug-gests that the most satisfactory resolution of the problem of his-tory lies in a direction which these other approaches have not pursued. If theologians are to take history seriously in their work,

15 For a survey of this school, see Gerhard Bauer, *"Geschichtlichkeit"-Wege und Irrwege eines Begriffs* (Berlin: Walter de Gruyter, 1963).

16 S. C. Alexander, *Space, Time, and Deity*, 2 vols. (London: Macmillan, 1920). See also his "The Historicity of Things" in Raymond Klibansky and H. J. Paton, eds., *Philosophy and History* (London: Oxford, 1936), pp. 19 ff.

17 Alfred North Whitehead, *Process and Reality* (New York: Macmillan, 1929).

18 *Infra*, pp. 140–152.

they must ponder the significance of the empirical history (or tradition) of the Christian community for their theological methodology, and they must give much more attention than they are now giving to the vitalities of life which serve as history's matrix and from which history takes its course. If this study has any contribution at all to make to this problem, it lies in the assertion that: The history of God's people is constituted by God's redemptive presence which is in turn his action of self-revelation; the totality of this history, as it is focused in any present moment, constitutes the only adequate principle of knowledge and certainty that the Christian theologian has at his disposal.

The thesis that Ritschl's theological achievement owes its shape to his preoccupation with a certain historical continuity pertains essentially to this discussion of theological methodology. We must deal with the questions: Of what does this preoccupation consist? What does it mean to be "preoccupied" with a certain historical continuity? The answers given to these questions here recur again and again in this study,[19] providing a key for understanding Ritschl's theological work and demonstrating one way in which history comes to play a role in systematic theology.

This preoccupation certainly consists of participation in the reality of the continuity—participation in its reality as *indicative* and as *imperative*. To participate in the reality of the continuity as *indicative* can mean several things. It means that the man's theology is informed as to its substance, purpose, and justification by the heritage as he understands it. Proof that any man's thought is genuinely informed by a certain heritage must always remain problematical. It is most likely to remain a matter of the interpreter's opinion. The discussion of such larger considerations is postponed to Chapter 3. It is a somewhat easier undertaking to demonstrate that Ritschl's explicit purpose consists in the positive enunciation of a certain theological heritage, as well as in the polemical argumentation which he believed to be necessary against those who either rejected or misunderstood the heritage to which he was beholden. This demonstration finds its appropriate place in Chapter 2. It is appropriate in that place also to show how Ritschl found the chief source for the justification of his theological achievement in the heritage of thought and faith which was conveyed by the historical continuity in which he stood.

A man's participation in the reality of an historical continuity as indicative is precisely the most difficult sort of thing to nail down in an academic discussion, because the indicative is always given. It is prior to reflection; it does not need to be talked about

[19] See, for example, *infra*, Chap. 4.

or demonstrated or justified; it is the base from which talk, demonstration, and justification all proceed in a man's work.

To participate in the reality of the historical continuity as *imperative* is another matter. As imperative, the historical continuity is not a thing possessed, but rather a thing to be grasped. This means that there must be probing, reflection, definition, interrelating, analysis—all of the activities which are not necessary when continuity is given as indicative. Inasmuch as these activities under the imperative are for the most part explicit, one should expect to find them rather clearly visible in Ritschl's work. If the thesis is to be established persuasively, there can be little ambiguity —such as was argued above—about the presence of these activities in his work.

These activities which reflect Ritschl's participation in a certain historical continuity as imperative are clearly visible in Ritschl's work, and Chapters 1 and 2 demonstrate their presence. These activities manifest themselves in two forms. The first deals with the category within which the historical continuity is to be located and by means of which discontinuities are to be distinguished. No imperative can be heeded, no reality grasped, unless there exists a key or category or some sort of understanding of just what is sought or to be obeyed. The fact that Ritschl took great pains to elaborate just such a category enhances our appreciation of the depth of his preoccupation with historical continuity. Secondly, activity under the presence of continuity as imperative must include extensive effort spent in demonstrating that the continuity in question does indeed exist empirically and that it has existed in the past. It has been all too little noted by students of Ritschl that a considerable portion of his output and of his years were dedicated to the meticulous demonstration (one might even call it an exhausting tour de force) that the continuity of which he spoke was in fact an empirical reality. Chapter 1 documents Ritschl's efforts to develop a category which could bear the weight of the historical continuity and his efforts to prove the existence of this continuity in respect to his interpretation of the history of early Christianity.[20] Chapter 2 performs this same task in respect to his interpretation of Catholicism, the Reformation, and Lutheranism. Chapter 3 attempts a thorough-going criticism of Ritschl's efforts.

Chapters 4 and 5 bring the chief facets of Ritschl's theological methodology—life and history—into explicit accompaniment with

[20] Throughout this study the term "early Christianity" coincides with Ritschl's own periodization, covering that period up to the latter half of the third century which is marked by the appearance of the *Apostolic Constitutions*.

contemporary problems of methodology, where my own programmatic suggestions are applied to the very issues that seem to have caused greatest embarrassment for Ritschl. In these chapters it becomes obvious that this is an essay in theology rather than in ecclesiastical history or Christian biography. It also becomes obvious that the two aspects of this study—the theologian and the theological problem—belong together. If it is true that the first consideration outlined above leads to an appreciation of history as the system-shaping factor in Ritschl's theological work, then it becomes equally clear that his work can be neither properly evaluated nor appropriated by the contemporary theological discussion unless the second consideration—the problem of history—is pursued to a satisfactory conclusion. This, in short, describes the goal and method of this book, as well as the shape which it has assumed in the pages that follow.

I

The Movement of History:
From Apostolic Faith to Catholic Church

THE SOURCES for a study of Ritschl's interpretation of early Christianity are the two editions of *The Emergence of the Old Catholic Church (Die Entstehung der altkatholischen Kirche)*[1] and the second volume of *The Christian Doctrine of Justification and Reconciliation (Die christliche Lehre von der Rechtfertigung und Versoehnung, whose subtitle is "Der biblische Stoff der Lehre")*.[2]

The former work is an almost perfect example of Ritschl's activity under the historical continuity as imperative. In it he applies a clear, though imprecisely formulated, category of the continuity in a determined effort to document its empirical reality.[3] The second volume of *Justification and Reconciliation*, coming twenty-five years later, is marked by a different purpose. It is a good example of Ritschl's stance within the continuity as indicative. He has attained precision and maturity in the formulation of the category which designates and expresses the historical continuity, but he is not so much concerned with proving that the continuity exists as he is devoted to the positive enunciation of the heritage of the continuity as it is refracted through his categories of thought, respectively, the Reformation *Lebensfuehrung*.[4] This essay does not

[1] Albrecht Ritschl, *Die Entstehung der altkatholischen Kirche* (Bonn: Adolph Marcus, 1850 and 1857). Hereafter cited as *Entstehung*. Unless otherwise noted, citations are from the second edition, 1857.

[2] Albrecht Ritschl, *Die christliche Lehre von der Rechtfertigung und Versoehnung*, 3 vols. (Bonn: Adolph Marcus, 1870, 1882, 1889), Vol. II. Hereafter cited as *R.u.V. I* (citations from the first edition, 1870), *R.u.V. II* (citations from the second edition, 1882) and as *R.u.V. III* (citations from the third edition, 1889).

[3] Ritschl, *Entstehung*, pp. 4–5.

[4] The term *Lebensfuehrung* occurs frequently in this discussion. Its mean-

undertake to analyze the second volume of *Justification and Reconciliation*, because it presupposes precisely that which this study seeks to demonstrate, namely, the preoccupation with historical continuity which gives shape to Ritschl's work. Therefore, it does not lend itself to the careful documentation of Ritschl's underlying concerns. *The Emergence of the Old Catholic Church* does lend itself to such documentation. Nor does the second volume of *Justification and Reconciliation* add anything to our understanding of Ritschl's preoccupation. It is important, however, to call attention to the fact that it is taken up completely with the positive enunciation, out of the biblical materials, of the continuity which is central to Ritschl's work.[5]

ing is set forth in detail elsewhere (*infra*, pp. 54–56), but it deserves explanation here. For the purposes of this study, *Lebensfuehrung* is considered to be synonymous with the term *Lebensideal*, which Ritschl uses more frequently in his own work. This discussion employs the less familiar term for the simple reason that *Lebensideal* has been so loaded with pejorative connotations—notably in Karl Barth (see *supra*, p. 40, note 6), pp. 601–605—that it is nearly unusable in this discussion. Barth interprets the term as referring chiefly to the ideal which man has constructed by his own powers as the goal for his life, towards the realization of which he bends every effort. For Barth, the term is nearly synonymous with bourgeois morality. In the present writer's opinion, the terms represent Ritschl's existential concern. They refer to the fact that the Christian faith characteristically deals with the direction and mode of human existence rather than with either doctrine or ecclesiastical institution. The root *fuehren* denotes this concern; the notion of *Ideal* also points to this concern, insofar as it refers to the concrete goal that man's will sets for his life. The difference between the various manifestations of Christianity (Roman Catholicism, Pietism, and so on) is measured in terms of the different configurations of existence (that is, *Lebensfuehrungen*, or *Lebensidealen*) which they engender. Ritschl's propensity for personalizing the Christian faith led him to discuss *Lebensfuehrung* in terms which emphasize individual vocation (*Beruf*). This emphasis is no doubt the source of Barth's interpretation. Barth's error lies in his overemphasis on the particular forms which this vocation takes, as if Ritschl were canonizing nineteenth-century German *buergerlich* modes of life. A more balanced reading suggests that Ritschl's use of terms did not intend any such glorification of particular forms, but that it meant to emphasize the significance of the Christian religion for the concrete realities of human existence. Ritschl conceived of the most satisfactory Christian *Lebensfuehrung* as the life which commits itself wholly to the responsibilities of this world—chiefly love for fellowman and a vocation in society—while trusting completely in God's providence for one's ultimate justification and redemption. (See *infra*, quotation and note 56, p. 59). Throughout this study, I argue that this concept of *Lebensfuehrung* constitutes the category by which Ritschl evaluates the historical development of the Christian community.

[5] This purpose is particularly well expressed in the introductory remarks to *R.u.V. III*, especially pp. 9–20, 24–25. In these places, Ritschl makes it clear that he is attempting to trace the biblical understanding of the Christian *Lebensfuehrung* which centers in reconciliation with God, as he himself has defined that reconciliation. He allows for the fact that the Bible and the Reformation may not hold identical beliefs on this issue, but he also affirms the fact that they are essentially one.

THE BAURIAN BACKGROUND

Ritschl's investigation of early Christianity cannot be interpreted adequately apart from the background furnished by the work in this area which was undertaken by Ferdinand Christian Baur. It was Baur who stimulated Ritschl to his first genuinely scientific theological work.[6] In respect to the investigation of early Christianity, Ritschl accepted Baur's basic approach in spite of fundamental differences of opinion which led to his final repudiation of the Baurian hypotheses.[7] It can be said that even Ritschl's independence and mature reflections upon early Christianity are in some sense dependent on Baur, because Ritschl reached those reflections by grappling with Baur's work, ultimately rejecting it in a decisive manner. In fact, Ritschl's preoccupation with Baur and the "Tuebingen school" that gathered around him was so great that one is justified in pointing to Baur as the dominant key to Ritschl's intellectual development. Particularly in regard to the concern for history (which is the most important key for our interpretation of Ritschl), Baur dominated Ritschl's thinking, as Ritschl first attached himself to his older colleague and then later worked out his own destiny in *Auseinandersetzung* with the Tuebingen school.

The reasons for Baur's influence are not hard to discern. When Ritschl entered the university, he was soon caught up in the search for a teacher who could guide him into genuinely critical and profound scientific work. He saw his entire vocation as an imperative to be faithful in his scientific study of theology. At Bonn and Halle, he found several important teachers, but none of them satisfied his desire for critical scientific study. His letters to his father indicate that Nitzsch, Tholuck, Thilo, and other lecturers left but little impression upon his development. When, in 1841, Ritschl read Baur's book on reconciliation,[8] he found that Baur, and through him Hegel, was the mentor he was searching for. So dominant was Baur in his career that no other figures deserve mention. Baur and Hegel led Ritschl to the sources of Christian history, because it was only in the thorough investigation of the concrete events of history that the famous dialectic could be discerned. This intense preoccupation with the sources led Ritschl to Baur and, eventually, beyond Baur. It was not another, more impressive, teacher that led Ritschl to reject the Tuebingen school,

6 See Otto Ritschl, *Albrecht Ritschls Leben,* 2 vols. (Freiburg i. B.: Akademische Verlagsbuchhandlung von J. C. B. Mohr, 1892), Vol. I, pp. 55 ff., 75–77. Hereafter cited as Otto Ritschl, *I.*

7 See *infra,* pp. oo ff., for a complete documentation of this fact.

8 Otto Ritschl, *I,* p. 55.

but rather a more diligent study of the very sources to which Baur
had led him. Therefore, it is natural that when he broke with Baur,
Ritschl defined his development over against the teacher who had
inspired his diligent scientific efforts.[9] As he wrote in a biographical
sketch in 1844 (one year after receiving his doctorate), "It was
through Baur that I first gained a conception of what history is."[10]

Baur set the stage for both his own work and Ritschl's when
he established continuity between the various historical manifestations as the chief concern of the historian of early Christianity.
He viewed these manifestations as antithetical to one another; thus
it follows that the chief problem is the rapprochement between
antitheses. His task is to explain how historical movement is possible, specifically, how the apostolic community could possibly
have developed into the Catholic ecclesiastical institution. Such an
approach raised the question of historical continuity from the
very beginning. It raises the question of how two different manifestations of Christianity can yet be continuous in one and the
same religion; and it asks how two different historical phenomena
can yet be continuous in one and the same historical continuum.
This Baurian approach also holds within itself an important interpretive bias that ought not go unexamined. It begins with the
assumption that apostolic and catholic Christianity are in some
sense *discontinuous*.[11]

Baur elaborates his interpretation of early Christianity in his
book, *The Church History of the First Three Centuries* (*Das Christenthum und die christliche Kirche des drei ersten Jahrhunderts*).[12]
In this work he lays down his basic understanding of the history
of early Christianity as the development of a root-principle which
entered the Judeo-Hellenistic world and grew, by overcoming
several sets of mutually destructive antitheses, into the Catholic
church.

The Roman Empire provided the spirit of universalism;[13] Greek
philosophy had developed a high degree of moral consciousness;[14]
Judaistic religion had arrived religiously at the stage of full
monotheism, with an emphasis on God's holiness;[15]—thus the

9 *Ibid.*, I, pp. 271–278.

10 *Ibid.*, I, p. 430. Also I, pp. 55, 69, 105.

11 *Infra*, pp. 17–18.

12 F. C. Baur, *Das Christenthum und die christliche Kirche der drei ersten
Jahrhunderts*, 1st ed. (Tuebingen: L. Fr. Fues, 1853), 2nd ed. (Tuebingen:
L. Fr. Fues, 1860), hereafter cited as *Christenthum*; citations are from the 1st
German ed., unless otherwise noted. English translation, *The Church History
of the First Three Centuries*, 2 vols. (London and Edinburgh: Williams and
Norgate, 1878), hereafter cited as *ET, I/II*.

13 *Ibid.*, pp. 4–5.

14 *Ibid.*, pp. 11–16.

15 *Ibid.*, p. 17.

stage was set for Christianity. That is to say, the spirit of mankind had developed to the point at which the recognizable character-istics of Christianity could enter into history and win a reception. Christianity entered this matrix as a unique moral principle enun-ciated by Jesus. Baur writes, in his interpretation of the Sermon on the Mount:

The beatitudes of the Sermon on the Mount express, in an absolute manner, what constitutes the inmost self-consciousness of the Christian, as it is in itself, and apart from external relations. The original and radical element of Christianity appears further in the form of absolute moral command in the controversial part of the discourse which is directed against the Pharisees, and in other parts of it. In the Sermon on the Mount Jesus insists emphatically on purity and singleness of heart, on a morality which does not consist merely in the outward act, but in the inner disposition; and upon such an earnest and moral observance of the law as can admit of no arbitrary exception or divided-ness or want of singleness of heart. . . . But though there is no enuncia-tion of a general principle which is to apply to all cases alike, yet when we consider what is said to be the true fulfilling of the law in each separate instance, and see how in each instance what is done is to contrast the outward with the inward, to disregard the mere act as such, and lay stress on the disposition as that which alone confers any moral value on a man's acts, we cannot but recognize in this a new principle, and one which differs essentially from Mosaism. What the law contained, it is true, but only implicitly, is now said to be of most importance, and enunciated as the principle of morality. The expansion of the law quantitatively amounts to a qualitative difference. The inner is opposed to the outer, the disposition to the act, the spirit to the letter. *This is the essential root-principle of Christianity; and, in insisting that the absolute moral value of a man depends simply and solely on his disposition, Christianity was essentially original.*[16]

Having isolated this as Christianity's root-principle, Baur ob-serves that if it were to "enter on the path of historical develop-ment," it needed to assume concrete form.[17] This it did in the person of Jesus as the fulfilment of Jewish Messianic hope; and this "consciousness of Jesus as Messiah was taken up in the national consciousness and enabled to spread and become the general consciousness of the world."[18]

Even in this concrete form, however, Christianity would have been no more than a particularistic Jewish sect, if a basis for believing in Jesus' higher significance had not been introduced

16 *Ibid.*, pp. 28–29. *ET, I*, pp. 29–30. Italics added.
17 *Ibid.*, p. 36.
18 *Ibid.*

into the situation. Such a factor was introduced in the person of the Apostle Paul and his doctrines. Paulinism became an antithesis to Jewish particularistic Christianity (represented by James and Peter). And with the introduction of Paulinism begins the unending dynamic development of Christianity, which Baur charts as the continual struggle of antitheses within Christianity, which are transcended by a series of Christian syntheses. In the period which holds our present attention, Baur traces this dynamic through two stages: Pauline and Jewish Christianity, transcended in an incipient form of the Catholic church; Gnosticism and Montanism, transcended in the firmly established Catholic church.

Paul and Paulinism represent for Baur the high spirituality of the Christian faith, freedom, and liberty; whereas Peter and Jewish Christianity represent the material and particular aspect of it.[19] Petrinism and Paulinism represent the famous Baurian "double gospel." As such they present microcosmically the dialectic between universalism and particularism whose macrocosmic features I shall discuss at a later point.[20] Within the New Testament canon, this conflict is represented in the Paulinizing tendencies of the authentic Pauline epistles and Gospel of Luke (with the later influence of Marcion) pitted against the Judaizing tendencies of the Apocalypse and the Gospel of Matthew, abetted by the post-apostolic Pseudo-Clementine literature.[21]

This first sharp antithesis was maintained by the unresolved personal enmity between Paul and Peter. But after their deaths a final *rapprochement* was achieved through a continuing, gradual accommodation by both parties as they interacted upon each other. Within the canon, the Epistle to the Hebrews, Ephesians, Colossians, Philippians, James, I Peter, the Pastoral Epistles, and the Acts of the Apostles are to be classified as mediating works.[22] This *rapprochement* results in a microcosmic unification of the universal and the particular in that the organizational forms of the emerging Catholic church are Jewish, whereas the ongoing spirit of the church, universalistic in its defiance of the legalistic claims of these forms, is Pauline.[23] The result is a Catholic church of gentiles whom Paul has converted and whom the Jews have organized.

The culmination of this first Catholic *rapprochement* is preserved in the Johannine Gospel. Here, under the pseudonym of the Jewish-Christian evangelist and eastern saint, a spiritual-uni-

---

[19] *Ibid.*, pp. 61–66.
[20] *Infra*, pp. 23–26.
[21] *Ibid.*, pp. 73–83.
[22] *Ibid.*, pp. 109–124.
[23] *Ibid.*, pp. 105–107.

versalistic theology (which exceeds even the Pauline, in this respect) and western practice (concerning the Paschal observance) are given a powerful and popular expression. This combination of the *church at Rome* with the *theology of the Fourth Gospel* represents for Baur Catholicism's final resolution and transcending of the antithesis between Peter and Paul, with its final exclusion of the Judaizing party.[24]

The issue in this first struggle between antitheses concerned Christianity as a *principle of salvation*—whether this salvation were to be tied literalistically to material particularities, or whether it could be a matter of the spirit, free and universal. The second antithesis raises the controversy to the level of cosmic issues, namely, how Christianity is to be conceived of as *a world principle*.[25] Both members of the antithesis, Gnosticism and Montanism, pursue their interests, Baur holds, at this cosmic level. He writes, after concluding his discussion of both heresies:

When we have once clearly conceived the idea on which Montanism is based, and so seen what its essential nature is, we recognize the justness of the parallel that has been drawn between it and Gnosticism. Each adopts a transcendental mode of view. Each conceives the true essence of Christianity as lying far away, beyond the actual present. The Gnostic, however, looks back to a past whence all derives its first absolute beginning; the Montanist looks forward to a future wherein all reaches its end, and the present world vanishes before the world beyond. For both Christ is the absolute principle of the world; but while the Gnostic uses this principle in order to construct a whole world-development, its operation with the Montanist is only the destruction of the world. . . . In both systems, Christ, as the principle determining the process of world-development, is the turning-point, to which everything leads up in such a way that the end unites with the beginning; but while Gnosticism allows all its processes to continue through a limitless period, Montanism sees the final catastrophe arriving as soon as possible. . . . Different as the notions were which the Gnostics and the Montanists associated with the terms spirit and spiritual, in both systems what was sought after was that Christians should be pure organs of the spiritual principle. The Gnostics considered themselves to be pre-eminently the spiritual natures, and assigned all other Christians to the stage of mere psychical life. The Montanists found in their distinction of the *pneumatikoi* and *psychikoi* a vantage-ground from which they could look down with disdain on the catholic Christians who did not confess their doctrine of the

24 *Ibid.*, pp. 172–174.
25 *Ibid.*, p. 175.

Paraclete. The same antithesis comprises both systems; but in the case of the Montanists its sphere is much more limited.[26]

This passage reveals with unusual clarity the way in which Baur sets up his antitheses, shows their interrelations, and points the way towards a new synthesis.

Baur classifies five schools of thought as Gnostic: Valentinus, Basilides, Marcion, Pseudo-Clement, and the Docetics. He relates these schools and their individual characteristics in several ways. But they all serve to demonstrate that Gnosticism was speculative-philosophical in origin; it sought to illumine the principle of the world's development; as it did so, it revealed itself basically to be a very transparent rationalism, founded on the immanent relations of the self-consciousness of the spirit, wrapped in "symbolic myth-ical clothing."[27]

Gnosticism posed the danger for Christianity of dissolving its specific historical character into the thin element of a general transcendental view of the world.[28] It played up to that aspect of catholicity which sought to rise above everything particular and merge it into the universality of the Christian principle; but it ran afoul of catholicity's insistence that the positive historical elements of Christianity should be maintained.[29]

Montanism threatened the complementary danger of particu-larism. Millenarianism, coupled with ecstatic prophecy and rigor-istic morality characterized its reactionary effort to re-implement primitive Christian views. If its emphases were carried out con-sistently, particularism would reach its culmination in complete withdrawal from society. Further *development* in Christianity would be precluded. Catholicism at this point had to react in a way complementary to its reaction over against Gnosticism. It had to break open this separatistic closure, so that Christianity could plant itself firmly in the world and develop as broadly as was necessary for its healthy survival.[30]

Catholic Christianity presented, to use Baur's terms, both a dogmatic and a hierarchical antithesis to these two heresies; but the dogmatic antithesis could never have been victorious without the hierarchical antithesis. The dogmatic antithesis to Gnosticism was not, in the final analysis, brought off by the more subtle Alexandrian theologians—they sympathized too much with it. Rather, the dialectical antithesis to Gnosticism was erected by Tertullian and Irenaeus, because of their unyielding efforts to lay

26 *Ibid.*, pp. 244–245. ET, I, pp. 254–255.
27 *Ibid.*, pp. 233–234.
28 *Ibid.*, p. 234.
29 *Ibid.*, p. 176.
30 *Ibid.*, p. 247.

bare the essentially non-Christian character of Gnostic religious-philosophical speculation.[31] This antithesis, however, was never in itself more than a rhetorical alternative to Gnosticism; it could not overwhelm its foe, because its keystones—Scripture and apostolic insight—were effectively neutralized by the Gnostic's own claims to secret apostolic wisdom which could alone interpret Scripture adequately. In order to fasten their claims, the Catholics fashioned two other arguments: the orthodox content of apostolic teaching, which was preserved in the *regula fidei*; and the legitimate transmission of that teaching, in the episcopal succession. These two arguments made it possible to link the present Catholics with the past—with Christ and the apostles—and to give objectivity to their doctrines. Only with objectivity and tradition in their hands was it possible for the Catholics to brand the Gnostics as heretical.[32]

The Montanist antithesis was almost wholly political in character and its resolution, inasmuch as there was little or no dogmatic disagreement involved. The Montanist drive to purify the church denied forgiveness to the large number of *lapsi* that emerged from the persecutions. The Montanists would use this denial of forgiveness as a means of tightening discipline and withdrawing from the world to await the eschaton. This ran counter to the whole tone of permanence which underlay the notion of the episcopate and its succession; the bishops anticipated no sudden eschaton, and they were eager to lay the basis for continued existence within the world. The power of the keys, proclaimed by the Roman bishop (either Victor or Zephyrinus) granted forgivenes and set the stage for penance. Baur concludes:

> The pure ideality of the Church was thus lost, but the idea of the Church became practical . . . an important step was taken, that of guiding the Church into a path in which its continuous realization was not to be hindered by the sinful nature of its members.[33]

Rigorism and millenarianism were thereby rejected; morality was humanized; the Holy Spirit was institutionalized.

The Catholic church is thus firmly established in the episcopate which holds the *regula fidei* and the power of the keys. This Catholic development can be understood as a product of religious development in which the church as a whole symbolizes its unity of pure teaching in the company of these episcopal successors to the apostles, and in which the individual congregation symbolizes its

31 *Ibid.*, pp. 249–252.
32 *Ibid.*, pp. 257–258.
33 *Ibid.*, pp. 268, 270. *ET, II*, pp. 49, 51.

unity in Christ under the governance of its episcopal representative.[34] It is a very simple hierarchical and theocentric relationship
between congregation and leader, but at the same time it is a
flexible relationship which adjusts easily to pressure from the outside. The heart of Baur's interpretation of this Catholic hierarchy
is contained in these words:

Through the episcopate the Church acquired its determinate form;
it was in the bishops that men were first found, upon whom it could
be conceived that the highest privileges conferred by Christ himself
on his apostles had passed in all their fulness. What the Church as a
whole was, in its essence and its peculiar principle, concentrated and
showed forth itself in them.[35]

Christianity has thus evolved into the Catholic church. Historical continuity has been established in meticulous detail between
first- and third-century Christianity. As Baur charts the course of
this continuity it has been the essence or peculiar principle of the
church, moving from root-principle, embodied in the concrete
form of belief in Jesus as the Messiah, through the antithesis of
Christianity as the universal or particularistic principle of salvation, and through a final antithesis of Christianity as the universal
or particularistic principle of world development—culminating in
catholicity which is both cosmic and soteriological, universal and
particular. The significance of Baur's treatment of historical continuity in this manner must be elaborated in more detail. Baur's
historical investigations into early Christianity and the approach
which he introduced must be clearly understood; only then is one
able to understand the situation in which Albrecht Ritschl stood
when he undertook the foundational studies of his youth which
shaped his entire theological achievement; only then can one
grasp the Baurian method which Ritschl wholeheartedly shared,
as well as the Baurian historical judgments which he just as vigorously rejected.

Baur set the question of the interpretation of early Christianity
in the framework of the problem of historical continuity. This followed inescapably from his concern for *movement* in the history
of the church. The movement of events and their continuity was
the chief concern of the church historian, in Baur's opinion. The
category which served as the basis for the continuity in the history
of Christianity was the *Idee* of the church—its essence, or *Geist*.
This is clear from what Baur writes in a book which appeared one
year before his history of the first three centuries: *The Development of the Writing of Church History (Die Epochen der kirch-*

[34] *Ibid.*, pp. 260–261, 278–279.
[35] *Ibid.*, pp. 274–275. ET, II, p. 56.

lichen Geschichtschreibung), a book which he considered to be an introduction to the *Christenthum*.[36] In a memorable passage, Baur observes that historians generally fail to grasp the *meaning* of the church's history. He goes on to suggest the reason for this failing:

In a word, it lies in the defective way of relating the Idea to the appearances in which the historical development of those appearances presents itself. The Idea hovers at a great distance and in an uncertain form over the appearances to which it must be related; the Idea is not powerful or dynamic enough to permeate the historical materials as the soul permeates the body, to vivify and in this organic unity to be the animating principle of the whole range of appearances in which the history of the Christian Church runs its course. Or is there still doubt whether the history of the Christian Church is the movement of the Idea of the Church? And therefore not comprised just of a series of alterations that follow upon one another accidentally? If one can speak of an Idea of the Church, then this Idea (like every other Idea) must have the dynamic within it to go out from itself and actualize itself in a range of appearances; and these appearances can be considered only as another aspect of the relationship which obtains in general between the Idea and its appearances.[37]

In the *Christenthum*, likewise (although more implicitly than in the methodological introduction just quoted), Baur attributes the origin and movement of the church's history to the Hegelianesque *Geist*, or *Idee*.[38] This movement of *Geist*, or the *Idee*, of the church explains how the Christian community moved from Jesus' teaching to the Catholic ecclesiastical institution.

From this application of the Hegelian category to the historical continuity of Christianity, one can conclude that Baur's interpretation of early Christianity is *ontological and religious*. It is ontological, because the category of the *Idee* in history is ultimately identical with the general philosophical problem of the relation of the universal and the particular. And when he traces the continuity in the movement from apostolic to Catholic Christianity, it is a continuity rooted in the movement of being or the universal within the particular.[39]

This movement of the *Idee*, the Hegelian *Geist*, within the particularities of history is also the career of the relation between

36 F. C. Baur, *Die Epochen der kirchlichen Geschichtschreibung* (Tuebingen: Ludwig Fues, 1852). Hereafter cited as *Epochen*. See Baur, *Christenthum*, pp. iv–v.

37 *Ibid.*, pp. 247–249.

38 Baur, *Christenthum*, pp. 9–10.

39 See, for example, Baur, *Epochen*, pp. 267–268.

spirit and letter. As documented above,[40] a relation between spirit and letter constituted for Baur the essence of Christianity, as well as the basic structure of Jesus' message. In other terms, the relation between spirit and letter is the initial and central problem which faced early Christianity.[41] He located this problem and concern initially in Jesus' understanding of his own relationship to the Mosaic law.[42] He recognized that Jesus' preaching did in some way modify the external, literal applicability of that law upon himself and the members of his community. This modification is towards the pre-eminence of a spiritual authority over a literal, material one. Baur expresses it as the superordination of disposition and spirit over act and letter in such terms as imply an absolute demand that man bring his entire being—all of his moral and spiritual capabilities—into consonance with the spirit (or ultimate intention) of the law.[43] What is at stake is a fundamental distinction between that which is material and enslaving, the product of man's own endeavors, on the one hand, and that which is spiritual and liberating, the work of God, on the other. As Baur prosecutes his historical investigation, he traces what is in effect the ongoing tension and interrelation between these two factors.[44]

The category which bears and expresses the historical continuity of the phenomena of early Christianity in Baur's scheme is the *Idee* of the church, the *Geist*, whose movement does in fact establish the continuity of history. Its movement manifests itself in the career of spirit and letter (or matter) as they interrelate one with the other. But, inasmuch as this category is at the same time an ontological one as well as a religious one—being identical with the general philosophical problem of the universal and the particular—broader ramifications come immediately into focus. These ramifications are to be seen in the fact that Baur understands himself to be dealing simultaneously with three inseparably related conceptions in his preoccupation with the above-mentioned category of continuity.

In the first place, he understands himself to be dealing with the *constitutive principle* of history. Baur makes this especially clear

---

[40] *Supra*, p. 16.

[41] It may prove helpful if the reader keeps in mind that at a later point I will demonstrate a notable similarity in the manner in which Ritschl conceives of this central problem of early Christianity, even though he attaches a quite different significance to it. See *infra*, pp. 28 ff., 34 ff.

[42] *Supra*, p. 16.

[43] Baur, *Christenthum* (2nd ed.), pp. 28–29.

[44] See, for example, the manner in which Baur renders the Peter-Paul conflict plausible by relating it to the spirit-letter conflict within the preaching of Jesus himself, *ibid.*, pp. 46–47. Ritschl did this, too, in the first edition of his *Entstehung*, p. 108.

in *Epochen*. History *is* the movement of the universal (the *Idee*, or *das Allgemeine*) as it relates itself to the particular (*die Erscheinungen*); in the case of the history of Christianity, this is the universal *Idee* of the church.[45] In a most helpful passage, Baur asserts that Christianity can be nothing else but the concrete form that the *Idee* of the church assumes in the visible manifestations of history:

The substantial content of the historical development of the Christian Church cannot be anything else except this same unity [that is, the unity of absolute and particular, respectively, as expressed in the unity of the divine and human in Christ]. Everything must aim at this: so to actualize this unity in the Christian consciousness, within the different forms in which that unity can be conceived, that the Christian consciousness itself is nothing but the form for this absolute content.[46]

Secondly, Baur is dealing with the *constitutive process of the self-actualizing of being*, or *Geist*. The *Geist* actualizes itself by the very process of going out from itself into the *Erscheinungen* which constitute history.[47] This is the familiar Hegelian framework in which Baur works. In his *Lehrbuch der Dogmengeschichte*, Baur expresses this explicitly in his positive evaluation of Hegel. He writes that Schleiermacher made a step towards understanding the proper relation between the absolute and the particular, the objective and the particular, in Christianity. But he never overcame subjectivity; this remained for Hegel to accomplish. Hegel made it clear that Christianity is:

the self-explicating absolute Idea itself. The absolute Idea is God as the absolute Geist, as it mediates itself to itself in the process of thought (*Denken*). *Christianity is therefore essentially this process itself, namely, the self-explicating life-process of God in thought, since thinking is the nature of the Geist.*[48]

He goes on to say that the Christian consciousness is the subjective side of the "process by which the absolute *Geist* mediates itself to itself, to the end of attaining its subjective consciousness."[49] He concludes with the assertion that Christianity is not just feel-

45 Baur, *Epochen*, p. 249. Note that Baur's assessment of the catholic episcopate is that it represents a natural stage of the development of the church's understanding of itself, that is, of its *Idee*. See *infra*, p. 25.
46 *Ibid.*, p. 251.
47 Baur, *Lehrbuch der christlichen Dogmengeschichte* (Tuebingen: L. Fr. Fues, 1847, 1858), p. 251. All citations are from the 1858 (2nd) edition. Hereafter cited as *Dogmengeschichte*.
48 *Ibid.*, p. 355. Italics added.
49 *Ibid.*

ing (*Gefuehl*), but thought (*Denken*), "the self-determining of the *Geist*."[50]

Thirdly, in dealing with the relationship of the universal and the particular, Baur is dealing with the *essence of Christianity*. In Christ, the Christian community has seen the perfect unity of the two, the unity of the divine and the human. The history of the Christian church is the history of the attempt by the Christian consciousness to express this unity in an adequate manner.[51] The catholicizing tendency of the early centuries is a stage in this ongoing expression. Therefore, Baur can say of the final papal development of this Catholic episcopate:

> In the papacy, this same unity of God and man takes the absolute form in which the actualized Idea of the Church is visible; just as in Christology, the epitome of the dogmatic system, the absolute content of the religious consciousness is brought into one particular conception. Everyone is aware of this sanctifying unity with God, if he has faithfully accepted the dogma of the Church and submitted himself faithfully and willingly to the Pope as the vicar of God and Christ. The entire body of the Catholic Church binds itself together in both—in dogma and in papacy—to an absolute unity with God.[52]

These three conceptions must be held together as we assess Baur's own understanding of what is involved in his historical study of early Christianity. With all of this in mind, it can be said that for Baur, Christianity's initial and ongoing concern for the relationship between spirit and the letter describes the primal thrust which is actually constitutive of the historical process. This ongoing relationship can be said to be *in* history, but even more, for Baur, it *is* history. History is nothing other than the career of *Geist* (or *Idee*, or God) as it comes to actuality through the process of self-objectification. This process does indeed constitute history's own entelechy, and this is the source of its continuity. This career of actualization is constituted by the recurring action which brings spirit and matter, idea and appearance, divinity and humanity, into relationship. Therefore, for Baur to trace this continuous action of relating the universal and the particular is simultaneously to *interpret* history and to *account* for its being; but to interpret and account for history is at the same time to lay bare the actualization of being, or *Geist*. So that finally, when Baur asserts that *the* root-principle of Christianity and the motive power of Christian history is this continuous actualization of a relationship between spirit and letter, he is saying the Christian history is the

50 *Ibid.*
51 Baur, *Epochen*, p. 251.
52 *Ibid.*, p. 253.

consummate revelation of the career and being of *Geist*-itself, or
being-itself.

Therefore, it can be said that when Baur prosecutes his concerns
within the context of a historical investigation, that investigation
automatically becomes an enterprise of accounting for the constitutive factors of history and its being. That is, it becomes an
aetiology of history. This aetiology in *Geist* provides the key to the
meaning of the problem of spirit versus matter, as well as the source
of the unity which apostolic and catholic Christianity share as
events within the same historical continuum.

RITSCHL ON EARLY CHRISTIANITY

Baur, then, clarifies the movement of Christian history, specifically its early history, by referring its continuity to the career of an
"essence," or "*Grundprincip*," of Christianity (or of the church)
which is simultaneously the principle of being and of history, their
unity lying in the fact that the principle of being drives towards actualization in and through history, and consummately in
Christianity because in Christ (and in the church) spirit and matter
are perfectly united. It is important to understand that Albrecht
Ritschl accepted this basic framework for his historical investigations. The various historical manifestations of early Christianity,
because of their *apparent* irreconcilability, pose the problem which
historical investigation must resolve. As it did with Baur, the
attempt to resolve this problem involves Ritschl with the fundamental issue of continuity. Ritschl's considerable differences of
opinion with Baur cannot hide this genuine agreement in *Fragestellung*. The next few pages will concentrate on these considerable
differences; contributing as well to an understanding of the unity
of approach that exists between these two men. In this unity lies
that feature of Ritschl's thought which this study attempts to illumine.[53]

Within this overarching unity in approach, Ritschl differs from

[53] At this point, a word is in order concerning the two editions of *Entstehung*.
Generally speaking, one can compare the two editions thus; the first edition
(1850) expresses as clearly as the second (1857) Ritschl's preoccupation
with historical continuity and his intention to demonstrate the physical unity
of the historical continuum in its movement from the first to the third century,
as well as the discontinuity in belief and practice between these two epochs
(see *infra*, pp. 43–44).

The 1850 edition differs from that of 1857 in that it interprets Catholicism
as a product of Paulinism, in its victorious struggle against *Judenchristentum*
(see 1st ed., Chap. IV, pp. 264–327, 602–604). This means that Ritschl
accepted Baur's general notion of the antitheses between Pauline and Jewish
Christianity. A look at the table of contents of the two editions reveals the
way in which this interpretation affected the first edition. Instead of a chapter
on the *diverse* character of Jewish Christianity, one strand of which is termed
Judenchristentum, the first edition groups all Jewish Christians under that

Baur in a decisive manner. This sharp difference has its basis in the manner in which Ritschl understood the several issues that arose within the framework of historical investigation that Baur established.

The most decisive difference between Ritschl and Baur centers in their understandings of the *category* which bears and expresses the historical continuity in Christian history. Baur had understood this category to consist of the *Idee* of the church, or the *Geist*. Ritschl understands this continuity to consist of the *Lebensfuehrung* which he considered to be central to Reformation Christianity.[54] This is his category of historical continuity. This is the criterion by which he measures varying historical manifestations of Christianity and compares them for continuity or discontinuity. Therefore, it must be concluded that when Ritschl pursues the same historical investigation of the same problem in early Christianity as Baur did, he does not do so at all from an ontological concern. His concern, in distinction from Baur's, is *personal and religious*.

This personal and religious concern is revealed in the fact that

term (see *infra*, pp. 36–37). This chapter is followed in the 1850 edition with a chapter on Paulinism, as it developed in antithesis to *Judenchristentum*. The 1857 edition speaks rather of Gentile Christianity. The conclusion is to be drawn that the 1850 edition sees only the two Baurian antitheses, *Judenchristentum* and Paulinism. The 1857 edition sees in the same historical material two very diverse groups, Gentile Christians and Jewish Christians; the former are by no means all Pauline, and the latter are not all Judaizers. Another important difference is that the 1850 edition still uses Baur's notion of dialectical movement as the category of continuity, whereas the 1857 edition uses the category of *Lebensfuehrung*. It should be noted that Ritschl emphatically rejected the Baurian overtones of the 1850 edition (see *Vorrede* to 1857 edition, and Otto Ritschl, *I*, pp. 272 ff.). In the light of all this, the Baurian elements of the first edition can be overlooked, inasmuch as they hold little significance for the purposes of our study.

Furthermore, we must remember that even the 1850 edition evidences a critical stance over against Baur's school; indeed, Otto Ritschl dates his father's criticism of Baur as early as 1846 (see Otto Ritschl's summary in the biography *I*, pp. 124–126, 164–166).

The apparent ease with which Ritschl laid aside this Baurian influence is not surprising. He had been attracted to Baur, not because of an interest in metaphysics or speculation, but because of his admiration for Baur's disciplined, scientific approach to the study of history. He first read Baur in his days at Halle, in connection with his already well-delineated interest in history, particularly the history of the doctrine of *Versoehnung*. (See Otto Ritschl, *I*, pp. 54–55, 75–77.) Baur helped Ritschl define his vocation as a scientific historian—not his philosophical position; there is no record that Ritschl's attachment to Baur was part of a search for a philosophical mentor. The differences between the two editions of *Entstehung* represent a jettisoning of that aspect of Baur's work that was never of primary importance to Ritschl. He never did depart from Baur's example of disciplined, scientific study of history. For a summary of the innumerable differences in detail between the editions, see Otto Ritschl, *I*, pp. 286–294.

[54] *Supra*, note 4, p. 12.

Ritschl's historical investigations push continually *not* towards the elucidation of the ontological career of *Geist,* but rather towards an illumination of the personal relation between God and man, the relation of reconciliation. Like Baur, Ritschl locates this problem of reconciliation initially in the distinction between spirit and letter (or matter), as it is expressed in Jesus' own understanding of his relationship to the Mosaic law. Ritschl, too, understood that Jesus' preaching modified the literal, external applicability of that law in a way that gave pre-eminence to a spiritual authority over a literal or material one. Ritschl expressed this in terms of man's acknowledging the ultimate claims which his own highest end places upon him; these ultimate claims are found in those parts of the Mosaic law which embody the highest end, namely, love for God and man. Finally, like Baur, Ritschl considers that the issue at stake is the fundamental distinction between that which is material and enslaving, the product of man's endeavors, on the one hand, and that which is spiritual and liberating, the work of God, on the other. His historical investigation traces the ongoing inter-relation of these two factors. But, as I have already said, this interrelationship does not constitute the career of being; rather, it concerns the individual's relationship to God.

For Ritschl, the chief problem posed by the interrelation of these two elements (the activity of God and the activity of man) is the maintenance of a proper equilibrium between divine and human factors within the God-man relationship, the personal religious concern which resolves into the question, "Upon what basis can the individual be reconciled with God?" The distinction between spirit and letter (or matter) is the distinction between what God does for man and what man is thereby impelled to do on his own. The *Grundprincip* of Christianity for Ritschl (and for his own theology, as noted below) is the assertion that the God-man relation of reconciliation is grounded in the spirit (in faith, or trust in God) rather than in the literal or legal works which man can effect in his own behalf.

Just as Baur's formulation of the central problem of early Christianity implied ramifications which extended far beyond a simple tabulation of historical data, so when Ritschl enunciates this problem as being that of man's reconciliation with God, he sees a significance in this enunciation which reaches beyond the plain data of first- and second-century history.

First, the question of reconciliation is the *central religious question which faces man;* it directs all of his life's activity.[55] And the

---

[55] This is the sort of sweeping consideration that runs through a great deal of Ritschl's work. I have discussed and documented it in detail in "Albrecht Ritschl and His Current Critics," *The Lutheran Quarterly,* 13:103–112, 1961.

decision concerning what is the proper equilibrium between divine and human factors in this relationship of reconciliation ultimately determines the individual's attitude towards what that life-activity is and amounts to.

Secondly, inasmuch as the question of reconciliation is inseparable from the question of *how* man is related to God and how God's salvation is appropriated, it is *the center of the Christian revelation*.[56] Ritschl does not say, as Baur does, that his formulation of the central concern of early Christianity is identical to the essence of Christianity. But it is so decisive a factor in the Christian revelation that Ritschl can often pursue his historical investigations as if it were that essence.[57]

Thirdly, as he was to point out thirteen years later in the first volume of *Die christliche Lehre von der Rechtfertigung und Versoehnung,* the problem of reconciliation constitutes *the center of the Christian theological system*.[58] Ritschl's conviction that reconciliation is so central to the Christian revelation and theological system is demonstrated in his lifelong study of this issue; he himself dates this concern from his student days.[59]

This, then, is what Ritschl had in mind when he isolated the problem of the relationship between spirit and letter as the initial and central concern in early Christianity. It should be clear that Ritschl's understanding of the problem of early Christianity is so different from Baur's that it transmutes the material interpretation of this historical epoch so as very nearly to obscure the common *Fragestellung* which the two men share. Ritschl applies the *Lebensfuehrung,* a category of Christian existence, which emerges from the interrelation of spirit and matter which he terms "reconciliation," as the principle which serves as the bearer and expression of historical continuity. This brings an attitude towards history and continuity which is markedly different from Baur's. For Ritschl, history is not a process of being which is constituted by the ongoing relationship of spirit and matter. Rather, it is a given continuum about whose provenance Ritschl cares not and says very little. But within this continuum there has been an ongoing attempt by the Christian community to express what it knows through relevation to be the proper relationship of spirit and letter. Within this continuum the Christian church has sought

[56] For appropriate materials, see footnotes 55 and 58.

[57] So, for example, he can almost ignore Gnosticism in his study of early Christianity, presumably because he thinks that it does not touch on what he considers to be central in Christianity. He devotes about twenty pages to it in his *Entstehung.* Consider also his idiosyncratic interpretation of the antignostic fathers; see *infra,* pp. 39–42.

[58] *R.u.V. II,* p. 1; see *supra,* p. 12, note 2.

[59] *Ibid.,* "*Vorrede zur ersten Auflage.*"

to express its understanding of this central problem of how man is related to God; but this expression does not thereby constitute the total continuum of history. If history is a continuum which is given, within which there is presumably more than one tendency discernible, then Ritschl's assertion that his formulation constitutes the central problem of that continuum entails *a value-judgment and selectivity* in a way that does not arise in Baur's historical investigations.[60] In effect, then, Ritschl's historical investigation of early Christianity is a study of Christianity's ongoing expression of this one reality, of reconciliation, a tracing of its changing comprehension of this one reality; just as for Baur, proceeding from his ontological outlook, the history of early Christianity is the unfolding of *Geist*, or the *Idee*, of the church as it actualizes itself in the matter of history. Ritschl's analysis is not simply a neutral analysis, because Ritschl selects one particular expression of Christianity's position to be normative, namely, Jesus'. So, Ritschl's history of the emergence of the old Catholic church is actually an investigation of the community's changing understanding of the God-man relationship, one stage of which justifies the adjective, *Catholic*.[61] Because it is an investigation of the *change* in that understanding from epoch to epoch, one of which is normative, it is at the same time an *assessment* of that Catholic stage.

With all of this in mind, it must be concluded that when Ritschl, turning his attention to the same initial problem as Baur, within the same *Fragestellung* concerning continuity in history, prosecutes his own concern within the context of a historical investigation, that investigation becomes an enterprise of evaluating history; that is, it becomes *an axiology of history*. The axiological key of the *Lebensfuehrung* which emerges from reconciliation with God provides the meaning to the problem of spirit versus matter, as well as the source of the unity and difference which exists between apostolic and Catholic Christianity as events within the same historical continuum.

But there is still another issue at play in Ritschl's approach to historical continuity and to early Christianity. His propensity for axiology leads him to use the category of *Lebensfuehrung* just as effectively as a criterion of *discontinuity* in history. This stems from the fact that he has made a commitment to Reformation

60 *Infra*, p. 43.

61 Ritsch's use of the term "Catholic" is ambiguous. When he uses the term in contradistinction to apostolic and Reformation Christianity, it is a pejorative term. However, it is clear that when he uses it to designate the main stream of Christian tradition (see *infra*, pp. oo–oo), it is a term of approbation. The proper connotation of such usage in this study is generally evident from the context in which it appears.

Christianity which compels him to assume an emphatically Protestant position, which for him entails documenting a *discontinuity* between apostolic and catholic Christianity. Thus, Ritschl writes in the introduction to *Entstehung*:

We believe that we can gain clarity in our knowledge of the shadowy post-apostolic age most reliably if we conceive of our task as the *history of the emergence of the old Catholic Church from primitive Christianity.* . . . We hope with this investigation on the one hand to fill a gap in the history of dogma, but on the other hand also *to pay a debt which Protestant historical research owes.* . . . The fulfilling of our responsibility (to trace the emergence of the *one* old Catholic Church from the simple core of the Gospel through the manifold forms of the primitive Christian ideas and tendencies) is *a scientific obligation, which Protestant theology since its inception has not yet fulfilled over against the Catholic view of history.* In light of the claim of the Roman Catholic Church that its essential forms were established by Christ and the apostles, the theologians of the Reformation have two tasks to perform: to dismiss this claim as contradicting historical fact; and to comprehend historically the fact that the form of the Catholic religious consciousness and church organization deviates from the original meaning of the Gospel and from the forms of the apostolic teaching and practices.[62]

Unless he can document this discontinuity, he can carry out neither his program of positive enunciation of the Reformation *Lebensfuehrung* nor his program of polemic against its foes—chief of whom are the Roman Catholics.

Ritschl will not designate this discontinuity as a "fall of the church,"[63] because he is emphatic that there is a certain kind of continuity between first- and third-century Christianity. This is a simple, almost physical, unity of the historical continuum. Such a continuity is necessary if historical movement is to be explicable; without it historical writing could not be scientific, because alterations in the continuum should have to be ascribed to accident or to some sort of supernaturalism.[64] *Theologically,* however, this continuity is *not* significant (note the contrast to Baur, for whom this physical continuity was the whole significance, because it was ontologically related to the *Idee* of the church). More important is the continuity in understanding reconciliation, and at this point catholicism, specifically in its third-century roots, cannot pass

[62] See Ritschl, *Entstehung,* pp. 3–4. Italics added in part only. This quotation occurs in *both* editions.
[63] For a full discussion of this, see Ritschl, *Entstehung,* pp. 4–10, and *R.u.V. II,* pp. 12–14.
[64] See preceding footnote.

muster, in Ritschl's judgment. Ritschl insists that the historian must be fair and objective in his openness to the movement and physical continuity within the historical continuum. But his thelogical commitment to the Reformation, or, we might say, his propensity for axiological judgment, overpowers this objectivity in the final analysis.

Baur, too, had made a commitment to the Reformation, as well as a contradictory commitment to the Hegelian dialectic. But he handled this conflict of interests more adroitly than Ritschl, with the result that he did not have to posit a discontinuity between apostolic and catholic Christianity—even though he began from the *ex parte* distinction that the two are not one. He modified this *ex parte* starting-point in a way that Ritschl could not—by his commitment to ontological continuity in the movement of *Geist*. He had to be concerned with movement, but he did not have to oppose first-century Christianity to third-century Christianity in the way that Ritschl was driven to by his historical commitments. Baur superordinated this commitment to ontological continuity over his Reformation commitment to discontinuity. His dialectical propensity did not prevent him, however, from assessing the Reformation as a higher level of the self-actualization of *Geist,* even as the *telos* of that self-actualization.[65] Thus, he was able to satisfy both his Reformation commitment and his Hegelian *Tendenz.*

We now turn to a summary of Ritschl's historical interpretation of early Christianity, in which the theological considerations to which I have just pointed will assume concrete form. For Ritschl, as for Baur, the problem posed by the history of early Christianity was the transition from apostolic Christianity to the old Catholic church.[66] But for him that transition is not comprised by a dialectical Catholic synthesis of the antithetical components of a "double gospel." Rather, the Ritschlian scheme recognizes one fundamental Hebraic-oriented message which appeared in Christ and permeated the apostolic preaching; then, because of a combination of external and internal pressures, this gospel and its community became estranged from their Jewish heritage; this estrangement, coupled with cultural and political pressures, brought the alteration of belief and polity whose consequence was the old Catholic church.

On the basis of this general scheme, and because of the theological considerations discussed above, Ritschl took specific issue with the predisposition of Baur and his colleague, Albert Schwegler.[67] Specifically, Ritschl insists that this dialectical reading of

65 See Baur, *Epochen,* pp. 248–252 for his understanding of the Protestant position vis-à-vis Roman Catholicism.

66 Ritschl, *Entstehung,* pp. 3–4.

67 Schwegler died in 1857. Ritschl was reacting in particular against his *Das nachapostolische Zeitalter in den Hauptmomenten seiner Entwicklung,* 2 vols. (Tuebingen: L. F. Fues, 1846).

history: (1) violates the integrity of the Pauline literature (both canonical and post-canonical), by interpreting it as incipient Catholicism, and thereby fails to show how Paulinism could actually develop into Catholicism;[68] (2) violates the integrity of Catholicism by failing to recognize its non-Pauline, yet nevertheless *apostolic,* elements;[69] (3) violates the integrity of Jewish Christians, not all of whom were Judaistic;[70] (4) engages in a circular argument by presupposing that all Jewish elements in Christianity are antithetical to Pauline Christianity and then using the presence of these elements in subapostolic Christianity to prove the existence of an anti-Pauline party;[71] (5) emphasizes so much the antagonism between the antithetical elements in Christianity that their final reconciliation can only be accidental and contrived, so that although the dialectic can account easily for the inner diversity of Christianity, it cannot account for its inner *unity;*[72] (6) imposes an unrealistic burden upon the historian by insisting that the rise of Catholicism be explained solely by internal causes to the exclusion of external ones.[73] And, in what is finally its greatest distortion, the predisposition of the dialectic for synthesis forces it to misread the entire movement of this period, namely, as a bringing together of both Jewish and Gentile elements; whereas the nub of Ritschl's whole interpretation is to insist that Catholicism represents the culmination of Gentile Christianity's estrangement and final divorce from its Hebraic-Judaistic heritage.[74]

It must be noted that the task that Ritschl set for himself does not entail for him a full-blown discussion of the beginnings of the Christian community, the essence of its faith, and its historical development. It does entail charting the career of one particular problem in the history of early Christianity. This one problem is what Ritschl is interested in (which is, as we have seen,[75] the central problem for Christianity), and it is in the church's changing stance towards this problem that the transition from apostolic community to Catholic church is to be grasped. This is where the impact of Ritschl's personal and religious concern, as opposed to Baur's ontological and religious concern, is to be seen most clearly.

This problem is first described in the question: "What is Christianity's attitude towards the Mosaic law and practices and morals

[68] Ritschl, *Entstehung,* pp. 13–14.
[69] *Ibid.,* p. 23.
[70] *Ibid.,* pp. 22–23.
[71] *Ibid.,* p. 17.
[72] *Ibid.,* pp. 18–20.
[73] *Ibid.,* p. 23.
[74] These criticisms, of course, represent the mature opinions of the second edition of his *Entstehung.*
[75] *Supra,* pp. 28 ff.

grounded on that law?"[76] However, as his discussion moves on, it is clear that this is but one formulation of a more general problem, namely, *that of the basis upon which the relationship between God and man is to be established*—in other words, this is Ritschl's first, imprecise, formulation of the category of *Lebensfuehrung*. The changing understanding Christians had of this basic reality traces the movement from apostolic to catholic Christianity. There are five phases in this movement, as Ritschl charts it: (1) Jesus' attitude towards the Mosaic law; (2) the attitudes of the first Christians—Pauline, Jewish, and Judaistic; (3) the estrangement of Gentile Christianity from Jewish Christianity, culminating in rapid de-Judaization by A.D. 150 and a new legalism; (4) the Catholicism of the antignostic fathers—intensification of Christianity as a new law; (5) the struggle with Montanism—the firmly established episcopate. I shall discuss each of these phases briefly.

1. *Jesus' attitude towards the Mosaic law:* Ritschl is of the opinion that Jesus did *not* solve the problem of what should be the Christian attitude towards the Mosaic law (nor did he intend to), nevertheless, his own attitude can serve as the basis for a more thoroughgoing Christian attitude. The key to Jesus' own attitude is the distinction between *that for which man exists* (that is, man's highest end) and *that which exists for man*. Insofar as the Mosaic law pertains to the latter, it is adiaphoron for Christians; but to the extent that it pertains to man's highest end, it is binding even for Jesus himself.[77] Man's highest end, according to Jesus, is love to God and to man, with the result that this love becomes the principle or essence of all the law. Laws which do not serve this end must be set aside;[78] laws which do serve it are in fact laws applying in the kingdom of God.[79] (This could include circumcision and Mosaic worship.) Jesus himself did not explicate a new law in detail, because it was not his first purpose to do so; his first task was to establish the kingdom of God on the basis of his own personal worthiness as the Son of Man, and to awaken faith in himself as such.[80] Jesus' attitude towards the Mosaic law is summarized by Ritschl thus:

Jesus acknowledged the Law and the Prophets insofar as they contained in themselves the command to love God and man, since this command expresses man's highest goal. He fulfilled the Law and the Prophets in respect to the idea of righteousness they expressed, by referring the principle of the Law to the Kingdom of God. *Thus, he*

76 Ritschl, *Entstehung*, p. 27.
77 *Ibid.*, pp. 31–41 and *passim*.
78 *Ibid.*, pp. 45–46.
79 *Ibid.*, p. 47.
80 *Ibid.*, p. 46.

rejected the validity of the Mosaic Law for the Kingdom of God except where it corresponded to the highest goal of man. That is to say, he suspended not only the Sabbath rules, the sacrifice, and the cleansings, but also the rules for divorce, the *ius talionis*, the restriction of the obligation of love solely to friends, and the commands concerning oaths. Nevertheless, he did not do away with circumcision or the privileged position of the Israelitic people within the Kingdom of God; nor did he release his disciples from the actual observance of the Mosaic cultic customs.[81]

We shall note in a later place how this attitude of Jesus was incorporated into the norm by which Ritschl evaluates all later attitudes.[82]

2. *The attitudes of the first Christians—Pauline, Jewish, and Judaistic:* Ritschl contends that the apostolic generation held to the basic lines of Jesus' own thinking in their relation to the Mosaic law. There were tensions and variations among the apostles, but they were relative and not substantial. As they handed down the faith that they had received, they maintained two broad emphases—without which they would have betrayed Christ: the *autonomy* of Christianity—they made faith in Christ the only condition of salvation and entrance into the kingdom of God; and the *universality* of Christianity—they recognized the right of both Jews and Gentiles to become a part of the kingdom of God.[83] Ritschl insists that none of the original apostles betrayed this basic attitude, and that several of them (not just Paul) developed it dogmatically to some length.[84]

Paul differs from Christ in the *form* of his dogmatic development, not however in the *content* of his belief. He separates righteousness into two concepts—righteousness before God and righteousness before man, whereas Christ held them in one concept. He redefines the term righteousness to refer only to the relationship of faith to God. Finally, Paul abrogates the Mosaic law, asserting that love alone directs the new life. But Paul does affirm the close relationship between faith and the resultant ethical response (between love to God and love to man), and he finds, furthermore, that although love directs the new life, ethical (even Mosaic) injunctions are necessary for the lives of his Christian friends. Ritschl is emphatic in his insistence that Old Testament images and patterns are basic to Paul's preaching, not just because Paul wanted to relate his Gentile converts to the Jewish community, but because the Chris-

81 *Ibid.*, pp. 46–47.
82 *Infra*, p. 78.
83 *Ibid.*, pp. 47–48.
84 *Ibid.*, p. 48.

tian message would have been unintelligible without its Old Testament orientation.[85] I shall indicate below how important this Old Testament orientation is in the totality of Ritschl's argument.[86]

One of Ritschl's sharpest clashes with Baur is to be seen in his evaluation of Jewish Christianity. He denies that it is either monolithic or anti-Pauline. Paul held that Christianity is continuous and in agreement with the divine promise, but in opposition to the Mosaic law.[87] In order for any group to justify the "anti-Pauline" label, there must be direct opposition to this Pauline premise. Some groups did oppose this premise; they held that Christianity is continuous and in agreement with the Mosaic law, and that Christianity's promise depends on the legal status of a man. Such groups are anti-Pauline, not because they are racially or nationally Jewish, but because they hold that Judaism and Chrisianity are identical. Ritschl calls them "Judaistic Christians" (*Judenchristen*).[88]

The Jewish Christianity which is represented by the epistle of James, the first epistle of Peter, and the Revelation stands in the authentic line of Jesus' message, but it can be termed neither "Pauline" nor "Judaistic." The conceptions of the relationship between faith and works are not Pauline, but neither are they in opposition to Christ. The authors must be evaluated as original, thoroughly Christian thinkers, whose ideas were not reproduced widely in the second century because they did not lend themselves to the post-apostolic enterprise of dogma.[89] Ritschl summarizes the unity within variation which is found in Paul, James, and Peter, as follows: Paul holds that works are a *consequence* of faith; James, that works are the *concrete stuff* of faith; Peter, that they are the *test* of the utter confidence of faith.[90]

It is significant to note two things in this interpretation which Ritschl gives to apostolic Christianity: first, he has taken great pains, specifically against Baur, to assert the *continuity* of the apostles with Christ and their unity with one another; and second, the criterion by which he judges this continuity and unity to exist is the category of the *Lebensfuehrung* which emerges from reconciliation. At this point it would be a mistake to exaggerate the category of *Lebensfuehrung;* nevertheless, it is obvious that it does, in an incipient form, underlie Ritschl's analysis in the *Entstehung.*

For Baur, the decrees of the Council of Jerusalem represent a compromise between warring factions, whose consequence is an

85 *Ibid.*, pp. 102–103.
86 *Infra.*, pp. 61 ff.
87 *Ibid.*, p. 107.
88 *Ibid.*
89 *Ibid.*, p. 116.
90 *Ibid.*, p. 119.

authoritative recognition of a "double gospel" for Jews and Gentiles. Ritschl sees things quite differently. The Jerusalem decrees are primarily *sociological* in nature rather than religious. They are portions of the Jewish proselyte law, observance of which by Gentiles would make social intercourse possible between Jewish and Gentile Christians.[91] It may be true that Judaistic Christians turned this decree to their own discriminatory purposes, but the party of Peter and James considered it in no wise a condition for salvation or entrance into the kingdom of God. Therefore, this decree cannot be subsumed under the rubric of anti-Paulinism. Paul did later break with the decrees, because he considered even sociological distinctions to be a violation of the spirit of eucharistic fellowship.[92] Ritschl believes that Peter and James ultimately joined with Paul in rejecting the decree after the destruction of the temple of Jerusalem.[93] Ritschl summarizes the conflict between Paul and the other apostles as one which concerned the division and relationship of the Jewish mission to the Gentile mission. Paul differentiated them along geographical lines; James, along ethnographical.[94]

In the post-apostolic period, Ritschl classifies the Nazarites and the epistle to the Hebrews as representing the Jewish Christian position of the early apostles; while those of the community represented by the pseudo-Clementine literature, whom he terms "Christianized Essenes," he classifies as Jewish Christians who represent the position of Peter at Antioch.[95] As Judaistic Christians, Ritschl includes another group of Essene Ebionites, namely, the Syrian Elkesaites, whom he terms "pharisaic Ebionites" to distinguish them from the Ebionites of Epiphanius.[96] It is clear from this that he ascribes much more diversity to Jewish Christianity than does Baur, and he considers the Ebionites to be much less a force in second century Christianity.

3. *The estrangement of Gentile Christianity from Jewish Christianity, culminating in rapid de-Judaization by* A.D. *150:* A combination of internal and external forces brought about the reaction against Jewish Christianity which lays the foundation of Ritschl's claim that the old Catholic church is a product of Gentile Christianity. These forces account for the shift from the subapostolic unity of Gentile and Jewish Christians to the late second-century state-

[91] *Ibid.*, pp. 130 ff.
[92] *Ibid.*, pp. 146–147.
[93] *Ibid.*
[94] *Ibid.*, p. 152.
[95] These include the Ebionites of Epiphanius and the Elkesaites, *ibid.*, pp. 204–205.
[96] *Ibid.*, pp. 154–155, 248.

ment of Irenaeus, that Jewish Christianity is confined to "Ebionite sects, outside the church."[97] The responsibility for this shift, says Ritschl, lies chiefly with the Jewish Christians, because they placed inordinate demands upon the Gentile Christians. The Judaistic Christians demanded that the Gentiles submit to the whole Mosaic law, as proselytes; the Clementine-Essene-Ebionites insisted, more moderately, only on certain purificatory rites; the Jerusalem apostles and Nazarenes insisted on invoking the four decrees of the proselyte law, for reasons of social contacts.[98] Justin Martyr's attitude stands as a testimony that Jewish-Gentile Christian inter-course had not broken down completely.[99] But the Jews' demands, coupled with a second-century cultural and political situation that demanded increasing uniformity in practice, brought conditions to the point where even moderate Jewish Christian demands had to be rejected.[100] Ritschl considers the events surrounding the rise of Bar Kochba—his persecution of Jewish Christians, Hadrian's establishment of the Aelia Capitolina, the prohibition of circum-cision, and the installation of a Gentile bishop in Jerusalem—to be decisive external factors in the de-Judaization of Christianity, even more than Titus' destruction of the temple.[101] The significance of this de-Judaization in Ritschl's interpretation of early Christian-ity is considerable; for it means that the church was forced to consider as heretical a position which the apostles themselves had held, and it means that the Old Testament presuppositions, without which apostolic Christianity is unintelligible, were gradually fading from the church's understanding.[102] The consequence is what Ritschl terms "the Christian legalism of the Apostolic Fathers."[103]

The elaboration of this interpretation entails the rejection of the notion that early second-century Gentile Christianity was exclu-sively Pauline. Paulinism, Ritschl claims, never assumed con-fessional status in Gentile Christianity, and it was in fact of subordinate importance in several areas.[104] In fact, the apostolic fathers, although they held to a notion of catholicism which was a sort of "average" of apostolic teaching, distorted both the Pauline and Petrine teaching rather decisively. Their failure to grasp the genuine Old Testament basis of the Christian message led them to distort the concept of sacrifice, the relationship of faith to ethics,

97 *Ibid.*, p. 248.
98 *Ibid.*, pp. 250–252.
99 *Ibid.*, p. 255.
100 *Ibid.*, pp. 256–257.
101 *Ibid.*, pp. 258–259.
102 *Ibid.*, pp. 257, 281–282.
103 *Ibid.*, p. 274. This is a chapter title, see pp. 274–298. It does not appear in the first edition.
104 *Ibid.*, pp. 271–272.

and the entire understanding of how God and man are related.[105] Thus, for example, Clement of Rome and Polycarp cannot distinguish between faith and works;[106] and Justin Martyr totally misunderstands Christianity's relation to the Mosaic law when he proclaims Christ as a new lawgiver and Christianity as a new law.[107] Because he did not have access to the Old Testament background, Justin fails to distinguish between the "participation in a relationship that God himself has established, with the connotations of imperative, and the relationship that results because one has freely given himself to a desire to draw close to God."[108] This leads to a basic distortion of the notion of revelation as a new lawgiving. This assessment, Ritschl believes, not only demonstrates the distortion of the rising Catholic theology, but also reveals that the new legalism (contra Baur) originates in neither Pauline, Ebionite, nor Judaistic Christian circles.[109]

4. *The Catholicism of the antignostic fathers—intensification of Christianity as a new law:* Ritschl holds that Irenaeus, Tertullian, Clement of Alexandria, and Origen were the first genuinely Catholic theologians. His interpretation of these men is characterized by the notion that they intensify the trend of the apostolic fathers. The development of the *regula fidei* and the episcopal constitution in their struggle against Gnosticism is important, but for the purposes of Ritschl's investigation here it was much more important to him to note the culmination of their efforts against Judaistic Christianity in the legalistic conception of the relation between God and man. This represents their deviation from apostolic ways of believing, and this really is the only aspect of their theology that Ritschl pays attention to. This accords with our thesis that Ritschl narrows his interest to the historical continuity and discontinuity that can be established on the basis of his category of *Lebensfuehrung*. He writes:

It is generally acknowledged that Irenaeus, Tertullian, and the Alexandrians Clement and Origen are representatives of the old catholic church. It is customary, however, to stress their avowal of the apostolic rule of faith as the characteristic of their position, i.e., their opposition to heretical Gnosticism, together with their recognition of episcopal church order. At the very most, attention is called to the tendency towards works-righteousness which asserted itself in these teachers, quite con-

[105] *Ibid.*, pp. 280–284.
[106] *Ibid.*, pp. 283–284, 287–288.
[107] *Ibid.*, pp. 298–301. Note how Ritschl applies his category of *Lebensfuehrung* and reconciliation to establish a discontinuity between these figures and the teaching of Christ and the apostles.
[108] *Ibid.*, p. 304.
[109] *Ibid.*, pp. 310–311.

trary to the apostolic faith, without, however, clarifying the relationship of this tendency to their total position. It is indeed true that the rule of faith is one essential strand of the catholic-ecclesiastical perspective which these teachers of the church held. *The other important strand is, however, precisely their legalistic conception of the Christian's relationship to God.* As the rule of faith expressed opposition to the heretical Gnosticism, so also did the conception of Christianity under the category of the New Law mark opposition to Judaistic Christianity as well as deviation from the apostolic forms of understanding.[110]

At this point, Ritschl can draw tentative conclusions concerning the old Catholic church: It has lost the ability to assess properly the status of form in worship and law, chiefly because it has lost the proper criteria for assessing the Old Testament forms. It takes them literally rather than as ideas that comprise the Christian faith's consciousness of itself (*ideale Selbstgefuehl des christlichen Glaubens*).[111] This in turn reveals a deep misunderstanding of the relation between faith and works, a loss of the Pauline understanding of justification by faith,[112] and, one might add, a loss of continuity in understanding the fundamental Christian *Lebensfuehrung* which stems from Christ himself and which is the Ritschlian criterion par excellence. The Montanist and Novatian schisms arose out of the attempt by these groups to restore the proper equilibrium between faith and works, the religious and the ethical.[113] This leads Ritschl directly to a discussion of Montanism, which in his mind directs the church's development away from belief or dogma to practice and church constitution (*Verfassung*).

5. *The struggle with Montanism—the firmly established episcopate:* The importance for Ritschl of Montanism and its impact on early church constitution is indicated by the fact that he devotes nearly two-hundred and fifty of the *Entstehung's* six hundred pages to it. His discussion is essentially a study of the career of the episcopal office as it moves from the apostolic congregational office through Montanism to the catholic ecclesiastical order. This is a movement towards a catholic office in which the episcopacy bears the two indispensable marks of *public-liturgical distinction* (*gottesdienstlich*), centering in the bishop's representative and mediatorial functions, and *priestly designation;* only when these two marks are found together can the catholic conception of the episcopacy be said to be at work.[114] The apostolic office of bishop contrasts sharply with the catholic. The former is chiefly a political

110 *Ibid.*, p. 312. Italics added.
111 *Ibid.*, p. 332.
112 *Ibid.*, p. 333.
113 *Ibid.*, p. 336.
114 *Ibid.*, p. 555.

office of the local congregation, for the supervision of good works;[115] it is a charismatic office;[116] the bishop mediates nothing, but rather performs his duties in behalf of the entire congregation —even after he assumes the discharge of liturgical and disciplinary matters.[117] Ritschl's discussion of this apostolic office is oriented towards demonstrating that whatever it is, it is *not* the catholic office of the mid-third century. He keeps his eyes on that which the episcopacy was to become. For example, in one of his early summaries, he writes:

Nothing presents itself in the oldest form of the community's ordering or in its original conception that would indicate the acknowledgment of a specific *liturgical or priestly character* to the community's leaders in distinction from the rest of the community.[118]

The gradual shift towards the public-liturgical and priestly emphases accompanied the rise of legalism and the loss of understanding of the notion of justification by faith.[119] This shift manifested itself in the growing understanding of the laying on of hands in forgiveness, in baptism, and in ordination as actually transmitting grace as an act of the bishop rather than of the congregation,[120] as well as in the notion that prayers and fasting could be meritorious in securing forgiveness.[121]

The emergence of the monarchical episcopate at the beginning of the second century in Antioch, Smyrna, and Ephesus—for which Ignatius is our earliest witness—does not yet represent a Catholic episcopal conception, but it is an important phase in the movement towards catholicity.[122] At this point, the subjection to the bishop is still understood as an ethical responsibility which is laid upon the congregation in the interests of good order.[123] Later, it becomes a religious, liturgical matter.[124] The emergence of the monarchical episcopate in the Gentile church is to be distinguished from that in the Jewish church, however; Ritschl goes so far as to say that these two developments constitute two different episcopates.[125] The Jewish Christian development is found only in Jerusalem (with some influence in Alexandria), where a strong bishop system

115 *Ibid.*, p. 353.
116 *Ibid.*, pp. 362–363.
117 *Ibid.*, pp. 366–375.
118 *Ibid.*, pp. 383–384. Italics added.
119 *Ibid.*, p. 399.
120 *Ibid.*, pp. 384–386.
121 *Ibid.*, p. 381.
122 *Ibid.*, pp. 407–410.
123 *Ibid.*, p. 407.
124 *Ibid.*
125 *Ibid.*, p. 418.

evolved early, the bishop representing Christ, surrounded by twelve presbyters who corresponded to the apostolate.[126] The Gentile development was slower, partly because the episcopate had to win its superiority over a presbyterate which was originally equal to it; and when it did emerge preeminent, it was a successor to the apostles.[127] The Jerusalem bishop immediately assumed the status of ecclesiastical authority extending over his province; the jurisdiction of his Gentile counterpart was powerful at first only as a congregational office (*Lokalamt*), and later assumed wider authority[128] (*Kirchenamt*). Ritschl believes that both the Pseudo-Clementine and the Pseudo-Ignatian literature sought to implement the Jewish-Christian episcopate, the former in Jewish-Christian, the latter in Gentile-Christian circles; but both were ahead of their times, expressing views that were by no means universally held.[129]

The thrust of Montanism itself is best summed up (as Ritschl interprets it) as a reactionary force in doctrine, morals, and discipline, which sought a return to more primitive beliefs and practices in the face of what it considered to be a widespread relaxing of standards and accommodation to the world.[130] The immediate point of controversy concerned the "second penance" for the *lapsi*. Ritschl asserts that both the Roman decree in this matter and its Montanist opposition constitute innovations from apostolic Christianity. Traditionally, penance and forgiveness had been matters over which the congregation alone had authority; now, the Catholics make them matters of ecclesiastical office by granting the power of the keys to the bishop, whereas the Montanists (for example, Tertullian) want to make them charismatic matters by granting this power to the so-called "new prophets."[131] Here the real nub of Montanist reaction is revealed as opposition to the burgeoning episcopate, coupled with an uncompromising schismatic temperament.[132]

The consequence of the Montanist opposition and its defeat is the firm establishment of the Catholic episcopate, as set forth in the opinions of Cyprian of Carthage and in the policies elaborated in the Apostolic Constitutions. The bishop becomes priest, enacting a sacrifice which amounts to a representation of Christ's sacrifice, and thus the bishop attains a unique public-liturgical status.[133] The episcopacy becomes the organizing principle of the church,

126 *Ibid.*, pp. 416–419.
127 *Ibid.*, pp. 419 ff.
128 *Ibid.*, p. 436.
129 *Ibid.*, pp. 460–461.
130 *Ibid.*, p. 518.
131 *Ibid.*, pp. 518–521.
132 *Ibid.*, pp. 519–520.
133 *Ibid.*, pp. 555 f.

highpriest and judge, as well as preserver of the *regula fidei,*
prophet, and mediator of divine grace.[134]

To summarize, Ritschl seeks by means of historical investigation,
to answer the question of how third-century (Catholic) Christianity
could emerge from first-century (apostolic) Christianity. The answer which he comes to is this: because of its alienation from
its Hebraic roots, Gentile Christianity reacted to the social and
political pressures of the first and second centuries in such a way
as to deviate both in belief and practice from the broad apostolic
understanding of the God-man relationship. This deviate reaction
did in fact constitute the old Catholic church. *A Gentile deviation
in understanding the basis of man's relationship to God* would be
Ritschl's *formal* assessment of the old Catholic church. His *material* assessment could be phrased as *a Roman-oriented episcopate
which has perversely subordinated the religious to the moral in a
new legalism.*[135]

The point that cannot be emphasized enough is Ritschl's preoccupation with historical continuity and discontinuity discussed
and evaluated in terms of the *Lebensfuehrung* emerging from
reconciliation, specifically, from a properly realized God-man
relationship. His study of early Christianity achieved certain ends
by way of pursuing this preoccupation: First, he has given emphatic, though imprecise and mostly implicit, status to the category
of *Lebensfuehrung.* He has used it at every step of the way in his
interpretation of early Christianity. He has shown that it concerns
the basic God-man relationship of reconciliation, which is constituted by a certain equilibrium of divine and human factors. This
reconciliation has to do with the understanding man has of his own
life and its total commitment; at its best, it is committed to God's
grace for its justification; at its worst, it is committed to man's
own literal legalistic works. In the next chapter, I shall indicate how
Ritschl gained clarity in his formulation of this category as he
gained in maturity, and how he associates it intimately with Reformation Christianity.

Second, he has not only demonstrated how thoroughgoing his
preoccupation with historical continuity is, but he has also taken
one great step towards fulfilling the responsibility which he believes to have devolved upon him as a result of his participation in
the reality of that continuity as imperative. That step is the dem-

---

134 *Ibid.,* pp. 570 ff.

135 It is instructive to compare this with Baur's assessment of the same
phenomena: formally, a natural stage of a necessary religious development,
synthesizing antithetical factors; materially, the spiritual self-consciousness
of the Christian church, which by synthesizing Jewish form with Pauline
content, expressed its essential nature in the unity of the episcopate.

onstration of the continuity and unity of *Lebensfuehrung* that existed among Jesus and his apostles, as well as the discontinuity between this apostolic community and the emerging Catholic church of the second and third centuries. In the demonstration of this continuity and discontinuity, Ritschl has revealed two principles at work, which correspond to his dual commitment as an historian.[136] He has employed a principle of openness to history and the contents of the historical continuum, and he has also employed a principle of selectivity, or axiology. The former is commensurate with his commitment to the physical continuity of the historical continuum. This principle of openness has forced Ritschl to reject the notion of a "double gospel" as well as the notion that Catholicism is the product of a compromise of conflicting antitheses, because both of these Baurian notions entail lacunae which Ritschl believes disrupt the physical continuity of the historical continuum. It has forced Ritschl to conclude that Catholicism is a Gentile Christian phenomenon. The principle of selectivity or axiology corresponds to Ritschl's commitment to Reformation Christianity. This principle has brought Ritschl to assess Catholicism as a *deviation* from apostolic Christianity. The practical application of this principle modifies (one could even say, *violates*) the principle of openness to history in two ways: it has narrowed the focus of the attention which Ritschl directs to the historical continuum, and it brings Ritschl to some rather brutal and injudicious judgments of the historical data.

Third, in his discussion of early Christianity, Ritschl has given the student an opportunity to see how closely constructive and historical factors are interrelated in his theological work. There is no question that constructive factors are at work in this historical investigation of early Christianity, even if they tend to be imprecisely articulated, more implicit than explicit. These constructive factors account for the notion of *Lebensfuehrung* as a category of selectivity and as a category which gives purpose and direction to the historical investigation. But there is no attempt to work with this constructive category except in the context of historical materials. The constructive point which Ritschl wants to make is a point about history and its implications for the theologian's task. We will have occasion to note that this is true in all of Ritschl's theological work, even in the work which is explicitly more constructive than the *Entstehung*.

Having accomplished this much, it remains for Ritschl to delineate the career of the *Lebensfuehrung* which he has come upon in early Christianity, clarify it, and relate it to Reformation Christianity. This phase of his work is taken up in the next chapter.

136 *Supra*, pp. 27 ff.

The Movement of History:
Reformation and Continuing Reformation

THE PRECEDING CHAPTER traced the preoccupation of the young Albrecht Ritschl with the problem of historical continuity. As a young man, between his twenty-eighth and thirty-fifth years, Ritschl prosecuted this concern with continuity in the context of a historical investigation of early Christianity, beginning with the Baurian framework but rejecting its answer to the question of how catholic Christianity emerged from apostolic Christianity. It is particularly important to note the category of *Lebensfuehrung*, which Ritschl was beginning to formulate in order to locate and designate this continuity. The delineation and the defense of this continuity, described in terms of this category of Christian existence, the *Lebensfuehrung*, was deeply rooted in Ritschl's conception of his vocation as a Protestant theologian.

This chapter deals with the mature Ritschl, even interpreting material which he sent to the printer in his fifty-eighth year (he lived to the age of sixty-six). Between 1870 and 1880, Ritschl's output of materials dealing with the problem of historical continuity amounted to at least three thousand pages. In this massive output, he moved all the way from an interpretation of the biblical witness (in *R.u.V. I*) through the Medieval period, the Reformation, Pietism, and up to the Hegelian currents of his own day.[1]

Ritschl's interpretation of the Reformation merits particular attention here, with some summary attention to its relationship to Medieval and Pietist Christianity. This later work elaborates upon the main lines of theological development which were noted in

[1] He continued to revise these historical works up to the year of his death. A revised edition of *R.u.V. I* appeared in 1882; the third revised edition of *R.u.V. II* appeared in 1889, the year of Ritschl's death (see *supra*, p. 12, note 2.)

Ritschl's early work and brings these lines of development into sharper focus, while giving them more precise expression.

Ritschl's preoccupation with historical continuity did not lessen in his mature years; if anything, it became intensified. Ritschl's interest in the historical materials from Anselm to Hegel centers on only one thing, the delineation of their continuity or discontinuity, according to the criterion which he had formulated. This criterion continues to be the category of the *Lebensfuehrung* which emerges from man's relationship of reconciliation with God, which in turn presupposes a certain equilibrium between divine and human factors within this relationship. As before, Ritschl's historical investigations amount to an elaboration of the Christian community's ongoing understanding of this relationship of reconciliation. It is clear, however, that Ritschl attained greater clarity in the understanding and articulation of this category as he grew older. In the *Entstehung*, this category appeared to exert only an implicit force in his analysis; in this chapter, we shall note how explicit the force of this category became in his thought.

The one difference to be noted in this later work is the different question with which Ritschl approached the historical materials at hand. When he approached early Christianity, he had asked, "How did the apostolic community become the Catholic church?" In this later work he asks, "How did the Reformation emerge from Medieval Catholicism?" and "How did the Reformation become the Lutheran church?" Despite their differences, these questions are clearly parallel. Their very phrasing indicates that Ritschl is still operating within the Baurian framework which emphasized movement or continuity as the initial problem for consideration.

The sources for the argument of this chapter include the following: the first volume of *Die christliche Lehre von der Rechtfertigung und der Versoehnung*[2] (1870, 1882, 1889), whose subtitle is: "*Die Geschichte der Lehre*"; the essays[3] "*Die Entstehung der lutherischen Kirche*" (1878), "*Ueber die beiden Principien des Protestantismus*" (1876); and *Geschichte des Pietismus*[4] (1880–1886), specifically, the "*Prolegomena*" as found in Volume I.

Ritschl's historical analysis and interpretation of Medieval Christianity can be summarized as the attempt to demonstrate that an adequate understanding of reconciliation (which was taken up

2 All citations, in this chapter, are from the first German edition (Bonn: Adolph Marcus, 1870), unless otherwise noted. ET: *A Critical History of the Christian Doctrine of Justification and Reconciliation* (Edinburgh: Edmonston and Douglas, 1872). Hereafter cited as *R.u.V. I.*

3 The essays appear in *Gesammelte Aufsaetze* (Freiburg i. B. and Leipzig: Mohr, 1893).

4 Ritschl, *Geschichte des Pietismus*, 3 vols. (Bonn: Adolph Marcus, 1880–1886). Hereafter cited as *Pietismus.*

by the reformers) did persist in the church, even though this period generally reinforced the perversion which he had noted in the old Catholic church. The following quotations bring this out very clearly. They also reveal just how emphatically Ritschl uses the category of *Lebensfuehrung* as an axiological criterion for the interpretation of history. In these passages, he discusses the divine and human factors in the God-man relationship under the notions of justification and sanctification.

It is futile to try to document the Reformation doctrine of justification, that is the intentional differentiation between justification and regeneration, in the work of any medieval theologian.[5] . . . Nevertheless, the dominant Reformation idea of justification has a broad basis in the Church. One finds precursors of the Reformation idea explicitly and even intentionally emphasized even in the arguments of medieval men who just as intentionally and unambiguously endorse the catholic doctrine of justification. For the Reformers' idea of justification pertains, in the first place, not to an objective teaching in the theological system, but rather to the highest standard by which one who stands in the Christian church (and who in accordance with this standard is active in performing good works which proceed from the Holy Spirit) can judge himself. Indeed, for the Reformers justification has to do with the fact that the regenerate person does not hold his status before God and the certainty of his salvation on the basis of the good works that he actually performs, but rather through the grace of God, which justification through Christ guarantees to the Christian's faithful reliance. I have had to set forth this assertion here (which finds its demonstration in the next chapter), so that I can measure against this criterion the expressions of medieval piety which are rightly to be considered analogies to the Reformers' religious standpoint, and which to this extent reach out over the limits of the catholic doctrine of justification and its wretched teaching concerning merits.[6] . . . Where the manifest devotion of the Middle Ages lifted itself to the consideration that the value of the Christian life—even when it is fruitful in good works—is not grounded in works as human achievements, but rather in the mercy of God as that which makes these works possible in the first place and which at the same time outweighs the guilt of continuing sins; where this characteristic certainty of divine grace is present within the Christian community as the claim of the believers, which is preeminent over all possible and actual means of grace; there is the line along which the religious consciousness of our Reformers has proceeded powerfully to break through the existing structures of catholic doctrine and ecclesiastical institutions. Of course, it is true

[5] *R.u.V. I*, p. 93.
[6] *Ibid.*, pp. 94–95.

that other circumstances besides the understanding of grace have con-
tributed to this breakthrough. . . . Nevertheless, in that the religious
self-consciousness which denies in practice the value of theoretically
acknowledged merits was so pronounced among the heroes of the
medieval Church, we have proof that the dominant point of view of
our Reformation was indigenous to the Latin Church. The use which
the Reformers made of this idea of divine grace (which was superordinated to all other ideas) is simply a consistent application of the
idea itself.[7]

These quotations not only reveal Ritschl's rigorous use of the
category of *Lebensfuehrung* (as it emerges from reconciliation as
a criterion for interpreting history), they also illumine the force
which the preoccupation with historical continuity exerts in his
work. That is to say, Ritschl's historical investigation of Medieval
Christianity is undertaken in order to document the historical
continuity of a notion of reconciliation which finds its clearest expression in Reformation Christianity and in Ritschl's own formulations. This continuity is important for Ritschl because (if he is to
fulfill his vocation as theologian) this notion of reconciliation must
be rooted ultimately in apostolic Christianity, and its opposition to
ancient and Medieval Catholicism must be demonstrated. The
scientific demonstration of such continuity and discontinuity is impossible unless a fundamental, physical unity is posited as inherent
in the historical continuum.[8] This work of Ritschl's, then, as the
earlier work discussed above, grows out of his participation in
historical continuity as imperative.

There is another issue involved, however—besides continuity—
in Ritschl's interpretation of the Reformation and Reformation
Christianity. As Ritschl focuses his attention on the *emergence* of
Reformation Christianity *from* Medieval Christianity and its *development into* the Lutheran church, he is also concerned with
the task of elaborating his own constructive position. This elaboration, however, belongs within the context of the exposition and
polemic which grows out of his participation in the historical continuity which he is analyzing.[9]

As we observe this analysis of Reformation Christianity, we
should note the methodological scheme which Ritschl followed in
his interpretation of early Christianity and which is in force as he
compares the Reformation to Medieval Christianity and to the
Lutheran church. The first step in this method is the establishment
of the unity which exists as a simple physical factor within the

[7] *Ibid.,* pp. 96–97.
[8] *Supra,* pp. 43–44.
[9] For the significance of this elaboration, see *infra,* pp. 70 ff.

historical continuum.[10] This physical continuity is necessary if historical investigation is to proceed along scientific lines. Ritschl goes to great length to establish this continuity between Catholicism and apostolic Christianity, between the Reformation and the Medieval church, and between Lutheranism and the Reformation. But in each case this exercise constitutes only a propadeutic to the work that Ritschl really wants to perform, namely the evaluation of each of the historical phenomena in question in the light of a certain category of *Lebensfuehrung* which emerges from the God-man relation of reconciliation. In each case, this evaluation brings to light the theological continuities and discontinuities which hold ultimate significance for Ritschl. These continuities and discontinuities inform the chief purpose of Ritschl's work.

HOW REFORMATION CHRISTIANITY EMERGED FROM MEDIEVAL CHRISTIANITY

The long passages quoted above[11] indicate that Ritschl believes that the Reformation understanding of reconciliation is rooted in the best Medieval tradition of piety, which in turn can be traced back to the apostolic community. By insisting on this unity with the best of the traditional Christian piety, Ritschl is attempting to establish nothing less (by his own admission) than the *catholicity* of the reformers.

This catholicity seems to be constituted by *historical continuity*. In a revealing section of *R.u.V. I,* Ritschl lays down the maxim that no figure in the history of Christianity can be interpreted as if *his own personal* religious and scholarly experiences formed the sufficient basis for his theological position.[12] Particularly in the interpretation of the reformers, care must be taken to place each figure in the larger context of theological and ecclesiastical movements. One must adhere to the view that "it is in the *variation* and *development* of theological cognition that the logically necessary and self-caused movement of thought is to be demonstrated."[13] On the basis of this method, it is inadmissible to interpret the reformers —Luther, Zwingli, Melanchthon, and Calvin—as rebels who were on principle opposed to the "Catholic church as it had developed historically."[14] This is rather the characteristic of the Anabaptists, the heretics, and the sectarians.[15] Nor is it admissible to interpret

10 See note 8.
11 *Supra*, pp. 47–48.
12 Ritschl, *R.u.V. I*, p. 129.
13 *Ibid.*
14 *Ibid.*, p. 130.
15 *Ibid.*

the reformers as the founders of a new religion or as prophets who reached a perfection of knowledge and inspiration which heretofore had never been attained.[16] Again, these are characteristics only of the sectarians.[17] Rather, the interpreter must understand the grounds for the assertion that the reformers were more authentically Catholic than the Roman church, while at the same time unalterably opposed to the sectarians. Ritschl himself phrases the matter thus:

> In which historical events, therefore, can we perceive that our Reformation as such held the ground of the Church, that it confused this ground neither with that of the sect nor that of the "school"? What is the criterion for ascertaining that in their separation from the Roman form of the Church they did not at the same time bring about their alienation from the catholicity of the Church? The answer to this question will not be probed fully simply by indicating the intention of the Reformers to hold to the idea of the universal Church. For the Anabaptists and the Socinians also share this intention, in their own way; and yet the characteristics which these parties, each in its own way, ascribes to the concept of the Church run directly counter to the concept that has been in effect or indirectly presupposed up to this time in history.[18]

As he approaches the Reformation, Ritschl also approaches the theological position which he himself espouses. The passage just cited makes clear a crucial point: namely, that Ritschl is not simply interested in systematically elaborating his theological position, nor in demonstrating its existential or logical superiority over other positions. Rather, his interest here seems to be to demonstrate its catholicity, its historical continuity with the best of traditional Christian piety, back to apostolic times, including the teaching of Jesus Christ himself. This clarifies in an important way what it means for Ritschl to be preoccupied with historical continuity, even to the extent that that preoccupation shapes his theological achievement. This also clarifies our earlier statement that the constructive point which Ritschl wants to make is a point about history and its implications for the theologian's task.[19]

Ritschl adduces several specific arguments in behalf of his assertion that Reformation Christianity is authentically Catholic. The first, and perhaps the most massive, of these arguments centers in Ritschl's assertion that the reformers were neither mere appropriators of the traditional thought of reconciliation nor rebels who sought an open break with the church's tradition. Rather, the

16 *Ibid.*
17 *Ibid.*
18 *Ibid.*
19 *Supra*, pp. 43–44.

reformers mark a new stage in the church's development, and as such they introduce elements which are legitimate expressions of the Catholic tradition, but which are nevertheless new.[20] The task of the reformers—and that which gave their work a genuinely *reforming* turn—was to assert the claims of this new stage of development in such a way as to overwhelm and eliminate those institutions and forms which threatened to obstruct its expression.[21]

The Anabaptists and Socinians broke with the historical church in principle. In his attempt to distinguish their break from the reforming work of Luther, Ritschl enunciates once again his understanding of historical tradition and continuity with it:

In order, therefore, to differentiate the churchly character of the work of Luther and Zwingli qualitatively, from these other forms of radical and revolutionary reform, it is proper to say that Zwingli and Luther did not "discover" their basic reforming ideas, nor did they find them newly uncovered simply through the exegesis of Scripture. Rather, they received them from the internal tradition of the Church. One can also assert legitimately that the reforming application of the religious consciousness based on "grace alone" and "Christ alone" to set aside the institutions and school-like traditions which contradicted that consciousness—this application itself remained in the line of the Church's true character, because it stands in a reciprocal relation to the original, correct understanding of the Church as the community of those whom God has sanctified.[22]

The first argument, then, upon which Ritschl bases his claim that the Reformation Christianity is Catholic is the assertion that it represents a new, but nevertheless legitimate stage in the development of the church.

A second major argument which sustains the reformers' claim to be authentically Catholic centers in the fact that they professed the desire to remain within the limits of the Christian fellowship of the Holy Roman Empire. This not only sets them apart from those left-wing groups who withdrew from this fellowship; it also sets them apart from those who denied the doctrine of the Trinity and the ecumenical creeds of the ancient church.[23] Ritschl emphasizes this adherence to ancient dogma in the following manner:

Indeed, the Reformers themselves scarcely ever express a clear political awareness that through their acknowledgment of the doctrine of the Trinity they were keeping themselves on the legal ground of the Roman

[20] Ritschl, *R.u.V. I,* 171–172
[21] *Ibid.,* p. 172.
[22] *Ibid.,* pp. 172–173.
[23] *Ibid.,* pp. 134–136.

empire. *They were aware only that through their confession they stood on the ground of the catholic Church.* Without any doubt their own teaching seemed valid to the Reformers originally *by virtue of the authority of the Church's tradition and not that of the Holy Scripture.* . . . their opinion tended in that direction later maintained by Georg Calixtus, that the dogmatic consensus of the first five centuries is the criterion for the exposition of the Holy Scripture. The fact is, therefore, that in respect to the doctrine of the person of Christ and of the Trinity, the Reformers adhered to this consensus, and this chiefly because they kept their feet on the ground of the catholic Church of the Roman empire.[24]

This adherence to the Catholic tradition of dogma makes it clear, in Ritschl's mind, that the intention of the reformers was to *reintroduce* the church's *original* understanding of reconciliation, and thus they knew themselves to be acting in the spirit of the Catholic church.[25]

Finally, and this sets them off from the left-wing of the Reformation as much as it places them within the Catholic tradition, the reformers asserted the "priority of the church over every sign of redemption which manifested itself in individual persons."[26] This they held in practice, not just in theory, as is attested to by the fact that they laid down as the practical criterion of regeneration the notion of reconciliation which had been alive from apostolic times down through the best of Medieval tradition.[27] Ritschl is confident that even if the *public* doctrine of the Medieval church opposed the reformers, the "actual judgment that faithful Christians put into practice" (*geuebte, praktische Selbstbeurtheilung des Glaeubigen*) accorded with their notion of reconciliation and the God-man relationship.[28] (In other words, his confidence rests on the unity of *Lebensfuehrung.*)

If these are the grounds for asserting the fundamental unity and continuity between Reformation Christianity and the traditional Christianity of the ancient and Medieval periods—that is, the grounds for the assertion that the reformers were *Catholic*—the question next arises concerning the content of this Reformation Christianity, the content of this legitimate yet distinctively *new* stage of the church's development.

Ritschl interprets the Reformation as being concerned chiefly with the reality of the sinner's reconciliation with God. As he elaborates this concern, he is also filling out his own understanding

[24] *Ibid.*, pp. 135–136. Italics added.
[25] *Ibid.*, p. 138.
[26] *Ibid.*
[27] *Ibid.*
[28] *Ibid.*, p. 120; see also p. 97.

of reconciliation and the *Lebensfuehrung* which emerges from it. Up to this point we have not discussed the actual content of this *Lebensfuehrung*, because Ritschl's own discussion of the heart of Reformation Christianity gives us the opportunity to analyze in more detail this central category in his theology.

According to Ritschl, the heart of the Reformation emphasis is its insistence that the religious self-consciousness be oriented upon the reconciling, justifying work of Jesus Christ.[29] He writes, with specific reference to Luther and Zwingli:

The certainty of justification in faith through Christ (as this is grasped by the faithful persons who stand in the Church and who strive after God's will) is the lever for both men for the reformation of the Church. This is so because the Reformers united with their own subjective awareness of salvation the basic view of the Church as the community of the faithful who have been sanctified by God.[30]

As the believer enters into the God-man relationship, he recognizes that he does so only on the basis of God's grace in Christ, and not at all on the basis of his own efforts. For this reason Ritschl can assert that it is not really any specific doctrine of justification which stands at the center of Luther's theology, but rather, "Luther's theological principle is rather the idea of the revealed presence of love as the divine nature in Christ."[31]

Although he criticizes the reformers for neglecting its proper systematic elaboration,[32] Ritschl insists that this notion of justification and the love of God entails the understanding of sanctification (good works) as proceeding from the circumstance of being justified through Christ's righteousness.[33] In other words, the moral (or human factor) proceeds *from* the religious (or divine factor). For the purposes of this discussion, Ritschl's most succinct elaboration of this Reformation category appears in his comments on Bernard of Clairvaux:

. . . Bernard traced the totality of good works (as viewed religiously) back to divine grace, in his ethical consideration of the free will as freed by grace. In the form of an unmediated conviction, he grasped the two-fold idea *in which the practical foundation of evangelical Christianity is expressed. In this two-fold idea, evangelical theology also recognizes its task of demonstrating the harmony or the non-contradictory character of both aspects of the idea.* For, religiously, we

29 *Ibid.*, p. 160.
30 *Ibid.*, pp. 160–161.
31 *Ibid.*, p. 165.
32 *Infra*, p. 75.
33 *Ibid.*, pp. 173 ff.

place our good will in complete dependence upon God, without thereby granting any place for a meritorious position of man before God. Precisely for this reason, we are aware of the independence of our moral characters over against everything that is not of God, and therefore also over against the paternalism of the hierarchy of the church.[34]

On the basis of this analysis of the Reformation, Ritschl is emphatic that Reformation Christianity cannot be characterized as a doctrine or a set of doctrines. In the context of a discussion of Luther's principle of justification by faith, he writes:

One cannot point to this phrase [justification by faith] as a principle of *doctrine*. Rather it is simply a characteristic conclusion drawn from the principle of divine grace which, when related to other observations concerning the regulation of Christian life and the value judgments of that life, carries with it implications that are relevant for doctrine.[35]

This raises the provocative and instructive question of the validity of the traditional formal-material scheme for interpreting the Reformation. This scheme was formulated for the purpose of clarifying the essential proclamation of the Reformation theology; it was usually formulated with *sola scriptura* as the formal principle of the Reformation and with *sola fide* as the material principle. Ritschl devoted considerable attention to this question, and he was generally skeptical of this scheme's validity. He bases this skepticism on several grounds. In his essay, *"Ueber die beiden Principien des Protestantismus: Antwort auf eine 25 Jahre alte Frage"* (1876), Ritschl argues against the scheme on both historical and theological grounds. He objects to it historically simply because the designation, meaning, and usage of the two principles is so confused. In this essay, he points out that whereas some Lutheran theologians have designated *sola scriptura* as formal principle and *sola fide* as material principle (Bretschneider, Beck),[36] others have just reversed the designation (Baier, Wegscheider, de Wette).[37] Still others have substituted other designations entirely (Schleiermacher, Twesten).[38] On the basis of this evidence, Ritschl defies anyone to assert an historically consistent analysis of Reformation Christianity on the basis of this formal-material scheme. Furthermore, on historical grounds, such a scheme cannot even account for the distinctiveness of the Reformation. Even the Franciscans

---

34 *Ibid.*, pp. 99–100. Italics added. See also *supra*, pp. 47–48.

35 Ritschl, *Pietismus*, I, p. 37.

36 Ritschl, *"Ueber die beiden Principien des Protestantismus,"* in *Gesammelte Aufsaetze* (Freiburg i. B. and Leipzig: Mohr, 1893), pp. 234–237. Hereafter cited as *Aufsaetze*.

37 *Ibid.*, pp. 235, 237, 238.

38 *Ibid.*, pp. 240–243.

and the Anabaptists could adhere to these formulae, particularly to the principle of *sola scriptura*.[39]

Even more significant, however, for Ritschl, and more illuminating for our present study, are his theological objections to the formal-material scheme. He contends that the emphasis on Scripture alone fails to take into account the catholicity of the reformers and their reliance on tradition.[40] On the other hand, the emphasis on faith alone completely overlooks the fact that the reformers' work was meant to take place within the church, and that they conceived this faith to exist only within that community of saints.[41] Perhaps Ritschl's most vehement protest against this formal-material scheme is occasioned by what he considers to be its rationalistic tendency, which turns Reformation Christianity into a set of doctrines or into a school. Such a view stands in diametric opposition to Ritschl's own position.[42] At this point, it is sufficient to cite one passage from the *History of Pietism* which not only reveals Ritschl's opposition to the scheme in question, but also indicates the important role that the concept of *Lebensfuehrung* plays in his thought.

The formula of the two principles of the Reformation, as it is customarily used, expresses an unsatisfactory judgment concerning this epoch-making phenomenon. On the basis of the formula, one can only judge that the Reformation of Luther and the others has called into being a new form of theological "school." One would never suspect that the Reformation had set in motion a new phase of the Christian *Lebensfuehrung*. The upshot is that the formula has been put together in a very fortuitous manner, without extensive consideration of the facts. Schleiermacher has expressed the valid meaning and intention of the formula, namely, that within the diversity of Reformation theologians the acknowledgment of both principles [*sola scriptura* and *sola fide*] is the minimum that must be required of a man if he is to qualify as a Reformation theologian.[43]

In summary, Ritschl interprets the heart of the Reformation as consisting in a proclamation of God's love which reconciles man through Jesus Christ and his righteousness. This proclamation stands in the context of the religious self-consciousness of the believer, however, and this means that the impact of this divine love is conceived of as effecting a relationship of reconciliation between God and man in which sanctification or human moral

---

[39] Ritschl, *Pietismus*, I, p. 37.
[40] Ritschl, *R.u.V.* I, 164–165.
[41] *Ibid.*, pp. 162 f.; and Ritschl, *Aufsaetze*, pp. 246–247.
[42] *Infra*, p. 69.
[43] Ritschl, *Pietismus*, I, pp. 37–38.

activity is engendered by God's prevenient action of grace.[44] Reformation Christianity conceives all of this as taking place within the church. Reformation Christianity, then, is marked by a total human condition, a *Lebensfuehrung* or *Lebensideal,* in which God's prevenient reconciling action and man's subsequent ethical response are held together in equilibrium. If God's action is not always held to be *prevenient* to man's response, the equilibrium is disturbed. This content of Reformation Christianity will become still clearer as we note how Ritschl sets it in sharp opposition to the Medieval Christianity to which the Reformation is nevertheless so closely related.

With this assessment of the differences between Medieval and Reformation Christianity, Ritschl closes his investigation of how the Reformation emerged from Medieval Christianity. The opposition which Ritschl sees existing between these two stages in Christian development rests on two broad issues, both of which are traced back ultimately to the equilibrium in which divine and human factors are held within the God-man relation. These two issues are soteriology and ecclesiology. He has gone into great detail to assert the unity, within the historical continuum, between Medieval and Reformation Christianity. This unity is of great scientific significance; without it, Ritschl could not undertake his historical investigation. But it is not of ultimate *theological* significance. Ritschl cannot let his historical interpretation rest until he has applied his axiological category to the two parties in question. Ritschl applies this category in his discussion of soteriology and ecclesiology as these notions are understood within Medieval and Reformation Christianity, respectively. The application of this axiological category of *Lebensfuehrung* leads Ritschl to the conclusion that, within the physical continuity between these two epochs, there exists *a fundamental discontinuity.* And it is this fundamental discontinuity that is of ultimate theological significance to Ritschl (albeit within his larger concern for the fundamental *continuity*). It is the clear delineation of this discontinuity that informs the purpose of his historical interpretation.

The issue of soteriology is the issue of the God-man relation of reconciliation. And when Ritschl asserts an opposition between the two stages of Christian development on this issue, he clarifies that opposition in terms of *justification* (the action of God which establishes the relation of reconciliation) and in terms of *Lebensfuehrung* (the total condition of the believer's life which is engendered by this justifying action which reconciles). Finally, the source of this opposition lies in the two differing understandings of the equilibrium that should exist between divine and human

44 See Hefner, *Lutheran Quarterly,* 13:106–109, 1961.

factors within this God-man relation. And the evaluation of the relative desirability of the Reformation understanding over the Medieval is based on Ritschl's category of *Lebensfuehrung*, which defines what he believes to be the proper equilibrium.

The Medieval (Roman) and Reformation doctrines of justification differ both in definition and in intention. Ritschl's analysis of these differences reveals very clearly just what he believes is at stake in the opposition between these two forms of Christianity, as well as his conception of the essence of the Reformation faith. In the first place, one sees in the two doctrines of justification the tension between the Roman concern for dogmatic objectivity in the description of Christ's meritorious work and the subsequent work of God as against the Reformation concern for a description of the subjective religious experience upon which God has acted in his grace.

This formal alteration in the form of the problem is also a mark of an alteration in form and content of the idea of justification. First of all, in that Luther puts justification at the heart of the matter and emphasizes his own explanation as the decisive and inescapable truth, he intends justification through faith in Christ as a subjective religious experience of the faithful person who is in the Church, and not as an objective theological proposition of the Church's dogmatics.[45]

Luther is thus able to explain justification as "a total experience of the believer that has an integrity of its own."[46] The Roman doctrine can never serve to describe this unified experience, because of the dogmatic and ecclesiastical baggage which it carries with it in its doctrine of justification.[47]

This difference in approach and in the method of expressing the doctrine of justification is a manifestation of two fundamentally different understandings of the issue, which Ritschl describes thus:

The Roman Catholic doctrine of justification seeks to explain how and through what means a sinner becomes an actively righteous person who can be judged truly to be righteous by God. Contrary to this, the Reformation understanding of the religious experience of justification is that the faithful person (who as such is regenerate and a member of the Church), who is powerful and active through the Holy Spirit, can produce good works. On account of the continuing imperfection of the Christian, these good works are not made possible by the man himself, but rather only through the mediating and perfectly just work of Christ; the believer appropriates this work of Christ through faith

---

45 Ritschl, *R.u.V. I*, p. 126.
46 *Ibid.*, p. 127.
47 *Ibid.*

and finds therewith his standing before God, his righteousness, and the ground of his persisting certainty of salvation.[48]

This difference of perspectives on the doctrine of justification leads each of the respective parties to different understandings of sanctification or regeneration and its relation to justification. In this connection Ritschl makes judgments whose soundness has been underlined by current discussions between Protestants and Roman Catholics. He makes the judgment that the Roman perspective leads naturally to a concern for *gratia cooperans*. By this he means that the Roman (Medieval) doctrine does not necessarily deny God's prevenient grace in redeeming man; it does not emphasize merit as influencing God's initial action; but it *does* tend to allow merit a role in the *increase and continuance* of grace. And, as Ritschl points out in his discussion of Bernard, this confuses God's grace with man's freedom, thereby vitiating our awareness of divine grace.[49] This leads Ritschl to the observation that the Roman and Reformation understandings are so different that their respective doctrines of justification dare not be compared as if they referred to comparable realities, on a one-to-one basis. He sees evidence of this in the fact the Roman theologians can speak with perfect consistency of justification *and* regeneration, whereas the Reformation theology must speak of justification *or* regeneration.[50] Ritschl identifies the really anti-evangelical tendency of Roman Christianity with this preoccupation with *gratia cooperans*, in other words, with the influence of merit on the increase and continuance of grace, rather than with the notion of merit per se.[51]

Probably the most serious aspect of this opposition between Medieval and Reformation Christianity, at least in Ritschl's mind, is the different category of *Lebensfuehrung* which follows from the fundamental structure of the God-man relation as each party understands it. Ritschl considers it to be thoroughly consistent with its understanding of the God-man relation that the Medieval *Lebensideal* (or *Lebensfuehrung*) was that of the monastic existence. He writes in the *History of Pietism*:

Catholic Christianity sees the ideal for its life (*Lebensideal*) in monasticism, in binding certain obligations which follow from the universal law of God: poverty, chastity, and obedience (to the highest authority of the order). It is said that in these three virtues one can attain the supernatural destiny of man which is set forth in Christianity, a destiny

48 *Ibid.*, p. 127.
49 *Ibid.*, p. 101. See also the discussion of *gratia cooperans* in the theology of St. Thomas, pp. 69 ff.
50 *Ibid.*, p. 128.
51 *Ibid.*, p. 101.

that was not foreseen in man's original creation; one enters thus into the life of the angels. The vocation of the monk, so understood, is Christian perfection.[52]

This notion of the *Lebensideal* as including the perfect legal obedience finds a counterpart in the Roman contention that merit can insure the continuance and increase of grace, in the interaction between grace and freedom, and in the refusal to subordinate man's freedom to that grace.[53]

The Reformation *Lebensideal* (and this is also the heart of Ritschl's own position) stems from an understanding of the God-man relation which *does* superordinate the divine factor over the human, and which believes this to be the only proper equilibrium between the two factors. The human activity of regeneration can in no wise be identified with justification, even though that activity can be engendered by the justifying action of God.[54] Ritschl describes this Reformation *Ideal* in the following terms:

If Protestantism is to prevail against the practical weight that Catholicism carries by virtue of a high valuation of monasticism and the spread of monastic piety among the laity, then Protestantism too must exhibit a criterion of perfection that speaks in qualitative terms. But it does indeed exhibit such a criterion. Even as in the circumstances of sin man is characterized primarily by a failure to fear and trust God, so also perfection, according to the assertions of the Augsburg Confession, consists precisely in fear and trust of God in all the situations of life. This can be expressed more fully in terms of fear of God, trust in God's benevolent providence, prayer, and the faithful fulfillment of one's vocation.[55] . . . The meaning of justification by faith establishes itself in this connection, namely, that on the basis of this justification one can account for and actually trace back to its origin a trust in God's providence in all the circumstances of life—a trust that the sinner otherwise does not possess. This is the distinctive test of reconciliation with God, that one also becomes reconciled with the course of events that God brings to us, no matter how hard a blow these events deal us.[56]

This is perhaps Ritschl's clearest expression of the Christian *Lebensfuehrung* which forms the content of the axiological category which he applies so decisively in his historical investigations. This *Lebensfuehrung* is marked by diligence in one's vocation, accompanied by complete trust in God's providence.

[52] Ritschl, *Pietismus*, I, pp. 38–39.
[53] *Supra*, p. 58.
[54] Ritschl, *Pietismus*, I, pp. 40–41.
[55] *Ibid.*, p. 39.
[56] *Ibid.*, p. 40.

The opposition between Roman and Reformation Christianity on the issue of ecclesiology is not unrelated to this foregoing discussion of their opposition on the matter of soteriology. Briefly stated, the Roman position is that the legal community within the church is coterminous with the religious community, whereas the Reformation position holds that the legal community is an instrument of the religious community.[57]

This emphasis on the legal form of the church is directly correlated to the Medieval *Lebensideal*, which also emphasized, according to Ritschl, the regulated achievement of believers as an appropriate work before God.[58] The Reformation view, which subordinates the legal to the religious, parallels the Reformation understanding of the God-man relation, in which the ethical is subordinated to the religious, or the human is subordinated to the divine.

This concludes Ritschl's attempt to answer the question of how Reformation Christianity emerged from Medieval Christianity. His answer can be summarized thus: Within the given, physical continuity of the historical continuum, the Reformation constitutes a new stage in the historical development of Christianity. It implies a rupture with the previous stage, because, in reference to the heart of the Christian faith, namely, a certain *Lebensfuehrung* which emerges from reconciliation with God, Reformation Christianity insisted on maintaining the authentically traditional Christian understanding against the Roman Catholic perversion of it.

HOW THE REFORMATION OF LUTHER BECAME THE LUTHERAN CHURCH

One of the most cogent testimonies to the validity of the thesis that Ritschl's theological work is shaped by a preoccupation with historical continuity is the fact that Ritschl felt the necessity to come to terms with each of the major manifestations within Christian history whose support might be necessary for his purposes or whose opposition might constitute a threat to the validity of his own interpretation of Christianity. We have already examined his attempts to come to terms with apostolic, ancient Catholic, Medieval, and Reformation Christianity. In each case, by applying the category of a certain *Lebensfuehrung*, he has established either the continuity or the discontinuity which that category dictates. Now we turn to another of these historical entities with which Ritschl feels he must come to terms, orthodox Lutheranism.

Here, too, Ritschl follows the scheme discussed above, estab-

57 *Ibid.*, pp. 43–44.
58 *Ibid.*, p. 18.

lishing a simple physical unity within the historical continuum, as well as a more significant theological discontinuity. He establishes the continuity so that he can pursue his historical investigation on a valid, scientific basis. And he establishes a theological discontinuity so that he can reject an inadequate soteriology and, even more, an inadequate ecclesiology, which are occasioned by an improper understanding of the God-man relation. He followed the same procedure in his analysis of the relation between Medieval and Reformation Christianity. As Ritschl illumines the theology of the Reformation in contrast to later orthodox developments, he illumines the theological position which he came to identify with his own.

Before Ritschl can answer the question of how Luther's Reformation became the Lutheran church, he must demolish the opinion that the Lutheran church represents a "fall" from Luther. More specifically, he rejects the judgment of the nineteenth-century German historian, Heinrich Heppe (1820–1879), that this "fall" was personified in Melanchthon's deviation from Luther.[59] In combating this interpretation, Ritschl gives expression to a principle that we have already encountered several times, namely, the unsuitability of the notion of a "fall" as a category for the scientific historian:

Even if we granted that all this [tension between Melanchthon and Luther] were correct, we still could not be content with Heppe's explanation of the sudden change by which the German Reformation became the Lutheran church, *because the assumption of a simple "fall" from the earlier direction of Protestantism is opposed to the nature of the historical process.* From a preliminary view, something may appear to be a "fall" from the past or a break from it. *In historical research, however, one cannot accept this preliminary view as the complete fact of the matter, nor can he represent it as such in his work.* Rather, such a preliminary view calls forth the obligation to establish through more exact research into the facts a view that will counter and even set aside the preliminary view.[60]

The similarity of this analysis, formally, at least, with Ritschl's analysis of the emergence of the old Catholic church is striking. There, Ritschl rejected the notion of a historical "fall." But even more striking, he also rejected the notion that such a fall was personified in the disagreement between two men—Paul and Peter.[61]

[59] Heinrich Heppe, *Geschichte der deutschen Protestantismus in den Jahren 1555–1581*, 4 vols. (Marburg: N. G. Elwert, 1852–1859), Vol. I, 72–90.
[60] Ritschl, *"Die Entstehung der lutherischen Kirche,"* in *Aufsaetze*, pp. 171–172.
[61] *Supra*, pp. 35–37.

Rather than such a "fall," Ritschl believes that the changing conception of the church during the first years of the Reformation is a much more valid key to the interpretation of the development which culminated in the Lutheran church.[62] Even as he asserts this as the key for interpreting this development, Ritschl rejects the interpretation set forth by the group which he terms "contemporary exclusivistic Lutherans" (*die heutigen exclusiven Lutheraner*) to the effect that the emergence of the Lutheran church is to be dated from the presentation of the Augsburg Confession in 1530.[63] This position can be set forth by these "exclusivistic Lutherans" only because they insist on equating the doctrine elaborated in the Augsburg Confession with the Lutheran church; they do this on the basis of their interpretation of the seventh article of the Confession.[64]

Ritschl enumerates several reasons why he cannot accept the 1530 date for the emergence of the Lutheran church or the equation of the Augsburg Confession with Lutheranism. In the first place, Ritschl does not believe that the Lutheran reformers had any intention, in 1530, of establishing a separate church over against the Roman church. He writes:

First of all, as is borne out from the fact that the extent and import of the Reformation became clear only gradually even for Luther himself, the Reformation was from the very beginning oriented upon the total substance of the universal Church of the west; nothing was farther from its intention than the establishment of a sectarian church alongside the Roman church. The efforts which the Protestants had to undertake after 1525 to form such a church were necessitated because the bishops and pope rejected the Reformation; such efforts were not at the time looked upon as something final.[65]

Ritschl believes that the reformers wanted above all to reach a reconciliation with the Roman church even as late as 1555.[66]

Ritschl's most significant argument against the exclusivistic, Lutheran dating of the emergence of the Lutheran church in 1530 (and one which comes very close to the heart of his own theological position) is one in which he asserts that the reformers' understanding of the church rested on their understanding of the term *doctrina evangelii,* in article seven of the Augsburg Confession. Agreement on the *doctrina evangelii* is judged necessary for

---

62 Ritschl, *Aufsaetze,* pp. 173–174.
63 *Ibid.,* p. 175.
64 *Ibid.*
65 *Ibid.,* pp. 175–176.
66 *Ibid.,* p. 176.

church unity.[67] The problem posed by this term concerns which of the two words is to be deemed preeminent. Ritschl sets up the problem in the following manner:

The interpretation I have just cited [the interpretation of the exclusivistic Lutherans] is certainly a possibility for understanding the agreement concerning *doctrina evangelii* that is necessary for the untiy of the Church, if one takes that phrase out of all relationship to its context. But it is only one possibility, thus reading *doctrina* evangelii and understanding by those words the propositions of the Augsburg Confession. It is just as much a possibility to emphasize doctrina *evangelii*; and then the first word appears simply as an auxiliary to the second. On the basis of a number of considerations, the latter interpretation is the only possible and necessary one according to historical standards of judgment.[68]

Ritschl is insistent that this term must be read and understood as doctrina *evangelii,* because the Augustana goes on to speak of this *evangelium* as that of the preached word and of the sacrament. This can mean only one thing: "The illuminating of *God's* gracious will and not as a series of dogmas which stand as human perceptions."[69] In other words, *doctrina evangelii* refers to the reality of *sola gratia,* which must be understood, believed, and taught.[70] No specific doctrine and no specific view of the sacraments (as outlined in the tenth article of the Augustana) can meet these requirements of belief, and so they cannot be the referent of the seventh article.[71] It is clear that Ritschl is here rejecting what he considers to be an inadequate concept of the church because it makes the unity of the church dependent on doctrine in such a way as to exclude the category *Lebensfuehrung* which Ritschl believes to be central to the Christian faith. Ritschl's intent is made clear in the following quotation—he has just set down the principle that when Luther spoke of the marks of the church (the presence of which was necessary, and agreement on which

---

[67] In the *Confessio Augustana* itself, the terms *doctrina evangelii* are rendered by the German phrase, "*das . . . nach reinem Verstand das Evangelium gepredigt [wird].*" The term *doctrina* thus corresponds to *predigen*: see *Die Bekenntnisschriften der evangelisch-Lutherischen Kirche,* 2nd rev. ed. (Goettingen: Vandenhoeck und Ruprecht, 1952), p. 61. The *Augustana,* as well as the *Apologia,* seem to employ the word *doctores* at times with the connotation of *Prediger* (see *ibid.,* pp. 266, 269). This throws an interesting light on Ritschl's separation of *doctrina* from academic theology.

[68] *Ibid.,* p. 176.

[69] *Ibid.,* p. 177.

[70] *Ibid.,* pp. 177, 179.

[71] *Ibid.,* p. 178.

was a requisite for church unity) he referred to the reality of the religious life, in which God's grace is appropriated.

The conceptions [which the Augsburg Confession presupposes] of God, sin, etc., fade into the background when compared to the means for appropriating divine grace. That is to say, it [article VII of the Augsburg Confession] has nothing at all to do with the theoretical appropriation of a rule of faith in which each part is of equal value with every other part, as if an equal amount of theological effort has been expended on each. Quite the contrary, the pure understanding of the Gospel means human works of merit are excluded from any relationship to the representation and appropriation of God's grace.[72]

In accordance with this, the Torgau Articles clearly assert that the knowledge of Christ and faith in him is the foundation on which teachers erect doctrines of varying worth.[73] Ritschl summarizes by saying that the doctrine of the gospel that was held in early Lutheranism was the clear comprehension of God's grace in Christ; it was not equated with the Augustana.[74] There is therefore no basis for the claim that the presentation of the Augustana, in and of itself, marked the emergence of the Lutheran church.

This understanding of the *doctrina evangelii* of the Augustana (article VII) clarifies the real basis for the Lutheran opposition to the Roman church in 1530. This opposition is not based on the reformers' self-consciousness of themselves as one church pitted against another church. Rather, they opposed the Roman Catholics because they (the Romans) conceived of the church as coterminous with its existence as a legal entity.[75] This was diametrically opposed to Melanchthon's formulation in the Augustana that the church is not just a legal entity, but principally a community of faith and the Holy Spirit. The church is a legal entity, but this is not its chief mark. Much was at stake here, in view of the Lutheran understanding of *doctrina evangelii*, because the reliance on the external legal forms of the church is a denial of the *sola gratia* which constitutes the *doctrina evangelii* upon which there must be agreement if the church is to be one. To base the real existence of the church on the legalities of cultus and human relationships is to give such prominence to merit as to undermine the *sola gratia*.[76] Ritschl is not arguing for a notion of the church as *invisible*; he is arguing against a notion of the church which substitutes legal forms for the appropriation of God's grace as the decisively distinguishing mark of the church.[77]

72 *Ibid.*, p. 179.
73 *Ibid.*
74 *Ibid.*, p. 181.
75 *Ibid.*, pp. 181–182.
76 *Ibid.*
77 *Ibid.*, pp. 182–183.

Ritschl's final argument against the exclusivistic Lutheran hypothesis which dated the rise of the Lutheran church with the Augustana rests on his assertion that the Lutheran reformers do not (until after 1539) use the concept of the church in a substantive manner, but rather only in a critical way. By this, he means that they do not equate *the* church with their party, nor do they (except in the Schmalkald Articles) deny that the Roman Catholics are the church. Throughout the Augustana, the Apology, the Schmalkald Articles, and Luther's treatise, "On Councils and the Church," the Lutherans use the concept of the church in a negative, critical sense, in order to attack what they consider to be the Roman perversions of the church as the community of faith and of the Holy Spirit.[78] They leave the door open to the Romans, and they do not equate their own work with the church. Concerning the concept of the church as it appears in these documents, Ritschl writes:

> One can draw the conclusion from this concept of the Church [the concept in the documents mentioned above] that the Roman church, on the basis of its institutional organization and its doctrine of merit before God, is not the Church. On the contrary, however, there is not even a hint that the congregations that follow Luther's Reformation comprise the Church as it might be conceived ideally, with all of its essential marks. Such a claim is simply not considered, since the substance of the authentic Church can be traced only to the believers who are scattered all over the earth. This reluctance to claim that the Reformation is the only true Church reveals undeniably that the plan of the Reformation was to hold open the possibility of reconciliation with its opponents. This accounts also for the fact that the Augsburg Confession does not claim that its own teaching is the catholic rule of faith, but rather only that its teaching does not contradict the teaching of the catholic Church.[79]

Ritschl points out further, in order to buttress this argument, that the reformers did not call themselves "Lutherans," but preferred to be considered as "Catholics."[80]

All of this argumentation is aimed at demonstrating that the change in the reformers' understanding of the church did not emerge with the Confessio Augustana in 1530. His own theory is that the Reformation stance which was characterized by the understanding of *doctrina evangelii* as outlined above began to change in the years from 1537 to 1540. He believes that Melanchthon is the chief agent of this change. In 1537, writing in behalf of the

[78] *Ibid.*, pp. 184–186. Luther's treatise is available in *Works of Martin Luther*, 6 vols. (Philadelphia: A. J. Holman, 1931), Vol. V, 125–300.
[79] *Ibid.*, p. 184.
[80] *Ibid.*, pp. 184–185.

Schmalkald Confederation, Melanchthon asserts, for the first time, that the Roman church can no longer be considered to be Catholic, whereas the Schmalkaldic churches are the true Catholics.[81] Ritschl continues:

In order to legitimate this assertion [that the Roman church is no longer catholic], Melanchthon refers to the confession delivered to the emperor at Augsburg—a confession whose content is the pure teaching of the Gospel. We stand, he says, under the command of God as well as the moral obligation that follows from that command to hold fast to this confession of Christ, even if one thereby must break with the pope. We dare not leave the decision in this controversy to a council led by the pope, because such a council would hardly permit its doctrine to be tested by the Word of God (i.e., by the Gospel and the apostolic writings). The new step which this public pronouncement takes is the claim that *the church which is designated by the Augsburg Confession is the catholic Church.*[82]

From this assertion, says Ritschl, it was inevitable that the Augustana should be equated with the *doctrina evangelii.*[83]

Ritschl does not accuse Melanchthon of any evil intent in this alteration of the Reformation concept of the church. On the contrary, he considers Melanchthon's action "thoroughly correct and honorable."[84] His action was forced upon him by the turn of events in relations between the Lutherans and the Roman Catholics. The policies of the Roman church and the emperor during the years 1537–1540, if they had succeeded, would have destroyed precisely those emphases which the reformers considered central to their understanding of Christian faith and worship.[85] In the face of such consequences, the self-consciousness of the reformers was heightened, to the point where they had to insist that their insights were both Catholic and unchangeable.[86]

But, even though this alteration of the Reformation insights was unavoidable, it resulted in several perversions of those insights. In the first place, the church now comes to be empirically designated, that is, in the Schmalkaldic congregations (*"Gemeinde-complexen"*). Heretofore the reformers had acknowledged the *concept* of the church as the criterion for designating every em-

---

81 *Ibid.*, pp. 186–187. Ritschl is referring to Melanchthon's letter, "Reasons Why the Princes, Estates, and Imperial Cities Rejected the Synod Called by the Roman Pontiff Paul III, Thereby Publicly Confessing the Pure and Catholic Teaching of the Gospel." Epist. 1543b, *Corpus Reformatorum* III, 316–317, 322.

82 *Ibid.*, p. 187.

83 *Ibid.*

84 *Ibid.*, p. 198.

85 *Ibid.*, p. 197.

86 *Ibid.*, pp. 197–198.

pirical form. Now conditions are just reversed.[87] Secondly, the concept of *pura evangelii doctrina* undergoes a decisive alteration. *Materially*, the content and definition of the term is altered. The emphasis is now on the *doctrina*, rather than on the *evangelium*. The term no longer refers to the reality of the *sola gratia*, but rather to all of the articles of the Augsburg Confession.[88] *Formally*, the alteration is even greater, and even more serious, because the Reformation insights are becoming estranged from their previous rooting in a *Lebensfuehrung*. Ritschl writes:

. . . formally, this right understanding which the empirical Church held concerning the Gospel attains a more independent significance than before. In the seventh article of the Augsburg Confession, the pure understanding of the Gospel is brought into consideration only as a means for the inner purposes of the Church, namely, that through the Gospel of God the community of the sanctified is brought into existence. Now [in Melanchthon's letter], however, the pure *teaching* of the Gospel establishes itself as a sufficient criterion for differentiating the empirical Church from the false church, that is to say, pure teaching is turned to an *external* purpose.[89]

In other words, *doctrine* rather than commitment and faith becomes the distinguishing characteristic of the church.

Finally, Melanchthon adds an empirical mark of the church which had not been mentioned in the Augustana, namely, common worship of God.[90] Ritschl sees this as a considerable addition to Luther's simple statement that prayer is a mark of the church. Furthermore, he believes that Melanchthon continued steadfast in this insistence that empirical unity in worship is a mark of the church.[91]

These alterations made a profound impact on the subsequent development of the Lutheran Reformation. Ritschl distinguishes two elements in this development. The first is the trend towards differentiating between Lutherans and Roman Catholics solely on external marks, chiefly on the basis of theological statements, ecclesiastical polity, and ordinances for the conduct of the lives of their adherents.[92] The second important element at work in this later development is the character of Melanchthon and his theological work. Ritschl asserts that Melanchthon was insensitive to the distinction between the rational, polemical theological for-

[87] *Ibid.*, p. 188.
[88] *Ibid.*
[89] *Ibid.*
[90] *Ibid.*, pp. 188–189.
[91] *Ibid.*, p. 189.
[92] *Ibid.*

mulation which was necessary for the Lutheran church in its apologetic tasks in relation to the external world, and the thetic, unifying activity of the church's thought within its own community as it seeks a clearer understanding of the gospel of God's grace.[93] This insensitivity colored all of Melanchthon's work, and it rendered him incapable of doing justice to the positive, edifying aspect of the church's thinking activity within its own community. Ritschl emphasizes the importance of this weakness of Melanchthon's by asking the following questions:

What happens when Melanchthon applies that perspective, which was well suited to represent the external aspect of the Church, as the sufficient criterion for the internal relationships of the Church?— remembering that Melanchthon was unclear in his understanding of his own work, predominantly taken up (because of the course of events) with polemics, and therefore deprived of the possibility of peacefully pursuing dogmatic problems. Is it possible to maintain a correct doctrine of the Church when doctrinal confession, i.e., *pure teaching of the Gospel*, which is the criterion for differentiating the true Church from the false, replaces the *Gospel of God* and is elevated to an internal criterion and ground for the true Church?[94]

It is not difficult to understand why Ritschl is alarmed by these two elements in the development of the Lutheran Reformation. They were responsible for guiding that development in a direction that was diametrically opposed to Ritschl's own understanding of what the church should be. When the Lutherans accepted external forms as the distinguishing marks of the church, they entered upon a path that led to an ever greater formal similarity to the Catholicism which they were fighting. This is also the Catholicism that Ritschl found to be a perversion of authentic Christianity in his analysis of early Christianity,[95] and also in his investigation of the relation between Medieval and Reformation Christianity.[96] In these studies, he criticized Catholicism's polity, because it emphasized external legal forms so as to undermine the *sola gratia*. He levels the same criticism against the Lutheran tendency to raise up an ecclesiastical authority of doctrine and practice which became, in its formal authority, very like the Roman.[97] In the final analysis, then, Ritschl opposes this ecclesiological development in Lutheranism because it undermines a soteriological concern which he considers to be crucial.

93 *Ibid.*, pp. 189–190.
94 *Ibid.*, p. 190.
95 *Supra*, pp. 40–42.
96 *Supra*, pp. 49–60.
97 Ritschl, *Aufsaetze*, p. 196.

Ritschl opposes Melanchthon's confusion between *doctrina evangelii* and *evangelium* for similar reasons. This confusion continued to assert itself, to the extent that the Word of God came to be equivalent to ecclesiastical tradition. This made a mockery of the *sola scriptura* which the reformers had enunciated.[98] This development culminates in the Formula of Concord, where Melanchthon's attitude is accepted without reservation, in Ritschl's opinion.[99] Ritschl considers the same tendency to be at work when Flacius proclaims Luther as the "third Elijah," and when Luther's word, too, is accepted in some quarters as equivalent to the gospel itself.[100]

Ritschl summarizes the nature of this development in a term that is his most thoroughly pejorative epithet, *Schulmaessigkeit*, of "school-like character."[101] Ritschl opposes this phenomenon, because it is diametrically opposed to his understanding of the Christian faith as entailing, most profoundly, a *Lebensfuehrung*. He makes this clear in the following discussion of Melanchthon's "error."

Since the characteristics of scholastically "correct" concepts are employed more easily than others for distinguishing between the true Church and the false, Melanchthon thought that they should be the decisive characteristics, as well as the essential ground, of the internal substance and order of the true Church. But even if scholastically shaped doctrine can serve to present the Church's beliefs externally, there is no reason to believe that the Church in and of itself is a kind of school.[102]

The residue of the original reformation concept of the church militated against this *Schulmaessigkeit*, but Melanchthon stifled the force of this residual consciousness. His *Wittenberger Reformation*, written 1545, seems to confirm this judgment, according to Ritschl. Of it, he writes:

This much is clear, that in this document [the *Wittenberger Reformation*], the center of the Church's selfconsciousness resides in the

---

98 *Ibid.*, p. 207.
99 *Ibid.*, p. 208.
100 *Ibid.*, pp. 209–212.
101 This term remains untranslated throughout this study, because of the rich connotations included in the German usage. The root-word, *Schule*, signifies both "school" and "party." Thus, *Schulmaessigkeit* refers both to the intellectualism of the former and to the sectarian tendency of the latter. To translate the term as "scholasticism" would indicate the intellectual tendency, but not the sectarian.
102 *Ibid.*, p. 201.

Church's confessional statements and not in God's Gospel. This fact parallels the assertion that the Church is really a kind of school.[103]

When a theological document is equated with the gospel of God's grace, then the church has become a school. When the Lutheran church is distinguishable from the "false church" chiefly by its theological statements, then the two groups are not different churches, but rather different schools or parties, similar to the Medieval schools. This, says Ritschl, marks the real beginning of the *Lutheran* church, and this is the root of its error and perversion.[104] Its existence is itself a contradiction, because it makes the claim to be *the* Catholic church, but its comportment is apppropriate only to a school.[105]

This foregoing analysis accounts for the emergence of the Lutheran church from Luther's Reformation. Ritschl concludes that its founder is Melanchthon, even though he was later discredited on the grounds of deviation from the very *pura doctrina evangelii* that he had elevated to highest ecclesiastical authority as the chief mark of the church itself.[106] Ritschl even suggests that Melanchthon later reversed his position on the indispensability and unalterability of this *doctrina*; but, by the time he made this reversal, he had already fallen victim to his own earlier views.[107]

CONTINUING REFORMATION—A CRITIQUE AND A PROGRAM

We turn our attention to the theme of continuing Reformation in Ritschl's historical-theological work. The theme is crucial for Ritschl's theology. This notion of continuing Reformation constitutes the goal towards which all of Ritschl's historical investigation ultimately tended. It constitutes his effort to bring up-to-date the historical continuity as imperative and participation in it as indicative. As I argued in the Introduction,[108] this participation in the continuity as imperative was characterized by the activity of clarifying a category which could bear this continuity and give it expression, as well as the demonstration that this continuity does in fact exist, together with the elaboration of its content and meaning. This work is preparatory (at least it is preparatory if the theologian possesses a propensity for systematic thinking; and Ritschl did exhibit such a propensity) to the work which characterizes participation in the continuity as indicative, namely the

103 *Ibid.*, p. 202.
104 *Ibid.*
105 *Ibid.*, pp. 202–203.
106 *Ibid.*, pp. 214–216.
107 *Ibid.* pp. 216–217.
108 *Supra*, pp. 9–10.

positive expounding of the content and meaning of the continuity. The imperative in this instance tends to involve the theologian in *polemic*, whereas the indicative involves him in *proclamation*. The two are never wholly separated in any single work of Ritschl's, but one can be said to predominate over the other in various ways. In his notion of continuing Reformation, Ritschl summarizes the force of his polemical activity, and, in its historical dimension, at least, brings it to something of a conclusion. At the same time, he illumines the ongoing significance and intention of this continuity so as to set the stage for the proclamatory activity which characterizes his full participation in the continuity as indicative. This is not to suggest that Ritschl could not engage in the proclamatory activity until the polemical work had been brought to a conclusion. Indeed, he engaged in this positive activity long before his final polemical historical work was finished—if indeed, it was ever finished. The polemic is preparatory to the proclamation, *not* from an existential point of view, but rather from logical and systematic considerations. The same preoccupation with a certain historical continuity informs both activities. It remains central. In his systematic and scholarly thoroughness, Ritschl understood that he was called upon to enter into several types of activity in behalf of this continuity—exposition, legitimation, documentation, and defense. As he speaks of the continuing Reformation theology, all of these activities are brought together in an unusual manner.

Ritschl's notion of continuing Reformation includes both a critique and a program. On the basis of what he considers to be the essence of Reformation and apostolic Christianity—its understanding of the God-man relationship which emerges from reconciliation—Ritschl exercises a vigorous theological critique of the reformers. But the purpose of this critique is always to carry forward the reformers' own intention. And Ritschl devoted fully as much attention to the elaboration of this ongoing expression of Reformation Christianity as he did to the documentation of his critique. Ritschl identifies this attempt to carry forward the intention of the Reformation with his own theological purpose. His own theological achievement can, with some justification, be called an attempt at continuing Reformation. By this I mean that it is in the indicatives and imperatives contained in apostolic and Reformation Christianity that Ritschl finds the substance and strategy of his own theological career. Inasmuch as this is the case, it is in a discussion of "continuing" Reformation that we should see most clearly that Ritschl's own constructive theological work is shaped by his historical judgments and commitments.

There are three aspects to Ritschl's critique of the reformers, each of which leads to a program that Ritschl actually attempted to carry out. These three aspects are the historical, the systematic theological, and the religious. The historical aspect is one which we have already discussed; indeed, the larger part of this study is an elaboration of this historical critique and program. Ritschl charges that the reformers did not take full advantage of the possibilities for demonstrating that Reformation Christianity (specifically the doctrine of justification) was Catholic and in continuity with early Christianity, and that the Roman position was in fact an innovation. They failed to seize this opportunity largely because they were ignorant of the historical materials, or else because they were strangely unwilling to utilize them.[109] Most glaring of all is the reformers' failure to push strongly enough the foundation of their position which lay in the ecumenical dogmas of the Incarnation and the Trinity. These dogmas not only would have served as a basis for demonstrating the catholicity of the reformers, but would also have identified them indissolubly with the Holy Roman Empire. The following quotation illumines Ritschl's expectations of what the reformers could have accomplished if they had paid proper attention to pursuing their historical advantage.

The Protestants could demonstrate the claim that their church was the catholic Church only in a rather imprecise fashion. In our historical hindsight, it is clear that the Lutheran doctrine of justification is the formula for a line of thinking that is evident from the beginning in the western church as a corrective to opposing dogma. Further, it can be established that the chief institutions of the Roman church are innovation, compared with the ancient Church. Insofar as the Protestants established the validity of such criteria, they could in many instances designate their own "innovations" as the ancient substance.[110]

If it succeeds in demonstrating nothing else, this study should have made clear how much effort Ritschl devoted to the historical program that grew out of this critique of the reformers. That which, in his opinion, the reformers failed to do, he assumed as his theological and scholarly obligation to perform.[111] He devoted at least three major works (R.u.V. I, II, and Entstehung), composed during a period of twenty-five years, to filling this lacuna in the Protestant argument.

From considerations of systematic theology, Ritschl criticizes the reformers for systematic and scientific inadequacies. They did

109 Ritschl, "Die Entstehung der lutherischen Kirche," in Aufsaetze, pp. 191–192.
110 Ibid.
111 Supra, pp. 30–31.

not adequately elaborate the systematic whole with in which their practical religious insights belonged.[112] As a result they fell into unfortunate self-contradiction and ambiguity. In the *Geschichte des Pietismus*, Ritschl levels his criticism particularly at Melanchthon and his followers. He accuses them of a "defective scholarly disposition" (*"mangelhafte wissenschaftliche Disposition"*), which fails to relate religious insights systematically with the world, God, and man, so as to exhibit their fullness in a consistent manner.[113]

This "defective scholarly disposition" results in a rather considerable confusion, particularly in respect to the understanding of justification and regeneration. First of all, it led to the failure on the part of the reformers and their successors to grasp the real relationship between the Reformation and Roman Catholic doctrines of justification. The systematic defects of their theological exposition caused the reformers to overlook the significance of the fact that the Romans equated justification and regeneration, in contrast to the reformers themselves, who placed regeneration within the system as a response to justification.[114] The result is that the Reformation theological system must put into two or three doctrines what the Romans put into one. Not understanding this adequately, the reformers and their successors allowed themselves to fall into the "absurd" (*widersinnig*) situation in which their doctrine of justification was compared directly with its Roman counterpart, as if the two were univocal in meaning.[115]

Furthermore, their systematic confusion made it impossible for the proponents of Reformation Christianity to express clearly the grounds for the difference between their doctrine of justification and that of the Romans. Once they had been forced into the same plane of argumentation with the Romans, the Reformation theologians tried to validate their case on the same grounds as their opponents. This led to nothing short of perversion.[116] The Lutheran theologians failed to make it clear that their distinctive approach to justification was necessitated by religious realities,[117] rather than by the requirements of objective doctrinal formulations.[118] Ritschl summarizes the significance of this theological failure thus:

---

112 Ritschl, *R.u.V. I*, pp. 127–128.
113 Ritschl, *Pietismus, I*, p. 86.
114 Ritschl, *R.u.V. I*, pp. 127–129. See *Supra*, pp. 56 ff. for a full discussion of this issue.
115 *Ibid.*
116 *Ibid.*, pp. 129–130.
117 *Supra*, pp. 56 ff.
118 Ritschl, *R.u.V. I*, p. 130 f.

As the scholastic tradition raised itself to a dominant position in the Lutheran church, the doctrine of justification by faith, imperfectly shaped as it was, became unintelligible to the masses. This unintelligibility grew out of the practice of treating the doctrine as if it were primarily an objective doctrine, thereby its religious meaning dependent upon the acknowledgment of the objective formula.[119]

This means, in other words, that their systematic inadequacy led the reformers to isolate their insights from the realm of *Lebensfuehrung*—a betrayal of their own understanding of Christianity, as well as a deviation from what Ritschl considers to be central to the Christian faith.

This failure to elaborate their religious insights with systematic adequacy led also to unfortunate consequences in regard to the reformers' doctrine of regeneration. Luther, Melanchthon, and Zwingli, all come in for particular mention at this point in Ritschl's criticism. The gist of Ritschl's argument is as follows: By conforming to the Roman theological scheme, the reformers tried to make their doctrine of justification fit into a precise pigeon-hole in which it dealt chiefly with the easing of the believer's conscience by the communication of God's grace.[120] The doctrine was thus separated almost entirely from regeneration, which is dealt with primarily in terms of the gift of the Holy Spirit as enabling good works.[121] Both justification and regeneration are required by man's religious consciousness, so that his need for grace and God's demand for good works are both satisfied. However, Ritschl asserts, the fullness of the reformers' thought is not expressed when the two notions are wrenched apart into two isolated doctrines.[122] He writes:

The doctrine [of justification] which Luther and Melanchthon hold remains imperfect so long as the movement of these two related notions [justification and regeneration] is not united in one idea. Furthermore, a separation of the two notions takes away the full cogency of the concept of justification, namely, that it is calculated precisely to illumine the basis upon which the power to do meritorious works rests, the basis on which the needs of man as well as the demand of the divine law for man are satisfied.[123]

Ritschl's concern, then, is that the fullness and systematic unity of the chief elements of Reformation Christianity were never

119 *Ibid.*, p. 128.
120 *Ibid.*, pp. 177–178.
121 *Ibid.*
122 *Supra*, pp. 54 ff.
123 *Ibid.*, p. 178. For comments on Zwingli, see pp. 178–179.

adequately expressed by the reformers and their orthodox followers, nor were they brought to bear on the theological problems of
the time. The inadequacies of conception and formulation were
most immediately apparent in the doctrines of justification and
regeneration, but they affected other important elements of the
Reformation position as well. What Ritschl's criticism here amounts
to is ultimately the rejection of an inadequate soteriology that
engendered an inadequate ecclesiology.

As to soteriology, Ritschl contends that the confusion concerning the doctrines of justification and regeneration brought uncertainty to the understanding of just how Christ's saving work is
appropriated by the believer and at what point the believer is
declared righteous. The reformers and their orthodox followers
believed on the one hand that justification *precedes* the bestowal
of the spirit, and on the other hand that the faith which justification entails requires the *prior* possession of the Holy Spirit.[124]

The self-contradiction here is obvious. It should be noted that
the issue, as Ritschl sees it, is essentially that of the relation or
equilibrium of divine and human factors in the God-man relationship. Ritschl charges that the reformers, and more particularly
their orthodox followers were imprecise in expressing this relationship, with the result that on the one hand the divine action preceded
the human, while on the other hand the human action was presupposed in order that the divine might be efficacious.[125] Ritschl
considers that this dilemma in the Reformation formulation of its
position was never adequately dealt with. The result is an utter
perversion at the level of the relationship between law and gospel.
The question here is whether man must possess some rudiment
of faith *already* under the law, if that law is to bring him to the
gospel. Ritschl contends that the reformers chose to ignore this
rudimentary faith, restricting the discussion of faith to the full
justifying faith (*fides justificans*), in order to accommodate their
doctrine to the unlearned masses who could not understand the
complexities of this matter.[126] The consequence is that the masses
were exhorted to obey the law, God's command, and to fear God
—all activities under the law—with no attention at all being given
to the explanation of how this obedience was even possible unless
it, too, were conditioned by a measure of faith.[127] Ritschl seems
to believe that this state of affairs was initiated by Melanchthon
and agreed to by Luther simply because the latter reacted against
John Agricola's extreme criticism of Melanchthon (Agricola main-

[124] *Ibid.*, pp. 185–186.
[125] *Ibid.*
[126] *Ibid.*, pp. 188–189.
[127] *Ibid.*, p. 190.

tained that the law was superfluous).[128] Ritschl deplores the effects
of this perversion upon the masses; it led them either to a denial
of the law's efficacy, or to hypocritical acts of false penitence.[129]

It is unfortunate, in Ritschl's opinion, "that Luther entangled
himself even more firmly in a schema which deduced conversion
from law and gospel," because it seriously impaired the Reformation understanding of the church. The law does not work upon man
in splendid isolation from all previous conditioning of faith, as if
he could come to repentance as a solitary individual. Rather, the
word of God comes to man through the *ministerium verbi* which
is the instrumentality of the church, the community of believers
which is its ground.[130] The dilemma posed by rudimentary and
justifying faith can be resolved only by an adequate concept of
the church. The door was opened for an unevangelical understanding when the reformers began to look upon their congregations as
individuals who needed to be made the object of the word of God,
rather than the community which is the ground of the ministry
of that word.[131] Furthermore, such a depreciation of the role of
the church is a betrayal of the real intention of the reformers.[132]
Ritschl took these systematic theological inadequacies as direct
imperatives for his own work. He criticized the reformers for failing to give adequate systematic and scientific expression to their
practical religious insights. In his own work, he never tired of
emphasizing the precise systematic and scientific method which
he had evolved to express what he considered to be the essence
of the Christian religion. I cannot document this in detail here.
I shall, however, indicate certain pertinent lines of argument,
which the informed reader can immediately place in context so
as to test the validity of my thesis.

In the third volume of *Rechtfertigung und Versoehnung*, Ritschl
makes clear what he understands by "scientific" theology. His train
of reasoning proceeds along these lines:[133] Theology has the task
of describing the action of God in the life of the Christian believer
as he lives in the Holy Spirit;[134] this description must be taken
from the self-consciousness of the believer as it is caught up in

128 *Ibid.*
129 *Ibid.*
130 *Ibid.*, pp. 190–191. See also pp. 176–177.
131 *Ibid.*, p. 190.
132 *Ibid.*, pp. 176–178. See *supra*, pp. 55–56.
133 This discussion is to be found in the Introduction to Ritschl, *R.u.V. III,*
(4th ed., 1910). See also Hefner, *Lutheran Quarterly,* 13:108–109, 1961. Also
Dan L. Deegan, "Albrecht Ritschl as Critical Empiricist," *Journal of Religion,*
(2) 44: 149–160, 1964.
134 At a later point, I will make clear that this life takes place in the community of believers, in the church.

the twofold activity (religious and moral) which takes place in the Holy Spirit; these moral and religious acts and the self-consciousness which accompanies them are not to be equated with the action of God, but they are the inseparable correlates which always accompany that divine action; this relationship is analogous to the relationship that psychology has established between the sensations of noise in the ear and the vibrations in the air which give rise to that noise (the sensations of noise are not to be equated with the vibrations, and the form of each is quite different; but the sensations are inseparable from the vibrations, and they constitute the only means of knowledge that the average man can gain of those vibrations). From this train of reasoning, Ritschl summarizes the definition of scientific theology:

From this principle of psychology there arises the task of scientific theology, to refer all that is recognizable as the gracious action of God upon the Christian to the appropriate religious and moral acts that are stimulated through revelation as a whole and through the particular means that are included in that revelation.[135]

Whether or not Ritschl really achieved this scientific presentation of Christian theology is a question that can hardly be settled decisively to every critic's satisfaction. That this was his intention and that he exerted a great deal of disciplined effort to achieve it can hardly be denied by anyone who has worked through his closely reasoned three volumes on justification and reconciliation. The organization of the third volume itself illustrates the consistency of his endeavor. He works through four general categories —definitions, presuppositions, demonstrations, and religious-moral consequences—all with the purpose of describing the reconciling action of God from the perspective of the religious and moral self-consciousness of the Christian believer.[136]

The foregoing has described Ritschl's understanding of the scientific method appropriate to systematic theology. The systematic character of theology is constituted by the manner in which the material produced by the scientific method is arranged. Ritschl considers this arrangement to be crucial for systematic theology. The arrangement follows from one's understanding of the Christian religion.[137] Ritschl's understanding of Christianity involves his famous ellipse of the religious and the moral; it proceeds from the God-man relation of reconciliation in which the divine (religious) and human (moral) factors are held in a certain equili-

---

135 Ritschl, *R.u.V. III*, p. 22.
136 *Ibid.*, pp. v–viii.
137 *Ibid.*, pp. 8 f.

brium.[138] From this understanding follows the system of theology. Ritschl defines the Christian religion as follows:

Christianity is the monotheistic perfectly spiritual and moral religion, which, on the basis of its Founder's lifework of redemption and the establishing of the Kingdom of God, consists in the freedom of divine sonship, includes within itself the impulse toward the activity of love (which is directed toward the ethical organization of mankind), and grounds blessedness in sonship as well as in the Kingdom of God.[139]

From this elliptical view, the following systematic considerations follow (this quotation follows immediately after the definition of Christianity just cited):

This concept [of Christianity] is necessary for systematic theology, so that the material that has been correctly lifted from biblical conceptions can be used properly. The history of theology reveals only too many of examples of men who brought forth either only a doctrine of redemption or only a doctrine of morals. We must also observe that it is incorrect to say that dogmatics is grounded in the idea of redemption, whereas ethics is grounded in the idea of the Kingdom of God; rather, insofar as systematic theology participates in both of these disciplines, both ethics and dogmatics stand under the constitutive influence of both of those fundamental ideas. That is to say, dogmatics conceives of all of aspects of Christianity within the framework of God's action; ethics, presupposing the cognition of dogmatics, conceives of the realm of personal and corporate Christian life within the framework of the personal action of the self. Therefore, even as the revelation of God is oriented not only towards the intention to redeem men, but also towards the goal of the Kingdom of God, so also dogmatics cannot avoid this same orientation. Similarly, just as the spiritual activity of the self who has been called into God's Kingdom and redeemed is not limited simply to his ethical deeds for others, but in the distinctive functions of divine sonship, so also ethics is conditioned also by the idea of redemption.[140]

One could summarize this lengthy documentation by saying that, for Ritschl, a scientific and systematic theology was one which proceeded consistently and completely from that which is central to the Christian faith. Ritschl understood the God-man relation which emerged from reconciliation to be this center, and he made it central to his own work.[141] Because Ritschl saw this center in a God-man relation in which there were two factors, one

138 *Ibid.*, p. 1.
139 *Ibid.*, pp. 13–14.
140 *Ibid.*, p. 14.
141 *Ibid.*, p. 1. See also *supra*, p. 29.

of which corresponded to justification (the religious or divine) and the other to regeneration (the moral or human); and inasmuch as he insisted on a reciprocity between the two,[142] at least for the purposes of systematic theological methodology; therefore, he built into his very method a concern for both justification and regeneration which would seem to be able to obviate the incompleteness which he found in the reformers at this point. His definition of scientific theology also includes this safeguard.[143]

Furthermore, by interrelating the religious and the moral (justification and regeneration) so intimately as one total human response to one engendering act of God,[144] Ritschl seems to be laying the groundwork for a formulation of soteriology which obviates precisely the criticisms which he had leveled at the reformers.

I have left one affirmation unmentioned which Ritschl emphasized vigorously as a presupposition for scientific and systematic theology as he understood it. This presupposition has to do with Ritschl's conviction that the material of systematic theology is *the consciousness of the church.*[145] Theology has to describe the gracious action of God as it is mirrored in the religious-moral consciousness of the Christian believer, but that believer exists only in the community which has been founded by Christ and which accepts him as the forgiver of its sins.[146] Ritschl summarizes this opinion in emphatic tones:

Only as one consciously and purposely places himself in the community that Christ founded can he perceive and understand the Christian meaning of God, sin, conversion, and eternal life. Theology must assume this standpoint; only so can it succeed in elaborating a system of theology deserving of the name.[147]

Thus, once again, whether he has been successful or not in his achievement, it is clear that Ritschl has shaped his theological work in such a way as to avoid precisely the weaknesses which he saw in Reformation formulations. He harbors the hope not only that he can fill the lacunae of the Reformation theologies, but that he can also present a formulation which will oppose the Roman Catholics as well as the Pietists and the "exclusivistic" or "confessional" Lutherans.

There remains a third set of considerations, on the basis of

---

142 *Supra,* note 140, p. 78.
143 *Supra,* note 135, p. 77.
144 *Supra,* note 135, p. 77; note 140, p. 78.
145 Ritschl, *R.u.V. III,* p. 3.
146 *Ibid.,* p. 2.
147 *Ibid.,* p. 4. See also Dan L. Deegan, "Albrecht Ritschl as Critical Empiricist," *The Journal of Religion,* (2) 44:149–160, 1964.

which Ritschl leveled criticism at the reformers. These are religious considerations. The gist of Ritschl's concern here is that the reformers allowed the pressure towards *Schulmaessigkeit* to draw them away from the genius of Reformation (and apostolic) Christianity, to which the implications of *sola fide* lead directly, namely, of Christianity as *Lebensideal* or *Lebensfuehrung*. This criticism is directly related to what Ritschl considered to be the perversion of Lutheranism, so this discussion is an elaboration upon the analysis documented above.[148] There, in the context of his interpretation of the historical development from Luther to the Lutheran church, we considered the historical essay, *"Die Entstehung der lutherischen Kirche."* Here, we turn attention to the argument of *Geschichte des Pietismus*, where Ritschl is chiefly concerned to illumine the essence of Reformation Christianity in distinction from Roman Catholicism and Pietism; consequently, this argument is less historical and somewhat more systematic than the argument of the earlier essay.

Ritschl is obviously concerned with what he considers to be Protestantism's (that is to say, Lutheranism's and Calvinism's) self-contradictory existence, in which it claims to be *the* Catholic church but behaves as one party or school within the church. He considers this to constitute an occasion for the need of continuing reform;[149] indeed, it was this perversion which provided the immediate stimulus for the rise of Pietism within the Lutheran church.[150] This *Schulmaessigkeit* is a direct holdover from the Medieval heritage, in which differing interests within the church did often identify themselves as schools within the one church, presenting their insights in the form of theological propositions, and resolving disagreements through theological discussion.[151] The Lutherans and Calvinists behave (not only in regard to each other, but even more within themselves) as ecclesiastical parties in their waging of sharp polemical discussion with the concomitant emphasis on *reine Lehre, pura doctrina,* and (in the case of the former group) on the Confessio Augustana as the *doctrina evangelii.*[152] Ritschl even undertakes a bit of psychological analysis and lays this *Schulmaessigkeit* to the fact that "The men who lived during the century of the Reformation were burdened with a peculiarly limited spiritual disposition."[153] By this, he means their "lack of acquaintance with feeling (*Gefuehl*) in general and its

[148] *Supra*, pp. 69 ff.
[149] Ritschl, *Pietismus*, I, p. 81.
[150] *Ibid.*
[151] *Ibid.*, pp. 83–84.
[152] *Ibid.*
[153] *Ibid.*, p. 92.

demands and interrelations within the spiritual life."[154] This narrowness of disposition made it impossible for Reformation theologians to rise above and reject the tendencies towards *Schulmaessigkeit*.

This narrowness of spirit rendered these theologians apparently incapable of understanding that the differences which separated the Romans (and the Pietists) from Reformation Christianity were *not* preeminently matters of theology, but rather matters of *Lebensidealen*; the two groups opposed each other with total perspectives of Christian piety and existence, total Weltanschauungen.[155]

This *Schulmaessigkeit*, which alienated Reformation Christianity from its true base in *Lebensideal* or *Lebensfuehrung*, tended to vitiate the presentation of the Reformation case. Ritschl considers it to be one of the chief causes for the systematic inadequacies of the Reformation theologians.[156] These theologians were separated from the total perspective (*Totalanschauung*) or *Lebensideal* which really lay at the base of their position, and as a result, in typical school fashion, they argued on isolated points, rather than elaborating the systematic whole which proceeded from their *Lebensideal*.[157] This describes exactly the weakness into which Luther, Melanchthon, and Zwingli fell when elaborating their understanding of justification.[158]

The greatest blow of all, however, is the dissolution and misunderstanding to which the Reformation's total perspective was subjected by this rising *Schulmaessigkeit*, which was engendering its own "Christianity of reason" (*Verstandeschristenthum*).[159] Soteriologically, this meant that the perversions of Catholicism were reintroduced, inasmuch as a new legalistic *fides implicita* was set up to replace the Catholic counterpart. This new *fides implicita* was marked by the confidence in pure doctrine. It became no longer necessary to believe that God's reconciling action was indeed directed to one's own personal redemption; rather, it was enough to hold to the doctrine of this grace.[160] Ritschl summarizes the tendency as a proud feeling of possession, in which one holds fast to pure doctrine.[161]

Ecclesiologically, there was also a regression to Catholic per-

---

[154] *Ibid.*
[155] *Ibid.*, pp. 83–84.
[156] *Supra*, pp. 71–77.
[157] Ritschl, *Pietismus, I*, pp. 85.
[158] *Supra*, p. 74.
[159] Ritschl, *Pietismus, I*, pp. 92 ff.
[160] *Ibid.*, pp. 91–92. See also Ritschl's monograph, *Fides Implicita: Eine Untersuchung ueber Koehlerglauben. Wissen und Glauben, Glauben und Kirche* (Bonn: Adolph Marcus, 1890), esp. pp. 68 ff.
[161] *Ibid.*, p. 93.

versions. The symbol of this regression, in Ritschl's opinion, was the Lutheran confessional, which he considered to be only a modification of the Roman sacrament of penance, which in turn was merely an attempt to press the legalistic claims of the moral and religious authoritarianism of the church.[162] The consequence was a depreciation of the quality of religious life and an emphasis on the legal adherence to the authority of the church which could render men meritorious before God.[163]

This perversion occasioned by *Schulmaessigkeit* Ritschl calls "the rationalistic reductionism of Protestantism" (*die verstandes-maessige Einschraenkung des Protestantismus*).[164] This may be the greatest perversion of all, in his mind. Of this phenomenon, more than any other, he says repeatedly that it puts the Reformation church in need of continuing Reformation.[165]

Ritschl is not wholly unappreciative of the men who were responsible for this perversion of *Schulmaessigkeit*. Indeed, he believes that what they did was inevitable in its time. It served the purpose in the sixteenth century of preserving the Reformation insights against total eradication by the action of the Roman church.[166] Here Ritschl develops his theory as to the limitations of this usefulness. He likens the forms of this *Schulmaessigkeit* to *Keimblaettchen,* to the protective leaves of a young plant which are soon outgrown and discarded.[167] According to Ritschl's theory or organic cultural development, such reactionary forms are always needed to ease the transition between epochs.[168] The unfortunate thing, however, is the inability to recognize the transience of these forms, and the efforts to push for their maintenance when they are in fact outmoded.[169] The rise of these forms under Luther and Melanchthon was due to the necessity of circumstances; their maintenance, however, reflects a profound misunderstanding of the God-man relation, of the proper relationship of the religious and the moral, justification, and regeneration.

Once again, as in the case of his historical and systematic theological criticisms, Ritschl accepted the unfortunate religious tendencies of the reformers and their followers as imperatives for his own theological work. In the first place, he sought to eschew any "party" label or activity. Although he was apparently concerned to establish a Ritschlian "school,"[170] an enterprise in which he was

162 *Ibid.,* p. 95.
163 *Ibid.*
164 *Ibid.,* p. 93.
165 *Ibid.,* pp. 92, 95, 96.
166 *Ibid.,* pp. 93 ff.
167 *Ibid.,* p. 94.
168 *Ibid.,* pp. 94–95.
169 *Ibid.,* pp. 95–96.
170 See the comments by Wilhelm Hermann in *Festgabe . . . fuer Harnack* (Tuebingen: J. C. B. Mohr, 1921), pp. 405–406. But see Karl Heussi's objec-

quite successful, he had no intention that his work should portray a version of Christianity whose application extended no further than the academic environment in which he waged his battles. As he writes in the preface to the first edition of the third volume of *Rechtfertigung und Versoehnung*:

My pathway and goal have been pointed out for me in what I have presented as the biblical material of the doctrine [of justification and reconciliation] in the second volume. Beyond that, however, I meant to make it clear enough in the first volume that my theology can find no place in the work of theological "parties" that have been commonly recognized up to this time.[171]

The practical success of Ritschl's attempt to avoid the party-spirit of his day is attested to by a contemporary historian, who writes, ". . . he took much of the wind from the sails of the mediationist school and the right wing; the mediationists, in fact, largely abdicated to him."[172]

In both his historical and constructive work, Ritschl expends much effort to emphasize that Christianity represents above all a *Lebensfuehrung*. This study has indicated that at every important juncture in his historical investigations, Ritschl criticized efforts to remove the Christian faith from the practical realities of life. He distinguishes what he considers to be authentic Christianity from all its deviations—ancient Catholicism, Medieval Catholicism, Lutheranism, and Pietism—on the basis of its distinctive *Lebensfuehrung*. Indeed, it is clear that this understanding of Christianity as *Lebensfuehrung* is the category by means of which Ritschl locates and elaborates the historical continuity with which he is preoccupied. In his systematic work, also, Ritschl attempts to make this notion of Christianity as *Lebensfuehrung* pivotal for theological method. The following passage is worth quoting for the clarity in which it presents this concern of Ritschl's.

. . . it is much more the work [of the theologian] to point to life in the Holy Spirit—that faithful persons perceive the gracious gifts of God (I Cor. 2:12), that they call upon God as their father (Rom. 8:15), that they act in love and joy, in meekness and self-discipline (Gal. 5:22), that they guard themselves most of all against party spirit, but on the contrary practice a feeling for the community (I Cor. 3:1-4). In these affirmations the Holy Spirit is not denied, but

---

tions in *Kompendium der Kirchengeschichte*, 11th ed. (Tuebingen: J. C. B. Mohr, 1957), p. 482.

171 Ritschl, *R.u.V. III*, p. iii.

172 James Hastings Nichols, *History of Christianity, 1650–1950* (New York: Ronald Press, 1956), p. 285.

rather acknowledged and understood. This way of proceeding is not new; on the contrary, Schleiermacher followed it, and the presentation of justification by faith in the Apology to the Augsburg Confession employs this same scheme. This method alone must be followed if Christianity is to be concretely intelligible. Those formulae concerning the individual way of salvation—formulae which are arrived at and actually prescribed by faith—make Christianity unintelligible if their practical interrelations and authentication is not made clear.[173]

Finally, in regard to ecclesiology, I may repeat what I have said in regard to Ritschl's understanding of Christianity as *Lebensfuehrung*, immediately above. It is clear that Ritschl does not acknowledge *pura doctrina* as the chief mark of the church, nor as the chief vehicle of unity or disunity within it. On the contrary, he considers several marks more important, including prayer.[174] The chief mark, however, which distinguishes the church is its participation—first as a corporate entity, secondly as a group of individuals—in the reconciliation wrought by Christ.[175]

It appears legitimate to conclude from this survey of Ritschl's concern for continuing Reformation that what is at stake is the conception and establishment of a certain historical continuity. This is the continuity of Christianity understood as a certain notion of *Lebensfuehrung* (with all that term implies concerning the God-man relation, the equilibrium of divine and human factors within that relation, and the relation between justification and regeneration). In elaborating a notion of continuing Reformation, Ritschl seeks to establish this continuity of Christianity from the apostolic era, through the best Medieval tradition, to the Reformation, and thence to his own theological formulations, in a way that not only secures his own position within that continuity, but that also disqualifies those who oppose this thread of the historical movement.

Ritschl's concern for continuing Reformation also clarifies the fact that the continuity with which he is preoccupied is not simply an accumulation of past events, but rather a bearer of qualitative meaning. Ritschl has differentiated several epochs within this past tradition, and, with the help of the category of *Lebensfuehrung*, he has clarified their interrelations so as to give a qualitative content to the tradition in which he participates. In this study, three sets of transition, with their corresponding epochs, have come under discussion. In Chapter I, attention was given to Ritschl's differentiation between apostolic and third-century

173 Ritschl, *R.u.V. III*, pp. 22–23.
174 *Ibid.*, p. 608.
175 *Ibid.*, Sect. 56.

Catholic Christianity, with the transition between them located in the emerging old Catholic church. In this chapter, the discussion has centered on the transition from Medieval Catholicism to the Reformation and from the Reformation to the Lutheran church. In spite of the sheer physical continuity which Ritschl affirms between these epochs, it is clear that the Christianity of the third through the sixteenth centuries, together with the Lutheran orthodox period, are judged negatively in respect to apostolic and Reformation Christianity. This negative evaluation implies no suprahistorical metaphysical category of a "fall" from apostolic or Reformation Christianity, nor does it deny the sound motives and the necessities that prompted the shifts of history; but it does denote a definite turning away or deviation. On the other hand, a new resurgence of the apostolic faith is asserted in the Reformation epoch, as well as in Ritschl's own understanding of the Christian revelation. The picture of the continuous tradition takes on the following configuration: the constitutive and normative revelation of God's reconciling action is located in the initial epoch of Christianity, which is dominated by Jesus Christ and the apostolic testimony to him. Cultural and political pressures rendered succeeding epochs incapable of maintaining this testimony in its clarity and purity; the testimony of these Catholic centuries was not indeed wholly perverse, and the apostolic faith was never absent from it; but, publicly at least, its witness represents a confused understanding of God's reconciling activity on man's behalf. The significance of the Reformation lies in its ability to maintain the physical continuity with its immediate past, holding fast to the community of Medieval Catholicism and laying hold of its minimal witness to the apostolic faith, while at the same time freeing itself from the confusions of this immediate past and laying hold of the witness of its ultimate past, the age of Christ and his apostles. The successors to the reformers found themselves beset by cultural and political pressures which rendered them as inept as the Catholic successors to the apostles in the attempt to preserve an adequate testimony to God's gracious work among men. The Lutherans, therefore, were incapable of laying hold of either their immediate or ultimate past, in spite of their physical continuity with this past and in spite of their honorable intentions.

Ritschl's own continuing Reformation finds its task to be the same as Luther's, namely, that of retaining its continuity with the historical community and its intentions, while at the same time setting aside the perversions of its Lutheran-Pietist representatives and laying hold of the ultimate past which stands as judge and inspiration to every epoch of the Christian tradition. Attention has been called above to Ritschl's two-pronged approach to the historical continuity of the Christian tradition.[176] The significance of this approach can now be seen more clearly. By his affirmation of the sheer physical continuity of the successive epochs of Christian history—rooted in the physical unity of the historical continuum—he affirms his unity with the community which is concerned in one way or another to preserve the authentic testimony to God's gracious action for man. But by the application of his category of historical judgment—the *Lebensfuehrung*—he is able to assert that this tradition and its continuity is more than the simple accumulation of years and events. Rather, it is a continuity of man's encounter with and report concerning God's revelation; moreover, the report which is engendered by the encounter of certain epochs is qualitatively more significant than the testimony of other epochs. Those epochs which have articulated a witness which is most faithful to the action of God as proclaimed in the initial events of the Christian tradition—in the apostolic era—play a normative role in themselves, a guide to later generations encountering the same divine revelation. In their impact on later generations, these epochs overshadow those whose witness is less adequate, even though they never displace those lesser epochs completely.

In the light of these considerations it becomes clear that although Ritschl takes great pains to establish the physical continuity and identity of the various epochs which constitute the history of the Christian community, he is much more concerned to draw attention to what he considers to be the tradition of Christ, Paul, Luther, and Albrecht Ritschl. This is the background against which Ritschl's commitment to the Reformation takes on its real significance.[177] "Back to the Bible through the Reformation" expresses an authentic Ritschlian concern, not because Bible and Reformation are ends in themselves,[178] but rather because they represent epochs whose witness to God's revelation judges and inspires the faith and theology of all epochs and of all men within that tradition. The position set forth in this study holds that this oft-quoted aphorism represents Ritschl's concern for and evaluation of the historical continuity in which he participated and which shaped his work.

The notion of continuing Reformation has also dealt persistently

---

[176] *Supra*, p. 49.

[177] *Supra*, pp. 30–32, where Baur's position is contrasted to Ritschl's. The differences in Baur's axiological category (that is, *Geist*) made it possible for him to approach each epoch of the tradition more positively than Ritschl could.

[178] So, Ritschl (in *R.u.V. II*, pp. 13 ff.) asserts the primacy of the biblical witness, not on the basis of a theory of inspiration, but rather on the grounds that it represents the *initial*, or original, epoch in the Christian religion.

with soteriology and ecclesiology. Ritschl's soteriological concern has been to establish an understanding of Christian faith as a certain *Lebensfuehrung* over an understanding of intellectualistic *Verstandeschristenthum.* Parallel to this distinction, he has attempted to assert the preeminence of the divine reconciling action over the full moral response it engenders, against those who insist that this moral activity has some legal claim in itself upon God's grace. Once again, parallel to these distinctions, he has emphasized a notion of *gratia justificans* over a notion of *gratia cooperans.*

Ritschl's ecclesiological concern has been to undermine a position which is perversely individualistic, and which therefore cannot account for man's coming to faith and his possession of the Holy Spirit. Conversely, he seeks to establish an understanding of the church as the ground of the ministry of the word, which is its instrumentality for opening the possibility of grace, justification, to those in its midst. Concomitant to this concern has been the attempt to establish the preeminence of the concept of the church as the communion of saints, distinguished by its participation in God's reconciling act in Christ, over an understanding which gives priority to the church as an empirical, legal entity, and which assumes that its legal forms can somehow domesticate the gracious action of God.

More important for this study, however, is the fact that this critique and call for a continuing Reformation constitute a precise program which Ritschl adopted so meticulously in his own theological work. This underlines the fact that his constructive work does not find its elaboration except in the framework of historical judgments and commitments; indeed, it is shaped by them. There is no reason why Ritschl could not have cultivated the theological insights which he considered to be the continuation of the Reformation and simply elaborated them constructively quite apart from any historical investigations and demonstrations. The fact is that he devoted most of the years of his life, and many volumes, to the historical study which served to clarify his knowledge of these insights, justify them, and emphasize their significance. It is for this reason that in this concern for continuing Reformation, our thesis attains its clearest statement, namely, that his preoccupation with historical continuity shapes Ritschl's theological achievement. The next chapter turns to an assessment of the significance of Ritschl's preoccupation with this historical continuity.[179]

179 Even though I have referred to Ritschl's polemic against Pietism and confessional Lutheranism, I have not discussed it in detail. Such discussions are omitted because they would introduce no factors in Ritschl's argument which have not already been discussed. Ritschl attacks the Pietists on the grounds that they embrace a Medieval Catholic *Lebensfuehrung.* The confessionalists come under censure for dogmatic rationalism.

3

The Shift from History to Systematic Formulation

SUMMARY

THE DISCUSSION in the first two chapters has illumined three judgments in particular concerning Ritschl's theological career. The first of these is that the preoccupation with historical continuity played a considerable role in Ritschl's thought. This is clear from the simple fact that he devoted a great many years and not a few works to the documentation of a certain thread of historical continuity and its significance. The significance of this preoccupation for Ritschl's work will be discussed below.

The second judgment has to do with the substance of this continuity. The thread of historical continuity that Ritschl expended so much effort to document consists of a continuous Christian understanding of the Christian revelation as pertaining to a *Lebensfuehrung* which emerges from participation in a certain relationship with God; in this relationship, God's prevenient reconciling activity in Christ engenders a human moral response rooted in utter confidence in God's gracious providence—even in the midst of this life's greatest woes.

The third and most substantial judgment is that Ritschl's concern with this historical continuity is not one of detachment or complete objectivity. On the contrary, he *participated* in this continuity as a reality in his theological career, and he felt the full force of its impact. He participated in the reality of this continuity as imperative and as indicative. Under the impact of this continuity as imperative, he devoted his energies to the formulation of a category which can serve as the bearer and the expression of that continuity. It has been noted how, from his youthful days, Ritschl employed such a category, steadily growing in his understanding of it and in his ability to articulate it clearly. This category is that of

88

Lebensfuehrung or *Lebensideal,* as described above. Under the force of this continuity as imperative, Ritschl also expended much effort in demonstrating that this historical continuity, conceived in terms of this *Lebensfuehrung,* did in fact exist. We have seen the meticulous care with which he traces the existence of this continuity from the New Testament literature through ancient Catholicism, Medieval Christianity, the Reformation, and post-Reformation developments. This demonstration also involved Ritschl in polemical activity, in which he had to document the deviation of all the manifestations of Christianity other than those which supported his category of *Lebensfuehrung.* We have followed his polemic against ancient Catholicism, much of Medieval Roman Catholicism, and orthodox Lutheranism. Attention has been called also to his polemic against Pietism and nineteenth-century German Lutheran confessionalism.

Ritschl also participated in the reality of this continuity as indicative. Under the impact of the indicative, his thought was informed by the heritage which is borne along by this continuity— informed as to content and strategy. Ritschl incorporated the results of his historical investigations and polemics (activities under the impact of the community as imperative) into his own constructive theological work. He incorporated these results so as to carry on the thrust of the continuity while at the same time avoiding the perversions which the necessity of historical circumstances had from time to time occasioned in the career of this continuity of *Lebensfuehrung.* Thus, the continuity provided content for his theological thought. This participation under the impact of the continuity as indicative impelled Ritschl to follow a strategy in his career which included the historical demonstration of the reality of the continuity, the polemic against all who rejected or misunderstood its heritage, and the positive enunciation of its content to his own age.

All of this, I believe, may fairly and legitimately be concluded from our discussion in the preceding chapters, together with the sketch of the genesis of Ritschl's preoccupations under Ferdinand Christian Baur and the subsequent break with him.

If the foregoing is an accurate assessment of the argument so far, then it may be concluded that Ritschl's theological achievement was indeed shaped by his preoccupation with historical continuity. Another way of expressing this thesis is to say that Ritschl's theological achievement is to be understood in terms of his interpretation of history; or, that his theological work was engendered by his historical judgments and commitments. The activities which have been outlined in Ritschl's career as emerging from his participating in the reality of the historical continuity as imperative and indicative are in a sense activities determined by historical judgments and commitments. Each of these activities is beholden to historical judgments and commitments as a propadeutic for systematic understanding and elaboration, or as a source for the substance of that systematic elaboration, or as an end in itself to serve the purpose of demonstration or polemical defense.

This suggests a comprehensive scheme for interpreting Ritschl's work. The career of his theological work took the shape it did because he understood history as he did, because he was committed to that understanding, and because he accepted the responsibility for the theological activity which commitment to such an understanding of history would impel. This activity consists almost wholly of documentation (including historical investigation and biblical exegesis), defense, and proclamation (or even propagandizing) of a certain historical continuity and its heritage. His understanding of history demanded that this documentation be undertaken; the documentation led naturally to the polemic against hostile groups; and documentation and defense together immediately revealed the lines which systematic elaboration would have to take if Ritschl's understanding of history were to remain a live option in his own day (specifically, if the historical continuity were to be extended to his own age). In terms of his total published output, approximately eighty percent of his effort was expended in documentation and defense with the remaining twenty percent devoted to proclamation. This scheme for interpreting Ritschl's work takes into account more adequately than any other yet presented the structure and sequence of his own theological output, as well as his own statements concerning his task as a theologian of the ongoing Reformation. At this point we turn briefly to a discussion of other schemes which are presented in the secondary literature for the interpretation of Ritschl's theology.

The secondary literature on Ritschl is considerable, but by no means vast. Professor Gøsta Høk's exhaustive bibliography of this literature fills seventeen medium-sized pages.[1] This bibliography includes survey works in which only a few pages are devoted to Ritschl. A count reveals that only one-fourth of the works in Høk's listing appeared after 1900. So far as I have been able to survey this literature, there is no single work on Ritschl which deals with that aspect of the Ritschlian corpus which I have discussed in this dissertation. None of these works, so far as my acquaintance with them reaches, gives more than a passing reference to the role of history in Ritschl's theological work.[2] Rather, the secondary

[1] Gøsta Høk, *Die elliptische Theologie Albrecht Ritschls* (Uppsala: Universitets Arsskrift, 1942), pp. xviii–xxxiv.

[2] I have discovered three exceptions to this rule: André Jundt, *Le role de la métaphysique et de l'histoire dans la dogmatique protestante moderne:*

literature deals exclusively with Ritschl's systematic work: with *Rechtfertigung und Versoehnung*, III; *Theologie und Metaphysik; Die Christliche Vollkommenheit;* and *Unterricht in der christlichen Religion.* This literature approaches Ritschl from the point of view of his philosophical and philosophical-theological antecedents, or from the perspective of a single doctrine or group of doctrines which he discussed. Certain of the works do indeed acknowledge that Ritschl was an historian, and even that historical work was one of his dominant concerns.[3] But they either dismiss this historical work as an episode,[4] or fail to probe into the significance of this historical concern for Ritschl's entire career, particularly for his systematic theological work.

In the light of the character of this secondary literature, it is not particularly relevant or appropriate to argue with the specific interpretation which the critics offer of Ritschl's work; rather, it seems necessary to argue with the approach which they employ and to suggest the relation (and validity) of the approach set forth in this dissertation, over against theirs.

There is one fundamental question that must be put to the researchers who have attempted to interpret Ritschl's work without taking his historical concern and its significance into account: By choosing to ignore a segment of his work which is unquestionably so large and which was evidently so important in his own mind, how can these interpretations presume to provide a *comprehensive* understanding of the man's theological work and career? Although the significance of the various factors which make up Ritschl's work cannot be assessed by merely quantitative considerations, it appears to be unwise to interpret a man's work on the basis of only one-fifth of his published output. Even if the unpublished dogmatic and ethical materials, to which Professor Høk refers, are considered, the prevailing interpretations plainly ignore at least two-thirds of Ritschl's work.

More importantly, these critical interpretations fail to take into

---

Essai sur les principes de l'école Ritschl (Montbéliard: Société anonyme d'imprimerie Montbéliardaise, 1920); Robert Mackintosh, *Albrecht Ritschl and His School* (London: Chapman and Hall, Ltd., 1915); Albert Swing, *The Theology of Albrecht Ritschl* (London and Bombay: Longmans, 1901). But none of these works deals seriously with the significance of history in Ritschl's theology. Jundt describes Ritschl's historical work briefly, but chiefly in respect to the role which the historical Jesus plays in his work (see pp. 44–46). Mackintosh surveys Ritschl's historical output in more detail than any other commentator, but he assesses it as a passing phase of Ritschl's career, rather than as a constitutive element of his theology. Swing considers the historical figures from which Ritschl borrowed important ideas or methods; history is thus only a sort of proof-text for Ritschl's constructive work.

[3] Barth (see Supra, p. 4, note 6) p. 601. H. R. Mackintosh, *Types of Modern Theology* (New York: Scribner, n.d.), p. 139.

[4] Barth, p. 601.

account the explicit interrelation of historical commitments and constructive intention that has been illumined above in connection with the notion of continuing Reformation.[5] Thus, for example, such significant students as Otto Pfleiderer and Gøsta Høk discuss Ritschl's scientific theology solely from the perspective of its philosophical and philosophical-theological implications.[6] But they give no attention whatsoever to the historical judgments and commitments which may very well have impelled Ritschl's initial concern for scientific method in theology.[7] This indifference towards the impact of historical considerations in Ritschl's work becomes even more unsatisfactory when the critics claim to be making analyses of a *genetic* nature. So, Professor Høk (whose work is certainly one of the most responsible and impressive in this area) quite correctly isolates the elliptical concept of the God-man relation, with its distinctive interrelation of divine (religious) and human (ethical) factors, as the central category in Ritschl's theology. But he claims to have elucidated the genesis of this category, and Ritschl's systematic elaboration of it, on philosophical and philosophical-theological grounds alone.[8] Thus, Professor Høk completely overlooks the fact that (as the two previous chapters have indicated) Ritschl himself came upon this category in his encounter with the Christian tradition. And the biblical-historical witness to this God-man relation was fully as important for Ritschl's systematic elaboration of it as the philosophical and philosophical-theological tradition was.[9] Such an interpretation fails to take into account the fact that Ritschl *first* wrestled with historical and theological issues, that he continued to pursue these issues until he died,[10] and that he himself considered this preoccupation to be integral to his vocation as a theologian.[11] Karl Barth's assignment of determinative force to cultural factors in Ritschl's theology falls under the same critique.[12]

Several of the critical studies of Ritschl deserve careful attention and even incorporation into our over-all scheme for interpreting Ritschl. But they must be questioned in regard to their validity as

[5] Karl Barth, Robert Mackintosh, and H. R. Mackintosh mention this interrelation, but they make nothing of it.

[6] Otto Pfleiderer, *Die Ritschl'sche Theologie kritisch beleuchtet* (Braunschweig, 1891), pp. 1 ff. and *passim*. See also Høk, Chap. VII.

[7] *Supra*, pp. 77 ff.

[8] Høk, for example, Chap. I, pp. 174–176, 323–344.

[9] Høk himself indexes only three references to the historical works in his study. His discussion of Ritschl's *Geschichtsauffassung* (pp. 293–316) is wholly metaphysical and psychological in character.

[10] A list of his lectures and writings may be found in Otto Ritschl, *II*, pp. 526–535. (See *supra*, note 6).

[11] *Supra*, Chap. 2.

[12] Barth, pp. 598–600.

comprehensive and genetic interpretations because they leave so much of the man's work unaccounted for. On the other hand, the insights achieved by these studies can easily be incorporated into the scheme elaborated above.[13] This scheme suggests that Ritschl's theological work is to be understood as proceeding from his sense of responsibility for carrying out the theological activity which is entailed by his commitment to a certain understanding of history. This activity included the documentation, defense, and proclamation of a certain historical continuity and its heritage.

The psychological, philosophical, and philosophical-theological factors which the secondary literature has illumined can easily be subsumed under the proclamatory activity in which Ritschl engaged. When he turned from documentation to the systematic elaboration of the Christian faith understood in terms of his category of *Lebensfuehrung*, he utilized (consciously and unconsciously) every resource which was available.[14] This included the Kantianism of his *geistige Welt*, the logical treatises of Trendelenberg, the philosophy of his colleague Hermann Lotze, as well as other factors. The utilization of these factors must be recognized, but they must not blind the student to the fact that Ritschl was a theologian of the Christian tradition (as he understood it), and that he labored under the impact of this tradition. The secondary literature of the Ritschl scholars has not, to this date, made this clear.

This present study cannot discuss the psychological, philosophical, and philosophical-theological factors in Ritschl's theology, on which these scholars have concentrated. Its thesis aims at illumining, rather, the role of historical factors. But it should be clear that it *has* accounted for the role and importance of these non-historical factors by incorporating them within a more comprehensive scheme. On the other hand, the scholars who have concentrated their attention primarily on these non-historical factors have *not* accounted for the four-fifths of the Ritschlian corpus to which we have turned our attention, nor to the impact which this four-fifths has had on the one-fifth that does come within their purview.

This emphasis on the system-shaping force of historical factors in Ritschl's theology should not blind one to the power of his constructive insights. Ritschl's constructive thrust was extraordinarily strong. This constructive thrust is difficult, if not impossible, to analyze into its components, but it is omnipresent in his works. Its

13 *Supra*, p. 90.
14 This judgment finds general support in the remarks of Georg Wobbermin, in *Schleiermacher und Ritschl in ihrer Bedeutung fuer die heutige Theologische Lage und Aufgabe* (Tuebingen: J. C. B. Mohr, 1927), pp. 17–18.

provenance is equally difficult to trace.[15] It is clear that Ritschl brought these constructive insights *to* his historical perspective, even as the insights grew out of this perspective. This constructive thrust provided the drive within his historical stance. These constructive factors led to the formulation of the category of *Lebensideal* or *Lebensfuehrung*. This category gave purpose and point to Ritschl's historical investigations; without it he could never have undertaken these investigations, nor could he have dealt with the historical problem of continuity. This constructive category supplies what he considers to be the meaning of history. It compels him to his decisive interpretations of the "deviation" of the old Catholic church and to the repudiation of Pietism and confessional Lutheranism. This constructive thrust also served to limit drastically the breadth and objectivity of Ritschl's historical understanding.[16] Indeed, most of his inadequacies as a historian are traceable to the peculiar force which this constructive thrust exerted on him.[17]

Our analysis of Ritschl, therefore, does by no means intend to overlook or even to depreciate his powerful propensity towards construction in theology. It does mean to suggest that Ritschl's historical judgments and commitments seem to determine *almost exclusively* the manner in which he can utilize his constructive insights. There appear to be only four paths taken by Ritschl for utilizing his own constructive insights: (1) he located and amplified his constructive thought within the historical tradition of Christianity;[18] (2) he demonstrated its consonance with biblical-apostolic-Reformation Christianity; (3) he used it as a polemical tool against Catholics, Anabaptists, Pietists, and confessional Lutherans; (4) he systematized it in terms of the traditional theological materials.[19] Careful examination reveals *no* constructive utterance by Ritschl to fall outside these four areas. The conclusion seems to be that his constructive thought gives point to his theological work, but that Ritschl found it impossible to express this thought except as embodied in the material of his historical investigations.

Another way of stating this same point is to speak of the *service*

15 Otto Ritschl, *I,* 243–244.
16 For a fuller discussion of this point, see *infra,* pp. 98 f.
17 See previous note.
18 Even a work which is apparently as "constructive" as his *Theologie und Metaphysik* (1881) can be located plausibly under this rubric, inasmuch as approximately one-half of the work deals, either analytically or polemically, with traditional historical materials.
19 The so-called "systematic" works—*R.u.V. III,* (see *supra,* p. 95, note 9), *Unterricht,* and *Vollkommenheit*—work themselves out against the traditional theological materials much more than they do against philosophical materials. *R.u.V. III,* especially abounds in historical excursuses which are often ignored by those who are more interested in Ritschl's "Kantianism" or "Lotzeanism."

which history and historical investigation performed in respect to Ritschl's constructive insight, in respect to his notion of *Lebensfuehrung*. Or, this could be subsumed under the rubric of Ritschl's *use* of history. Four uses of history are summarized below.

1. *History serves as a principle of knowledge:*   Without history —in the form of the Bible, early Christianity, and the Reformation —Ritschl would not know what the constitutive factors of this *Lebensfuehrung* really were.

2. *History serves as a means of elaboration:*   Ritschl's historical works and, even more, the extensive historical excursuses in the systematic works (for example, *R.u.V.III*, and *Theologie und Metaphysik*) testify to his great dependence upon history as a means of amplifying and elaborating his constructive category of the *Lebensfuehrung*.

3. *History serves as a means of legitimation:*   Once again, the historical excursuses in the systematic works, not to mention the historical works themselves, indicate the need that Ritschl felt to justify his own position on the basis of the historical tradition.

4. *History serves as the source of the purpose of theology:*   We have noted above how Ritschl's commitment to a certain understanding of history shaped the career of his theological work both as to its content and its strategy. It was, in other words, the turns and shifts of the historical continuum, as he understood them, which determined the goal of Ritschl's work.

A CRITIQUE

Ritschl's preoccupation with history must be evaluated on two levels. The first level is constituted by the *general stance* which Ritschl assumed on the problem of the role of history in Christian theology. This stance is characterized by the assertion that no construction is possible except within the context of historical judgment and commitment. The second level is that of the *specific judgments and commitments* which Ritschl made, and which formed the material content and strategy of his work.

1. *The general stance:*   Ritschl's sensitivity to the role that history must play in Christian theology is impressive. The specific manner in which he conceived of this role raises problems, however. That Ritschl acknowledged the fundamental way in which the theologian is beholden to history seems beyond question. This study has shown, above, how he understood history to serve as a principle of knowledge, a means of elaboration, a means of legitimation, and as the source of the purpose in theology. Such a position is further demonstrated in two succinct statements which Ritschl

made in his early years concerning systematic theology. In his 1845 lectures on dogmatics, in a comparison of biblical and systematic theology, he writes that the former has the task of deriving *the* Christian principle from the New Testament, whereas the latter articulates this principle in the form which the general consciousness demands. To which he adds:

The continuity of the historical development is to be preserved in this way, *that every new form show itself to be the result of the entire historical development,* while at the same time demonstrating its agreement with and dependence upon the self-consciousness of Christ.[20]

And later, in 1853, as he attempted to outline an adequate methodology for systematic theology, he wrote to his father, most provocatively:

We are dealing here with the source and principle of knowledge for dogmatics. *In the final analysis, religious knowledge cannot avoid a proper concept of tradition;* that is, the portrayal of personal faith in its reciprocal interaction with the thought forms and ethical patterns of the community. The source of knowledge is Scripture as the document which contains the history of revelation. In regard to theological knowledge, one must observe that the Catholics used tradition as the principle of knowledge, whereas Protestant orthodoxy used Scripture as the *principium cognoscendi.* Both were in error. *The principle of theological knowledge must be a synthesis of personal religious knowledge with the full understanding of the history of the reciprocal relations of piety with Scripture and the understanding of the world.* . . . Therein lies the churchliness of theology; and my own theology must be churchly.[21]

Ritschl was very clearly aware of the constitutive force of history in systematic theology. He is able, therefore, to recognize the power for shaping the knowledge, truth, and certainty which history has in fact held in traditional Christian theology. But this awareness is vitiated rather decisively by one methodological blunder which makes it impossible for Ritschl to permit history to carry out other functions in his theology.

This blunder can be described in several ways. One way is to say that Ritschl has allowed history to make an impact on his work at a *material* level only, and not at a *formal* level,. Another way of putting it is to say that he has permitted a *material* formulation of the essence of Christianity to operate as a *formal* norm in his theology. The issue here is one in which the theologian is faced

---

20 Quoted in Otto Ritschl, *I*, p. 101. Italics added.
21 *Ibid.*, p. 229. Italics added.

with the problem not merely of using history but also with taking it seriously in its own integrity—of providing a place for history in one's theological methodology which will allow it to play a constitutive and regulative role at every point of the theological enterprise in its own right and not simply as a dynamic proof-text for the concerns which the theologian inevitably brings *to* his consideration of history. A theological methodology which does not allow history to play this constitutive and regulative role does not really take history seriously; it inevitably depreciates history to the status of means to some other constructive end.

In the final analysis, Ritschl could not allow history to play this basic role in his methodology. As a consequence, he ultimately violates the integrity of the very historical reality that he knows himself beholden to, because he places this history at the mercy of a constructive category which distorts it. In other words, in violating the integrity of the historical witness of the Christian community, Ritschl violates his own methodological intentions.

This inner incongruity in Ritschl's theological methodology manifests itself at several points, already evident in the discussion in Chapters 1 and 2. It crops out, for example, in Ritschl's recurring practice of positing a given, almost physical, continuity between historical epochs, only to render this continuity theologically insignificant by subjecting it to evaluation under a constructive category.[22] Ferdinand Christian Baur could evaluate this given unity of the historical continuum positively in its own right because he could relate it without exception to the life of God.[23] Ritschl cannot relate history *qua* history to the divine life. He cannot even relate Christian history to God directly. Time and again we have observed that he can evaluate positively only that history which passes muster in the light of his own distinctive category of judgment, specifically, the *Lebensfuehrung*.

This may explain why, in turn, Ritschl never really turned his attention to history except as he conceived it to be the history of this *Lebensfuehrung*. Gnosticism does not interest him, nor does Greek Christology, nor does the Greek Christian elaboration of the Trinity, nor does the Christian tradition of worship and cultus, nor do other large areas of Christian history—because he cannot conceive their being relevant to the *Lebensfuehrung*. This category, in the final analysis, is the overpowering norm in Ritschl's theology. To be sure, he cannot apply this norm except within the context of his preoccupation with history and its continuity; but the real constitutive and regulative power of history is nearly always, from a

[22] *Supra*, pp. 61–62, 84–85.
[23] Baur's difficulties arise because he is *selective*, and not because he fails to acknowledge the formally constitutive role of history. *Supra*, pp. 31–32.

methodological point of view, subordinated to this norm which is constituted by the category of *Lebensfuehrung*.

But this category is emphatically ill-suited to function at so crucial a level in Ritschl's theology, because it is a specific judgment which emerged from one idiosyncratic configuration of piety. Its idiosyncratic character constitutes its genius. Ritschl's normative category of *Lebensfuehrung* is not a formal category that embraces all forms of piety; on the contrary, it *excludes* all forms of piety save one (the implications of Ritschl's use of this norm are discussed in the next section). If it did not exclude these other forms, history would have no meaning for Ritschl.

The point of this criticism is not that Ritschl is selective, nor that he brings presuppositions to history. The contention is not that uninterpreted or presuppositionless history is or ought to be available to the theologian. Rather, I am suggesting that Ritschl's theological work is beset by incongruities which undermine his own intention to permit history to shape the content and strategy of that work. This incongruity arises from his inability to permit history to permeate his theological methodology as a factor which in its own integrity is worthy to function normatively; it arises from the fact that he permits too specific and too idiosyncratic a category to exercise a formally normative function in his work. This category (the *Lebensfuehrung*) represents the constructive factor in Ritschl's theology. He related it axiologically to the historical factors in his work so as to deny them any normative power except as their integrity has been altered to fit his understanding of *Lebensfuehrung*. So conceived and so altered, the historical factors could never bear the freight of normativeness that Ritschl apparently wanted to load upon them; because they had been deprived of the very characteristics which make history so appropriate a norm otherwise—breadth (which saves the theologian from the partiality of his own relativity) and independent integrity (which mitigates the subjectivism which besets every discriminating judgment that the theologian makes).[24]

[24] Traditionally, Christian theologians have taken refuge in the normative character of history by invoking it under one of two terms—either as the appeal to the "fathers and the brethren" or as the appeal to Scripture (or to the Word). Ritschl acknowledged the normativeness of history under both of these forms. But he rendered this normativeness ineffective by his methodological violation of the integrity of history. Of contemporary theologians, Wolfhart Pannenberg has perhaps spelled out most clearly the alternative to Ritschl's axiological relationship between historical and constructive factors, at least in terms of theological methodology. He suggests, in his *Offenbarung als Geschichte*, that God's truth is not simply within history (as Ritschl believed), but that in a sense history *is* revelation, inasmuch as the totality of the historical acts of God are, in their own integrity, the unfolding of God's being *ad extra*. Pannenberg thus repossesses Baur's openness to history

This methodological blunder rendered Ritschl incapable, with his understanding of history, of providing a formal principle of knowledge and truth without doing considerable violence to the primary datum of the Christian faith, namely, the living reality of the human confession which is engendered by God's redemptive activity. Ritschl recognized—and acknowledged—this primary datum. Indeed, his category of *Lebensfuehrung* aims precisely at preserving the importance of this datum of the living human confession.[25] But because he permitted one idiosyncratic form of this confession to exercise formally normative power in his work, he brutally violates the integrity of all human confessions—either rejecting them out of hand as perverse or by conforming them to *his* material formulation of *Lebensfuehrung*. (This will be discussed in more detail below.) This ironic perversion of the purpose for which he intended his category of *Lebensfuehrung* is a further manifestation of the internal incongruity which marks Ritschl's work.

This same blunder renders Ritschl's understanding of history incapable of presenting a viable understanding of history which can do justice to the dynamic movement of history while at the same time avoiding the meaninglessness of relativistic historicism. The source of this inability is simple to locate: Ritschl's constructive category imposed a unity on history, and his axiological propensity compelled him to reject as perverse all of the phenomena which fell outside this unity. Relativistic historicism could scarcely be a problem for his work, because his constructive category restricted so decisively the range of the dynamic relativizing movement of the historical continuum. Here again, the painful tension is manifested which arises from the internal incongruity of Ritschl's method. Within the movement of the historical continuum from epoch to epoch, Ritschl recognized the dynamic of change, with its great diversity. But he reduced the relativizing factor in this dynamic to the point where he did not even have to take it into account. In none of his methodological prefaces[26] does he come to grips with the problems of historical relativism that so exercise theologians today. He reduces the force of this relativizing movement because he subsumes all of the phenomena of history under one category, that of *Lebensfuehrung*. By means of this category he reduces the phenomena to *relevance* or *irrelevance*. Ignoring the latter (his omission of the concern for creeds among the

qua history, but he does so by means of a notion of God's revelatory activity, rather than by means of a metaphysical category. See *infra,* p. 133, and note 30, this chapter.

25 *Supra,* p. 12.

26 For example, the introductions to each of the volumes of *R.u.V.*

antignostic fathers, for example), he reduces the relevant phenomena to *adequacy* or *inadequacy*, whereupon he rejects the latter.
Otto Ritschl corroborates this analysis when he writes concerning
the methodology of the mature Albrecht Ritschl, "Therefore, the
historical continuity of religious development demonstrates itself,
more than anywhere else, in a continuity (or agreement) in piety"
(*"An der Uebereinstimmung in der Froemmigkeit also erwiest sich
ueberhaupt die geschichtliche Continuitaet der religioesen Entwicklung."*)[27] And for his purposes, there *was* no history except the
history of "religious development" interpreted in terms of *Froemmigkeit* or *Lebensfuehrung*.

In summary, concerning Ritschl's general stance, it must be ad-
mitted that he did acknowledge the role which history had to play
in systematic theological work. And in practice he committed
himself to the power of history to inform and sustain his work. But
both his insight and his commitment were vitiated by the methodological blunder outlined here. The foregoing has indicated how
this blunder affected Ritschl's basic insights. The following section
will turn to his material commitments.

2. *Specific judgments and commitments:* Several pertinent
questions arise for the systematic theologian, on the basis of certain specific judgments and commitments which Ritschl made as
he pursued his theological enterprise under the impact of history.
We can evaluate Ritschl by phrasing these questions and discussing
the problems which they raise so as to suggest both the strengths
and weaknesses of Ritschl's position. Some of the criticisms expressed here will become clearer in Chapter 4; the questions may
be phrased as follows:

Must the Protestant theologian commit himself to apostolic–
Reformation Christianity?

Must the Protestant theologian be, in principle, opposed to
Catholicism, as well as to other types of Christianity?

How is the Protestant theologian to account for the unity as well
as the divergence between his Christianity and that of Catholicism
and these other types of Christianity?

Must the Protestant theologian posit a deviation or "fall" in the
movement from apostolic to Catholic Christianity?

Is it satisfactory for the Protestant theologian to distinguish his
own type of Christianity and its opposition to Catholicism in terms
of piety (*Froemmigkeit*) or *Lebensfuehrung*?

Is historical continuity a central issue for the theologian? Is his
work in fact a grand attempt to establish certain kinds of continuities and to reject others?

[27] Otto Ritschl, *II*, 170–171.

If so, is *Lebensfuehrung,* or piety, an adequate category to serve as the locus, bearer, and expression of this continuity?

The theologian's approach to these questions depends ultimately on his understanding (be it implicit or explicit) of historical continuity and the role it plays in his work. Ritschl's own position holds that history serves certain crucial functions for the Christian theologian because it constitutes the principle of knowledge and of certainty (or legitimation) for his work. History has to serve this function if the theologian is to maintain the integrity of the primary datum of the Christian faith, the only datum that can justifiably function as the ultimate norm for theology—namely, the *Lebensfuehrung* which is engendered in human existence by virtue of God's redemptive activity in that existence. If this is an accurate assessment of the norm which confronts the theologian, then historical continuity must be a central issue for the theologian, as it certainly was for Ritschl. Theological methodology must be carefully shaped so that its structure allows for the constitutive and regulative force of history, specifically, as the historical witness of the Christian community.

Indeed, this shaping of the structure of theological methodology may be the most important (as well as the most difficult) methodological task which faces the systematic theologian today. In Ritschl's own words, the theologian must learn, methodologically, that every new form is itself the result of the entire historical development that precedes it and at the same time it must manifest its agreement with and its dependence on Jesus Christ.[28] The theologian must learn the methodological implications of Ritschl's judgment that religious knowledge (and theological reflection upon that knowledge) cannot avoid an adequate conception of *tradition.*[29] Or, in Wolfhart Pannenberg's terms, the theologian must wrestle with the *methodological* implications of the fact that only the totality of God's acts can be understood as the revelation of God; and since God is One, that means the totality of the events in God's history.[30]

These insights imply that the concern for continuity pertains to the *substance* of the theologian's task as well as to its methodology. The cruciality of historical continuity for the Christian theologian may be summed up thus: Unless he can be aware of a continuity between his own work and the Christian tradition which extends to the biblical witness, the Christian theologian cannot be confident as to the validity of *what* he says, nor of the means which he em-

28 *Supra,* p. 96.
29 *Ibid.*
30 Pannenberg, *Offenbarung als Geschichte* (Göttingen: Vandenhoeck and Ruprecht, 1961), p. 17.

ploys to *know* and to *verify* his message. The theologian is, therefore, always under the imperative (either consciously or unconsciously) to erect certain types of historical continuities. The
problems which arise at this point are formidable, and they are
largely unsolved, or insoluble—for example, the problems of diversity in history, of historical relativism, of the validity of Christian
history over against non-Christian religions, and so on.[31] But the
desirability, even the necessity, of implementing such a historical
methodology in systematic theology, makes one bold enough to
assert that the immensity of the problems is an indication of the
great importance of the issue in question.

Our argument has seriously questioned Ritschl's success in
working out a theological methodology that is adequate to this
understanding of historical continuity.[32] But there seems little
doubt, in view of the material that has been brought to light in
Chapters 1 and 2, that he was at least instinctively aware of the
validity of this methodology and that he did in fact implement it,
in spite of his theoretical blunders which unfortunately marred
his admirable sensitivity to the issues involved. As we shall note
below, this may indeed be the clue to Ritschl's power, to the significance that his work has held in the past four generations, and
to the importance which it holds for contemporary theology. It may
well be that the greatest weakness in the critical literature on
Ritschl to date is its failure to illumine this aspect and significance
of his work.

The question now arises concerning the way in which this historical continuity is to be identified. What sort of category can
serve to locate it and serve as its bearer and expression? The
answer to this question depends on the answer to the prior question: "By virtue of *what* does the continuity of Christian history
exist at all?"

The history of theology is instructive at this point, particularly
in its grappling with the notion of the "essence" of Christianity.
The most satisfactory suggestion appears to be the one which
affirms that this continuity is rooted in the action of a God who is
One and who is faithful.[33] This suggestion must be set in contradistinction to suggestions that the continuity is constituted by
structures of reason or of human religious experience.[34] This action
of the one, faithful God does not appear apart from reason and the
human existence whose confession of commitment it engenders.
And it follows that this confession is a statement concerning man,

[31] *Ibid.*, pp. 16–20 for a discussion of still other problems.

[32] *Supra*, pp. 96–99.

[33] See, for example, H. H. Rowley, *The Unity of the Bible* (Philadelphia:
The Westminster Press, 1955), Chap. 1.

[34] See the argument of Chaps. 4 and 5 for the elaboration of this comment.

even as it concerns God; the confession may indeed speak of God only in the language of human analogy. But the engendering *occasion* of the confession has to do with divine action rather than with human experience; and the ultimate explanation for the emergence and the existence of the confession is the meeting with God (however he may be conceived) which is the subject of the confession. All of this is to say that the tradition of Christian history is not primarily a history of human religious experience (although it is that); on the contrary, it is the history of *God's revelatory and redemptive action* (however that may be defined). The clear implication to be drawn from these comments is that history is related intimately, indeed we can say ontologically, to the life of God. The precise nature of this relation is open to speculation, but it remains a mystery. Its being a mystery does by no means lessen its reality, however—at least, this is the confession of the Christian community.

Ritschl understood this when he formulated his notion of *Lebensfuehrung*. We have surveyed his repeated emphasis that this *Lebensfuehrung* is characterized by the interrelation of human and divine factors; the latter, preeminent and superordinated to the former. And in his succinct statement of the methodology in systematic theology he makes it clear that he elaborates upon human religious experience in order to illumine "everything that can be perceived as the action of God's grace upon the Christian" (*"alles was als Gnadenwirkungen Gottes auf den Christen zu erkennen ist."*)[35] The category of *Lebensfuehrung* is a testimony to God's gracious action. But this category did not function as such a testimony when it was placed in the role of a formal theological norm. When Ritschl used it in this role he very plainly elevated the lineaments of human experience to the status of a criterion, and it was *in virtue of these lineaments* that he employed it as the bearer and expression of historical continuity. It was solely by virtue of these lineaments of human experience that the category functioned as a criterion, according to whose application Catholicism, Pietism and confessionalism were deemed *discontinuous* with the authentic Christian historical tradition, and by which the apostles, Luther, and Ritschl himself were deemed continuous with this tradition. Here again the internal incongruity is revealed which was occasioned by Ritschl's methodological blunder. The very divine action to which the category of *Lebensfuehrung* was supposed to testify was, in the final analysis, rendered methodologically inoperative when Ritschl attempted to put that category to a formally normative use for which it was structurally unsuited. This category became, when put to this use, an exceedingly dan-

[35] Ritschl, *R.u.V. III*, p. 22. *Supra*, p. 77.

gerous weapon. As a formal criterion, it came very close to identifying the authentic Christian revelation of God's life in history with a single idiosyncratic configuration of human religious experience. One may therefore conclude that, although the intention of this notion of *Lebensfuehrung* is helpful, its use as category for identifying, locating, and expressing the continuity of the historical action of God must be rejected.

The question remains: "What sort of category *can* function in Christian theology to designate this historical continuity?" This is an exceedingly difficult and complex problem. Some suggestions can be made, however. As we elaborate more fully in the next chapters, rather than locating the continuity, as Ritschl has done, in the piety (or *Lebensfuehrung*) alone of the individual believers who exist in the Christian community, it seems preferable to locate it in the total corporate life of the community, as well as in the total lives of its individual members. This total life includes piety, worship, canonical and later writings, dogma, theology, and actions (including internal and external institutional relationships, as well as personal ethical actions).

But how is the continuity, which occurs in the locus of this life, to be identified? This is the most difficult *methodological* question of all. It must be kept in mind that *this* methodological problem is not to be solved by intellection alone. It is, as H. Richard Niebuhr writes, "not an intellectual exercise but a moral event."[36] The decision the theologian makes here is, in part at least, a decision of faith.[37] Furthermore, it is a problem whose solution calls for

[36] H. Richard Niebuhr, *The Meaning of Revelation* (New York: Macmillan, 1941), pp. 75 ff.

[37] This is a consideration which deserves much more attention than it generally receives, particularly in respect to its force in the history of the Christian faith. One of the most striking testimonies to its importance is the pathos which has accompanied great transitions in the development of the faith, as a result of the difficulties which men have had in discerning just what constitutes historical continuity. For example, the study of the transition from the Mosaic to the Davidic religion is most instructive—see Gerhard von Rad, *Theologie des alten Testaments* (Munich: Chr. Kaiser, 1957), pp. 56–65; Albrecht Alt, *Kleine Schriften zur Geschichte des Volkes Israel*, 2 vols., (Munich: Beck'sche Verlagsbuchhandlung, 1953), Vol. II, pp. 60–65. Other transitions of similar import: the church's movement from Palestine to the West; the transition from first- to third-century ecclesiastical forms; the transition from Latin to Germanic forms, and so on. One of the clearest discussions of the relation of faith and theological methodology occurs in the works of Saint Irenaeus, first great post-apostolic Christian theologian. He makes it clear that the theologian must not expect to understand the force of the historical tradition unless he approaches it in faith; nor can he employ it in his work apart from faith. For this reason, it is important that the student of the traditional faith be diligent in prayer, meditation, study, and obedience. For this reason also, the proper theological methodology brings with it communion with God, love for God and man,

awareness at the level of sensibilities as much as it calls for intellectual acumen. These considerations account, in part, for the complexity of the problem; they account for the imprecision which must always accompany the discussion of this problem.

Subsequent chapters bear the responsibility of speaking constructively on these questions. Our analysis does indicate, however, that Ritschl apparently did not comprehend that if history plays the role he said it plays, then the theologian cannot be opposed in principle to any single confessional manifestation in Christian history.

He cannot justify any such preconceived opposition, in the first place, because this history is related so intimately (albeit mysteriously) with the career of the divine life itself. F. C. Baur and his fellow-Hegelians were able to understand this much better than Ritschl. Ritschl's insensitivity at this point may account for the brutality with which he could dismiss certain historical manifestations within Christian history—a flat contradiction of the care and appreciation with which he investigated these manifestations historically. Secondly, the Christian theologian cannot be opposed in principle to Catholicism or any other Christian manifestation because of the role these manifestations may play in his theological methodology (in regard to his methods of knowing and certification), as Ritschl himself understood. Finally, the very complexity of the methodological apparatus Ritschl employs compels the Christian theologian to move cautiously in his opposition to the historic and contemporary Christian confessions. But on the other hand, all of these considerations encourage the theologian to approach these confessions with openness, because of the constitutive and regulative function which they may serve in his work. This stance of openness is the one with which Ritschl instinctively approached Christian history and theology. But, as we have noted repeatedly, he always vitiated this stance by his propensity for judgments which proceeded along the lines dictated by his category of *Lebensfuehrung*.

In particular, it appears to be much too simplistic to point to a deviation or a "fall" between Catholic Christianity and apostolic Christianity. Such a deviation is not even necessary unless one's commitment to the Reformation hinges on a category of judgment which is as idiosyncratic as Ritschl's. Indeed, positing such a deviation, or fall, between these two epochs probably raises more problems than it solves. It is unsatisfactory *anthropologically*, because it censures late Hellenistic Christian man for responding to God's

---

and the authority to discern and refute heresy. See his *Adversus Haereses*, Book III, p. 5, Books I and IV, pp. 26–33 (particularly the comments on the *discipulus spiritalis*).

action in the only terms available to him, and because it suggests that he ought to have responded in terms which were at home only in an earlier or a later age. Such a procedure is unsatisfactory *theologically*, because it suggests a breach in the divine unity as well as in the divine faithfulness. Just how the Christian theologian —or the Christian community of faithful believers, for that matter —could proceed amid such chaos is difficult to imagine. Both Ritschl and his student, Adolph von Harnack, obviated this chaos by the devious suggestion that the confessions of certain men and epochs (for example, early Greek Catholicism), although inferior and perverse, were nevertheless sincere. This sincerity, coupled with an apparent confidence in God's ability to engender more adequate confessions at a later date (during the Reformation and the nineteenth century, for example) seems to suffice for Ritschl and Harnack. Actually, both Ritschl and Harnack knew better; and both of them erected impressive demonstrations of the unity of Christian history, only to undermine these demonstrations with their keen historical judgments.[38]

I am not suggesting that Ritschl or any theologian should be blind to the diversity that exists within Christian history, or to the divergence between his own confession and that of other types of Christianity. On the contrary, one is keenly aware of this diversity. It is *given* in awareness, perhaps even *prior* to all else, because the theologian recognizes the dynamic of the historical continuum and the relativity which accompanies the multiplicity of perspectives, both of time and place, that constitute this continuum. Indeed, in a real sense the diversity within history is the given, not the problem. *Rather*, the problem posed by history is likely to be its unity. This unity is and has been the postulate of faith. But in the light of the character of his God and of the methodological realities which confront him, this unity of God and the divine action is a postulate that the Christian theologian cannot avoid.

It is precisely at this point that the inadequacy—one might even say the perversity—of Ritschl's category of *Lebensfuehrung* becomes obvious, at least as a category for identifying and expressing the continuity of Christian history. Such a category cuts the very sinew of the community's understanding of God's gracious revelation—namely, its conception of the unity and faithfulness of divine grace which makes redemption a possibility *in spite* of the diversity of time, place, and the psychic idiosyncrasies within the range of human existence. Ritschl's insistence on a certain *Lebensfuehrung* or *Froemmigkeit* as the identifying category of the Christian historical continuity specifically undermines this grace, because it

[38] *Supra,* pp. 50 ff., 60 ff.

makes God's redemptive grace accessible within only *one* configuration of the human psyche. Only by running roughshod over the realities of human diversity and historical relativism is Ritschl able to affirm a continuity even of this *Lebensfuehrung*. If he had honestly wrestled with what we now know about the relativism of time and place, the idiosyncrasies of race and nation, he would have had to admit that this psychical configuration to which grace is alone accessible was very likely a present reality only to those who shared the idiosyncrasies of a Paul or a Luther or a Ritschl. And if he were rigorously consistent in his reasoning, he might have had to reconsider whether the commonality between these figures is sufficient to warrant the assumption that all three shared the same *Lebensfuehrung*. (One suspects that only the nineteenth-century German *bourgeois* would really meet the specifications of this category of piety.) Ritschl apparently could not allow for the same unity between differing *Lebensfuehrungen* which he had documented empirically in apostolic Christianity between the Jews of the Temple (James), the Jews of the Diaspora (Paul), and the Gentiles of Hellenistic origin.

A final question remains: "Must the Protestant theologian commit himself to apostolic–Reformation Christianity?" It follows from the critical position which I have been suggesting that the Christian theologian must indeed commit himself to the apostolic and Reformation confessions. This follows from the Ritschlian position also. But the reasoning behind these common commitments and the theological imperatives deriving from them could not be more different. Ritschl committed himself to the confessions which emerged from these epochs, because he believed that in them *alone* the normative revelation, expressed in a normative conception of piety, was to be found. The imperative which derived from this commitment demanded the demonstration of the continuity between these confessions, the rejection of all other Christian confessions, and the positive enunciation of the heritage of this continuity so as to extend its efficacy up to his own day.

The Christian theologian whether Protestant, Roman, or Orthodox—is beholden to these periods because God has acted in them mightily, engendering significant confessions therein—confessions which have in both cases been epoch-making in their impact upon the Christian community, even upon the Western world as a whole. Without recourse to these confessions, the theologian is in danger of cutting himself off from the fullest possible knowledge of God and from the means for verifying his knowledge of God in a responsible manner. Without the apostolic confession, it is doubtful that he would consider himself a *Christian* theologian at all. But the confessions of these ages do not constitute the totality of God's revelation, nor do they invite the theologian to reject all other Christian confessions. On the contrary, if it were not for the confessions of subsequent ages (and the faithfulness of God to which those confessions point), it is unlikely that we would be aware of either the apostles (and their Christ) or the reformers. The commitment to apostolic and Reformation Christianity rather impels the Christian theologian to turn to whatever source he can, wherever the divinely engendered human confession occurs which will give him the knowledge and the certainty of the grace which may take him and his age up into the divine life—by whatever mystery that can be accomplished. Disciplined reflection upon this grace and upon its interpretation and communication constitutes the Christian theologian's task.

A FINAL WORD

Almost thirty years ago, H. R. Mackintosh wrote, "Ritschl at the moment belongs, like Tennyson, to the 'middle distance': too far for gratitude, too near for reverence."[39] Jaroslav Pelikan, six years ago, expressed the opinion that Mackintosh's *bon mot* "is still valid."[40] "Perhaps," he adds, "a new emphasis upon historical honesty among theologians . . . will give Ritschl his due."[41] The present writer hopes, very frankly, that the interpretation expressed herein may constitute a step—be it ever so small—towards fulfilling the need Professors Mackintosh and Pelikan have called attention to.[42]

I have sketched here the lines which the new appreciation of Ritschl might follow. It is not along the lines of a profounder grasp of the psychological, philosophical, and philosophical-theological undertones in his work (although such a grasp is to be wished for as well). It is a tribute to the diligence of historical scholarship that we have at our disposal numerous exhaustive discussions of Ritschl's Kantianism, his Lotzeanism, his theory of value-judgments, and his ethically oriented understanding of the

<hr>

[39] H. R. Mackintosh, p. 141, note 1.
[40] In "Introduction" to Karl Barth, *Protestant Thought: From Rousseau to Ritschl* (New York: Harper & Row, 1959), p. 10.
[41] *Ibid.*
[42] From a slightly different perspective, the writings of Professor Dan L. Deegan also help to meet this need. See his "Albrecht Ritschl on the Historical Jesus," *Scottish Journal of Theology*, 15:133–150, 1962; and "The Ritschlian School, The Essence of Christianity, and Karl Barth," *Scottish Journal of Theology*, 16:390–414, 1963. See also the important dissertation by Michael Ryan, "The Function of the Discipline of History in the Theological Interpretation of Albrecht Ritschl," unpublished Ph.D. dissertation, Drew University, 1966.

Christian faith. What we do *not* have at our disposal is an adequate appreciation of Albrecht Ritschl as a theologian of the Christian tradition. I suggest that if the man holds any relevance at all for our day, it is in his role as a theologian whose concern was to understand the message which constitutes the heritage of the traditional Christian faith and to interpret and proclaim that message to his day. The search for understanding came more easily to him than the proclamation and it consumed the greater portion of his time and output; for this reason, Ritschl's efforts have produced fruit for students of theology rather than an apologetic to the age—although the material for an apologetic (to his own age, at least) is certainly to be found in his work.

Our thesis suggests that Ritschl was a Protestant theologian who sought in some way to be *Catholic* within the circumstances of his own abilities and of his own age, and that herein lies his significance to Christian theologians today. The term "Catholic," when applied to Ritschl, may seem inappropriate. Closer examination reveals, however, that the term may indeed fit Ritschl's intention rather well. Professor Pelikan has recently spoken of catholicity in the following terms, in connection with Friedrich Schleiermacher:

. . . Protestant theology has proved that it can supply alternatives to Thomism that are just as comprehensive and yet just as Christian. . . . Now it is becoming evident that in the thought of Schleiermacher Protestantism possesses a resource for a world view that is simultaneously comprehensive and Christian—comprehensive in the sense that it takes seriously what the sciences and the humanities have learned about reality, Christian in the sense that it relates all of this to the revelation of God in Jesus Christ. Since "comprehensive" in this context refers to "Universality" and "Christian" in this context refers to "identity," what this really means is that the theology of Schleiermacher is *catholic* in the best sense of the word.[43]

If the interpretation outlined in our study is correct, Ritschl might be considered a Catholic Christian theologian—by instinct and intention, if not in accomplishment. Although he was probably not so successful as Schleiermacher in attaining this catholicity, and although he surely does not attain to Schleiermacher's "com-

[43] Jaroslav Pelikan, *The Riddle of Roman Catholicism* (New York and Nashville: Abingdon, 1959), p. 229. Italics added. Pelikan's comments on Schleiermacher's being both comprehensive and Christian are remarkably similar to Ritschl's own description of the task of systematic theology. He writes that biblical theology has "the task to perceive and to develop the principle of Christianity" from the New Testament materials. Systematic theology has the task of giving this Christian principle the form "which the circumstances of the general world view and the present range of ethical and theoretical knowledge demand." See Otto Ritschl, *I*, p. 101.

prehensiveness" (as Pelikan uses this term), it may be that he surpasses Schleiermacher's catholicity in one aspect which is instructive for theologians today—he wrestled more seriously wtih the totality of the traditional Christian witness than his predecessor (whose follower he counted himself).

The term "Catholic" may perhaps be applied to Ritschl even more legitimately if we accept the categories of another contemporary theologian, Gustaf Aulen. Writing in the same year as Pelikan, he elaborates this understanding of the term:

Catholicity . . . is entirely dependent on the fact that Christ is the Lord of the church. Perhaps it could be said that the meaning of catholicity does not appear as immediately as that of unity, holiness, and apostolicity. The interpretation of its meaning has varied. But two fundamental aspects inevitably come to the fore: *universality* and *continuity*. The two are closely related and cannot be separated. The church could not be the universal church if it did not through the ages stand in unbroken relationship with the original church which had its origin in Christ, the church of Easter and Pentecost.[44]

According to this definition, in terms of universality and continuity, both the adequacies and the inadequacies of Ritschl's work, in its relevance for contemporary theology, come to light. He understood the cruciality for the Christian faith of the *universality* of God's grace as manifested in Christ and in his church. He makes this clear in his interpretation of early Christianity. But thereafter, his instinctive concern for universality is modified, as I have demonstrated above, by the strange internal incongruity that stems from a fundamental methodological blunder. Ritschl's real power, however, as I have also expressed it above, was his appreciation of the importance of *continuity* for the Christian faith and its theological enterprise.

Concomitant to this "Catholic" intention, one must note Ritschl's sensitivity to the issues of ecclesiology and soteriology. Although he did not resolve the problems which attend these issues, he had a clear vision of the fact that Christianity was true to its essential nature only when it proclaimed a redemption which could do justice to man's capabilities, as well as to his predicaments. He also saw with unusual clarity that such an understanding of redemption could not be implemented unless it were complemented by an understanding of the church which could provide for the circumstances of the initiation and sustaining of this redemption. Therefore, he was quick to reject any understanding of redemption which, in his opinion, depreciated either God's prevenience and

44 Gustaf Aulen, *Reformation and Catholicity,* Eric Wahlstrom, trans. (Philadelphia: Muhlenberg Press, 1961), pp. 182–183.

power or the reality of man's response and regeneration under the impact of God's grace.[45] On the other hand, he insisted that such a concept of redemption was inexplicable apart from an understanding of the church which could account for man's encounter with God, his ability to respond to the divine grace, and his ongoing sanctification.[46] These are truly Catholic concerns, and their significance is gaining increasing attention among theologians today.

In the final analysis, one must admire Ritschl more for the questions he raised and attempted to solve than for the positive answers he gave. This is another way of saying that he holds more relevance for students of theological methodology than for students of homiletics (although for three generations, Protestant preachers have been more Ritschlian than we might wish). To speak of Ritschl in this way is really more of a tribute than a criticism, because it constitutes a criticism which is built upon the very method and concern to which Ritschl dedicated his own theological career. And the greatest tribute to a teacher is that following generations should supersede him by pursuing his concerns and methods further than he could himself (because of the circumstances of his own propensities and the limitations of his age). It is in this light that I hope to have presented Albrecht Ritschl's theological work for renewed consideration and appreciation—as an instructive example of a theologian who attempted—and who did not fail utterly—to erect a genuinely *Catholic* Christian theological edifice in the setting of nineteenth-century, post-Schleiermacherian, Protestant German theology.

[45] *Supra,* pp. 75 ff. Ritschl was so concerned for the power of God *and* the integrity of man in his understanding of redemption that he *tended* to collapse justification and regeneration into one. By so doing, he approached the position of the Roman Catholic *gratia cooperans* (or *fides caritate formata*) which he opposed so bitterly. It is instructive that contemporary Protestant-Roman conversations are forcing Protestant theologians to reconsider their traditional opposition to the *gratia cooperans.*

[46] *Supra,* pp. 75 ff., 77 ff.

4

A System Rooted in the Vitalities of History

THE GROUND OF CHRISTIAN FAITH AND THEOLOGY

Up to this point our study has attempted to uncover the essential concerns that determined the thrust of Albrecht Ritschl's life work. In the last chapter, our evaluation suggested that while Ritschl's methodology allowed for the recognition of history as a powerful shaping factor in the theological investigation and articulation of the Christian faith, it could not escape violating the integrity of the vitalities of history by sacrificing that integrity to the demands of a norm coldly abstracted from a particular configuration of piety. Although Ritschl's concern for history forced him to grapple seriously with the problems of continuity in the historical process, he never successfully coped with the issues raised by relativism or by the necessity of formulating a norm that could locate and describe historical continuity. Ritschl was sensitive to the constitutive role of history and its continuities in his work, but he failed to relate history vigorously enough to the power of God's presence in the world, thereby restricting the scope of both history and divine presence to the confines of a very narrow piety or *Lebensfuehrung*.

Cut deeply as it might, however, the criticism raised in the last chapter cannot give a full enough picture of the strengths and weaknesses of Ritschl's methodological thrust. For a fuller understanding of the man's significance, we must give more attention to the two overarching realities with which he worked: the *historical process* and its continuities on the one hand, and the *vitalities of life* in which that historical process is embedded on the other. Neither Ritschl's strengths nor his weaknesses can be appreciated until we have some idea of the vastness of the canvas upon which he chose to work as he delved into the realm where life and history mingle. What follows in the next two chapters is an attempt to survey the breadth of Ritschl's canvas. That

Ritschl himself may have been unaware of this breadth does not undermine our suggestion that it can serve as a touchstone for evaluating his work. What follows then is an attempt to indicate the depth of the issues that grow inescapably out of our study of Ritschl, at the same time calling attention to the fruitful lines of inquiry that emerge when history is properly related to the vitalities in which it is rooted. What begins here as a discussion of the Ritschlian issues ends up as a set of programmatic suggestions that stand quite far removed from Ritschl. Such a discussion throws a distinctive light on Ritschl, demonstrating both his true stature as a seminal thinker—a Maker of Modern Theology—because of his sensitivity to the crucial issues of life and history, and the decisive limitations of his methodology when measured by the demands our search uncovers as requisites for an adequate resolution of the problems that arise when one seeks to relate life and history.

The detailed analysis and criticism in the preceding three chapters bears its fruit, therefore, in what follows, because in these final chapters we survey a range of possibilities that grow inescapably from a consideration of life and history in our time—a range of possibilities that, for the most part, Ritschl himself did not see. At this point our own theological commitments come out into the open, the commitments that determine our own relative position in theological time and space. To say that Ritschl's true placement as a theologian can be made only when *our* contemporary reflections upon *his* issues are made clear is to say that history and constructive theology are inseparable—an assertion that underlies both Ritschl's methodology and my own. Therefore, in the reflections that follow we are asserting the inseparability of theology and history, illustrating the natural consequence of this assertion by allowing our contemporary reflections to throw light upon Ritschl.

Ritschl knew that the realities of Christian faith involve a concern both for life and for history and its continuity. His insensitivity to the range and richness not to say the complexity and ambiguity of life (which ultimately shipwrecked his theological efforts) cannot eradicate his equally impressive preoccupation with *Lebensfuehrung*—a preoccupation which demonstrates a basic recognition that Christian faith has to do essentially with the concrete realities of life. The programmatic suggestions that follow accept Ritschl's insight that the Christian faith focuses and manifests itself in a configuration of life itself. We argue that from this concern for life[1] as the primary datum of Christian faith, theology

---

[1] The term *life* appears throughout this chapter to designate the locus of God's reconstructive presence. This term includes, intentionally, the implication that the locus of God's presence in this world is dynamic and irrepressible

is driven inescapably into the history of the Christian enterprise. If Ritschl's perversities are to be avoided, however, we must be sensitive to the wholeness and integrity of Christian life; only so can we remain open to the fullness and power of history. Perhaps one who is more historically inclined would argue, conversely, that it is the concern for history that drives the theologian to an escapable confrontation with the richness of Christian life. In the following pages, nevertheless, we insist (as scientifically as possible) that given the centrality of life in the Christian enterprise, a preoccupation with history and its continuity is unavoidable.

Ritschl's emphasis on *Lebensfuehrung* is itself open to misunderstanding. He could be interpreted as asserting a new *theologia regenitorum* on the basis that personal religious experience as expressed in the Reformation *Lebensfuehrung* is the necessary credential for theological reflection. At the worst, a callow sentimentality could seize upon Ritschl's emphasis and confuse it with a religion of the "heart." Although Ritschl himself did tend towards a personalistic piety, he can hardly be charged with sentimentality. His emphasis upon the category of *Lebensfuehrung* was set forth in the interest of disciplined scholarly thinking. This vulnerability to misinterpretation should not blind us, however, to the essential wisdom of placing the focus of Christian faith and theology within the vitalities of life. Indeed, it is not only the practitioners of Christian faith, but also the professional theologians who find this focusing on Christian life important. The most profound and realistic theological work will understand that its methodology must be built on the bedrock which the actualities

---

as life itself. Furthermore, the intention is to indicate that just as life is a category that is applicable to all ranges of reality, including nonhuman life, so God's presence must not be restricted in any perverse sense to human life. There is no question, however, but that our discussion centers primarily upon human life and the reconciling activity of God within the human community. Insofar as human life is what we ordinarily refer to in the following pages, one might expect that the term *life* is synonymous with the term *existence*. We have, however, studiously avoided the term existence in referring to the position that is introduced here, because it has become such a specialized concept in existentialist philosophy. And as the following pages indicate, our position seeks continually to avoid identifying human life with the abstract conceptuality of existence that the existentialist philosophers have erected. On the other hand, we do not mean to identify ourselves with the so-called "vitalists" of previous generations, as these were represented by Bergson and certain German idealists. These men imposed their own dialectic upon life, tending towards the conceptualization that we seek to avoid. Our position is, however, close to the vitalists in their concern to allow for the integrity of life and its primacy in all thinking about reality. At the same time, we eschew the term *experience* because of its predominantly psychological connotations, thereby avoiding some of the problems that have confronted theologies like Schleiermacher's which made experience a central category.

of life and history provide. This methodology will attend to the assertion that the Christian faith originates in a redemption that is embedded in life, or to put the matter conversely, in human existence that has been penetrated decisively by God's redemptive power.[2] Putting it this way brings the actuality and the happened-ness of this redemptive transfiguration of life into the foreground of our consideration. As inexplicable as it may seem, the actualities of reconstructed human existence form the inescapable and irre-ducible quantity that stands as the basis of all Christian life, be-lief, and reflection. The ground of all Christian thinking is the affirmation that realities are present in Christian lives which were previously unthinkable.

This newness is the redemptive presence of God's power in human lives, and it stands at the center of the root-assertions by which the Christian community has confessed its faith. From one perspective, this community speaks of the covenant that God has made with man, asserting that in this covenant God has taber-nacled with man, promising to be his sustainer, providing the enfolding ambiance outside of which there can be no genuinely human life. The earthiness of the Old Testament witness leaves no doubt as to the concrete, this-worldly character of the redemp-tive presence of God. The candidness with which the Old Testa-ment brings the most secular events into continuity with God's purposes makes it unambiguously clear that the Old Testament community believed that God's reconstruction was actual in all of life.

Christians have also given expression to the primary datum of their faith and life by asserting the reality of the Incarnation in

2 See my "Nature, Grace, and the Christian Indicative," in Philip Hefner, ed., *The Scope of Grace* (Philadelphia: Fortress Press, 1964), pp. 183–214. This beginning-point in the life that Christ has transformed may offer an option for Christological discussions today. Wolfhart Pannenberg, in his recent *Grundzuege der Christologie* (Guetersloh: Gerd Mohn, 1964) outlines the alternative approaches in Christology (pp. 15–23) as those that begin with the Church's proclamation (thereby erroneously equating Jesus with the apostolic preaching), those that begin with the historical Jesus (thereby exercising an unfortunate reductionism upon Christology), and those that begin with personal experience (thereby opening themselves to the dangers of illusion). Pannenberg himself suggests an approach that combines the historical origins of Christology in Jesus and the dogmatic elaborations of traditional Chris-tology. The category of transformed life that I suggest holds a concern for the historical Jesus as the source of transformation, while at the same time pointing to the total historical continuum in which Jesus' effects are to be empirically observed. This category cannot be equated with experience (al-though it includes it) and its subjective overtones, inasmuch as it always carries with it the signification of the corporateness comprised of all those whose life is reconstructed by Jesus' power. The reconstruction of life also opens up the cosmic aspects of Christology in a way that "experience" does not.

Jesus of Nazareth. As ambiguous as the discussion of the Incarnation has been and as problematical as contemporary modes of thought have made it, the Christian understanding of the incarnation has been a massive testimony to the conviction that the structures of nature have been penetrated by the presence of grace in Jesus. The one truth that shines through all of the Christological debate that exercised the Church for centuries is that the reality of this penetration remains unshakable in Christian awareness; the reality is prior to all reflection upon it, as well as to all attempts to demonstrate its plausibility. The formulations of Chalcedon have been found by many to be inadequate; it is commonplace for scholars to observe that Leo's *Tome* and the *Chalcedonense* do not resolve, but rather only restate, the questions to which they addressed themselves. None of this detracts, however, from the clear conviction that runs through these formulations (particularly when they are taken together with the Trinitarian reflections dating from the Council of Nicea, A.D. 325) of the reality of divine redemptive power in Jesus, a reality that is prior to theological and metaphysical speculation concerning the Incarnation in two natures. The very embarrassment that we note in these Chalcedonian documents (as well as in the patristic writings that preceded and followed after them) is itself testimony to the unshakable character of this conviction. The complex theological wrestling with the fact of the Incarnation leaves this one indelible testimony: The Church was caught up in the certainty that God had decisively entered this world, concretely; and Christian faith and life owe their dynamic to this concrete datum of God's presence as the presupposition of their development. The Christian witness to the Incarnation is luminous with the celebration of "that which we have heard, which we have seen with our eyes, which we have looked upon and touched with our hands, concerning the word of life . . . which was with the Father and was made manifest to us" in Jesus (I John 1:1–2); and this is the same word of life that was celebrated by Paul as "Christ Jesus, who though he was in the form of God . . . emptied himself . . . and became obedient unto death" (Philippians 2:6–7).[3]

Still another form in which the primacy of redeemed life has been put is the confession of Christians that they have found new life in this world through the Spirit who came at Pentecost and in the resurrection of Jesus of Nazareth to which that Spirit points. The resurrection announces the most shattering testimony of all:

---

3 Werner Elert indicates that this emptying aspect of the Incarnation can in some sense be employed as the criterion by which a proper understanding of Christology is to be measured. See his *Der Ausgang der altkirchlichen Christologie* (Berlin: Lutherisches Verlagshaus, 1957), especially Chap. 2.

The new age has dawned, an age in which the forces of God's reconstruction must be acknowledged. The words ascribed to Peter in Acts 3:32–33 sum up the essential Christian conviction: "This Jesus God raised up, and of that we all are witnesses. Being therefore exalted at the right hand of God, and having received from the Father the promise of Holy Spirit, he has poured out this which you see and hear." Similarly, the ancient Exsultet prayer from the Easter vigil speaks of the Christian confidence in the actuality of redemption in the resurrection:

Exult, O earth, made brilliant by such splendor; and illumined by the brightness of the eternal king, *know that darkness has everywhere been overcome.* . . .[4]

This is the heart of the Christian proposition: that somehow because of this man Jesus of Nazareth, there has been ushered in a new age; human existence has been decisively altered; there is now reconstructed life, where before death and ultimate frustration seemed to dominate.

These three primal assertions—concerning life in the covenant, the Incarnation in Jesus, and the power of Jesus' resurrection—illustrate how the Christian community, by its interpretation of its own career, places the reality of redemption in its life prior to reflection upon that redemption. The awareness of the reality of the resurrection preceded (and still precedes) apostolic perplexity about the resuscitation of a corpse.[5] Similarly, the conviction that God was in Christ was prior to the speculation concerning two natures in one substance in the man Jesus; and without the prior conviction that speculation would have been meaningless. Or, to add still another testimony from the early sources of Christianity, the "Son of Man" title seems to have been attached to Jesus in order to express the same conviction, namely that man's situation has been qualified by the presence of God in Jesus. For the first-century Christian, the "Son of Man" terminology could articulate this affirmation about Jesus in terms that were generally intelligible.[6] The early Christian affirmation of Jesus as living Lord or living Messiah points in the same direction. Form critics now surmise that the first Christological emphasis upon Jesus as coming Lord or Messiah, with futuristic connotations, was quickly ampli-

4 Godfrey Diekmann, O. S. B., ed. *The Masses of Holy Week and the Easter Vigil* (Collegeville, Minn.: Liturgical Press, 1957), pp. 133–136.

5 For a summary of the pertinent critical materials, see Pannenberg, *Christologie*, pp. 85–103.

6 See Ferdinand Hahn, *Christologische Hoheitstitel* (Goettingen: Vandenhoeck und Ruprecht, 1963), Chap. 1, esp. pp. 37–38.

fied by the emphasis on his living presence.[7] Presumably, such a development took place under the early Christian judgment that Christ's presence in redeeming power could not be allowed to fade under the impact of the disillusionment that met the Christian hope of an early Parousia. Such a development represents a correction of the earliest eschatologically oriented interpretations of Jesus, presumably because such interpretations were not fully adequate to articulate the *present* redemption that Christians found in their dealings with Jesus.

It is no surprise to us that such confessions stand early in the history of the Church, because the interior logic of the faith, rooted as it is in the indicative of redeemed life, would be utterly shipwrecked without the grounding which these affirmations provide. They give expression to the reality that engenders all Christian life and belief, which is the principle of its unfolding. Karl Rahner calls attention to this grounding of Christian life and belief in the vitalities of redeemed existence in his book on Mary:

> Perfect Christianity must consist in receiving this gift of the eternal God, God himself, in grace-given freedom, with body and soul and all the powers of the whole being, with all a man is and has, all he does and suffers, so that this receiving of God takes up his entire nature and his whole life-history in the eternal life of God. . . . Christianity means to receive God, not merely in some abstract realm of thought, but in an actual historical context . . . in man's corporeality.[8]

If this indicative that God has already set about his work of reconstructing human life stands at the heart of the Christian faith, and if it has been prior to all thinking about the faith, then this point of reconstruction in life is where the theologian must begin his reflection today.[9] The very simplicity of this statement is deceptive, because it smacks of pietism and sentimentality. It hardly seems a sound basis for reasonable and scientific discussion. But its consequences are so far-reaching that we cannot let

---

[7] *Ibid.*, pp. 189 ff. Hahn's work gives further corroboration for our thesis by pointing to a general trend in early Christology toward de-eschatologization, thereby, indicating that early Christian experience affirmed, above all else, the *present* victory of Jesus.

[8] Karl Rahner, *Mary, Mother of the Lord* (New York: Herder and Herder, 1963), pp. 36, 37–38. A position like the one outlined here that is rooted in the *indicative*, faces two immediate dilemmas: the problem of evil and the unfulfilled character of Christian life (the "already/not yet" dialectic of St. Paul and Luther). These issues cannot be discussed in this methodological essay, but I have suggested a way of dealing with them in *The Scope of Grace*, pp. 188–200.

[9] This assertion is the sure instinct that underlies Ritschl's insistence that *Lebensfuehrung* is central to theological methodology.

its deceptive appearance preclude its use. Rather, we must ask: "What does it mean for scientific theological work and thought to insist that the theologian's primary datum is the vitality of redeemed life?" Most importantly, it turns theology's starting-point away from an idea towards a reality, away from a book towards history, away from proposition towards life. "Essences," or "core-ideas," must inevitably be formulated in order to communicate the Christian faith, but these ideas are secondary to the bedrock incarnate redemption that engenders Christian faith. It is hardly necessary to dwell upon the decisive character of the Bible for Christian theology. The Bible stands, however, as the monument a community's life has erected, a testimony that takes on meaning when its roots in that community's life are laid bare.[10] Creedal and confessional formulations are similarly inescapable features of the theologian's inventory, but not as the foundation of his work; they stand as the articulations crystallized from generations of existence that have known the transfiguring power of God.[11] In place of idea, book, or proposition, we must set a reality, a reality that is inclusive of and constituted by actual life, a segment of the stuff that comprises the vitality of this world and its history.

Only a few anachronistic hangers-on from a past theological world will take exception to the excision of idea, book, and proposition from the primal position in the Christian faith. What may not be so clear, or so easily acknowledged, is that the primary datum of Christian faith and theology is neither an abstraction nor a formal conceptuality (as Ritschl perceived clearly and demonstrates in his insistence upon the centrality of *Lebensfuehrung*). Abstractions and formalizations are purposely and by nature removed from the actualities of life. This detachment is their genius; this removal or distance from life is what makes abstractions indispensable. This distance also marks an insurmountable barrier between these useful abstractions and life. Theology cannot do its work without employing abstractions and conceptualities, but it betrays its true nature in the instant that it succumbs to the temptation to make these inescapable instruments the ground of its reflection.

10 This insight, I take it, is essential to the manner in which the biblical materials are treated by, for example, Gerhard von Rad, *Theologie des alten Testaments*, 2 vols. (Munich: Chr. Kaiser Verlag, 1957, 1960); and Robert M. Grant, *Historical Introduction to the New Testament* (New York: Harper & Row, 1963).

11 This image is utilized by J. N. D. Kelly, *Early Christian Creeds* (London: Longmans, 1950), as a way of relating the history of theology in the first few centuries.

If the ground of theology is neither abstraction nor formal conceptuality, then the statement that Christian faith originates in the actuality of redeemed existence must not be construed as a statement of Christian existentialism. Existentialism (insofar as it is a philosophy rather than a casually thought-through attitude) is such a formal conceptuality, which purports to illumine all of human life. Its categories of lostness, despair, existential decision, and authentic existence form the loom upon which every human life is stretched. At a later point, we must show that this characteristic makes existentialism inadequate as a constitutive basis for Christian theology. (This is not to deny its usefulness as a tool for analysis in theology.) Here it is enough to call attention to the fact that the train of thought under discussion here does not present itself as a brand of existentialism. When we say that the stuff of actual life is the primary datum of Christian faith and theology, we are explicitly denying that there is a conceptuality that can serve as the loom upon which every Christian life can be stretched. We are declaring emphatically that human life has an integrity of its own that must be accepted as such. If the redemption that stands at the heart of Christian faith is incarnate within human life, or, to put it another way, if actual human life is constitutive of the reality that engenders Christian faith, then the preeminence of redeemed life over all conceptuality must be acknowledged. This does not mean that existence is formless, or that the basis of Christian faith is formless. We are not calling here for a return to vitalism. Rather, we are insisting that no single conceptuality of existence, or constellation of conceptualities, can claim to be the ground for Christian faith and theology. If Christian faith originates in a configuration formed of human life, then it is illogical to identify it with a conceptuality.

These reservations (as to the adequacy of idea, book, proposition, or abstract conceptuality to serve as primary datum of Christian faith) emerge from the conviction that Christian faith and theology have to do with the total organism of human life, whether that organism be an individual or a community. This is already implied in the statement that the actuality of reconstructed life is the ground of Christian faith. Discursive reason plays a very important role in this total organism of existence, but it is no more than one dimension of that existence. It is more adequate to say that the reality which stands at the beginning of faith and theology is a phenomenon within the dimension of the sensibilities. The dimension of sensibilities stands in contrast to the discursive intellect. This dimension of sensibilities is not primitive, nor is it anti-intellectual or irrational. The dimension of the sensibilities is permeated by reason, but it is a dimension of depth and seriousness where reality is too vivid and irrepressible to be tamed by the discursive intellect and its categories.[12]

The dimension of sensibilities is preeminently the dimension of myth, action, cultus, and piety. Myth is the depiction (usually narrative) or verbal ordering of man's encounter with reality that defies discursive, literal accounts. Historiography, astronomy, sociology, political science, economics, geology, psychology, physics, and the other precise sciences are erecting vast apparatuses for ordering the data that have emerged from man's transaction with the world in which he lives, but the reality that encounters man wears an aspect that defies the reports of these discursive, precise sciences. This aspect is recorded in man's symbolic enterprises, particularly his myths. The actuality of reconstructed life that comprises the primary datum of Christian theology does not stand in any fundamental contradiction to the precise, discursive sciences, but its deepest reaches are reflected on the screen of myth and symbol. Myth stands, then, not as a necessarily inadequate or subjective representation, but rather the most appropriate form of expression for certain dimensions of reality, including the dimension in which Christian faith is operative. The assertion that myth is appropriate where the precise sciences are not is thus itself a scientific conclusion.[13]

Human action fills another important role within the dimension of the sensibilities, because reality within this dimension so engages the whole man that expression inescapably takes the form of deeds. Deeds are not appendages at the end of a line of calculations. Rather, decisive action within the public realm, in the full sight of our fellows, is a mode of self-constitution, a constituting that grows naturally out of the most serious transactions between man and his environing world. Christian faith finds its being in the dimension where action is constitutive, and as a consequence, the expression of Christian faith incorporates action. In this aspect of its being, it is incorrect to say that Christian faith stimulates action, as if there were a set of Christian meanings that are separable from action. On the contrary, in this aspect of its being the meaning of Christian faith *is* action, because the action is an integral part of the configuration of human existence that has

[12] It may be useful to distinguish between reason and the discursive intellect. This distinction is similar to Tillich's differentiation between ontological and technical reason, or Whitehead's distinction between speculative and practical reason. Reason as the thrust towards meaning and order permeates all of life's dimensions; the discursive intellect is a more specialized function that subsumes its contact with reality under topical rubrics that permit operational efficiency.

[13] See Richard Grabau, "The Necessity of Myth: An Answer to Rudolph Bultmann," *Journal of Religion*, 44:113–122, 1964. Also Ernst Cassirer, *The Philosophy of Symbolic Forms* (New Haven: Yale, 1955), Vol. 2.

been penetrated by divine redemptive power. Another way to put it is to say that human action is not simply instrumental, but it is also expressive; it is expressive of the reality that man has encountered in his existence.

At the crucial points in human existence, man's action is no more subject to literal, discursive decoding than are his myths and symbols. In these crucial moments, the action that flows from man's transaction with external reality is itself symbolic, pointing beyond itself, testifying that it is loaded with a meaning that runs deeper than the surface shapes of its movement. Cultus is comprised of such symbolic actions. The inseparableness of meaning and action that we noted above obtains of cultus as well. Cultic action *is* the meaning of one aspect of existence. To the extent that Christian faith is incarnate within human existence, its meaning also *is* the cultus that has emerged from the Christian community's transaction with reality.

The dimension of sensibilities is also the dimension of piety. The term piety designates the concrete configuration of psychological, sociological, national, and historical factors which makes each group or individual distinctive in its apprehension and expression of the reality of God's redemptive presence. Cultus, action, and myth may be shared elements of the sensibilities, whereas "piety" designates the set of factors which makes each group's or individual's participation in these shared elements distinctive. Piety resists in a singular way any attempts to reduce itself to alien categories or to translate it into a strange idiom, because piety is an elemental pattern of perception and response that has no reality at all apart from the individuals in which it is focused and the concrete vestiges of piety they leave behind. Piety cannot be translated into discursive categories because it is itself the energy of spirit that produces categories. Piety cannot be exhausted by any analysis of its components, because it is precisely the constellation of those components which would lose its actuality if separated from the specific synthesis that those components have attained in any given moment. Piety possesses an integrity that cannot be comprised by any detached study of it, because its identity is as *sui generis* in character as the focusing of social, economic, psychological, historical, national, and geographical factors is peculiar in any given individual or group.[14]

This discussion of the primary datum of Christian faith and theology has been carried on in terms that are quite far removed from

[14] This concern for the integrity of piety is the same concern that enabled Louis Bouyer to reassess the Church's liturgy, *Liturgical Piety* (Notre Dame: University of Notre Dame Press, 1955) and Walther Voelker to make his important new insights into the character of Origen, *Das Vollkommenheitsideal des Origenes* (Tuebingen: J. C. B. Mohr, 1931).

the terms and categories that characterized Ritschl's theologizing, and the twentieth-century presuppositions that mark the present discussion stand in contrast to Ritschl's nineteenth-century stance. It seems clear, however, these differences notwithstanding, that a twentieth-century grappling with Ritschl's primary assertion about methodology, namely, that it is rooted in the category of *Lebensfuehrung*, must move inevitably to the issues that have just been raised concerning the starting-point of theology. If this is properly understood, then we are already well on the way to demonstrating how a consideration of contemporary issues that are related to the range of Ritschl's concerns can furnish a larger framework within which to place and evaluate him.

PROBLEMS OF METHODOLOGY

The foregoing discussion of the primary datum of Christian faith and theology is wholly innocuous if it is placed within the realm of pious desires for the preservation of an experiential base for theology. The genuinely programmatic character of that discussion looms before us, however, when we ask the scholarly question as to how this primary datum of redemption incarnate in human existence can be made available to theology at the level of methodology. It is in fact the reasoned, scholarly thrust of our program that wills the primary datum incorporated at the methodological level into theological effort. It is far too little for the theologian to be content with a pious acknowledgment that the datum which engenders his work is constituted by redeemed life. Such an acknowledgment encourages the dilettantism and inconsistency that is diametrically at odds with the reasoned thought that scientific theology demands.[15] It is not enough for the theologian to avail himself of the resources of myth, cultus, piety, and Christian action when it suits his purpose. On the contrary, he must fashion a methodology that will force him to shape every phase of his theology under the impact of the primary datum of life that has been outlined in the previous discussion.[16]

[15] It is misleading to use the term "science" except in reference to the natural and physical sciences, because the term has seen its connotations flattened so drastically in the past decades. In these pages, "scientific" is a synonym for the German *wissenschaftlich,* in its reference to the disciplined, scholarly use of reason that marks the academic disciplines. On the other hand, it is not desirable to refuse the designation "scientific" to theology simply because it cannot employ experimental methodologies. In light of such works as Harold Schilling's, *Science and Religion* (New York: Scribner, 1962), and Henry Margenau's, *The Nature of Physical Reality* (New York: McGraw-Hill, 1950) and *Ethics and Science* (Princeton: Van Nostrand, 1964), it seems useful to emphasize the unity and similarity of thought wherever it undertakes disciplined and scholarly activities.

[16] See *supra*, pp. 151–156.

The problems that attend the methodological incorporation of the primary datum of redeemed life into theology center on the inescapable need in theology to abstract, on the question of a norm in theology, on the dilemma of recognizing the primary datum of faith, and on appropriating that knowledge in theology. The following discussion will deal with each of these three problem areas.

Our earlier rejection of abstraction in theology is to a certain extent an exaggerated one, inasmuch as abstraction is inescapable in theology as a helpful tool of thought; and if one eschewed abstraction altogether, his only real alternative would be simple repetition of the proclamation that has attended the key events in Christian history. As useful as abstraction is, however, it must not be confused with the primary datum of theology. That datum, being as it is a manifestation of life possesses a quality of untranslatable givenness that defies the abstractions of thought. Abstraction is unavoidable if one is to escape blind repetition, but inevitably (it seems) in theology abstraction becomes a bloodless categorizing that violates the fullness, the integrity, of the concrete datum of redeemed life in Jesus Christ. The theologian tends to forget that he must continually fall back on the full life and history of the Christian community for his work; he forgets that his recourse is this life and history, not abstractions from life. He bestows too great an honor on his abstractions by permitting those abstractions to function as the "essence" of Christianity. It is precisely here, as we have already had occasion to observe. that Ritschl committed his error, inasmuch as he permitted his normative category of *Lebensfuehrung* to function so abstractly that he violated the integrity of the life that stands at the heart of the Christian faith.

The problem of abstraction, or essence, goes hand in hand with the question of norms, because theologians inevitably permit their abstractions to become their norms. A norm must be abstract, because it functions as the abstraction from the data of the Christian faith which permits the theologian to be selective in his treatment of his materials, freeing him to make his own distinctive point with regard to those materials, while at the same time enabling him to remain faithful to the whole of the Christian faith. Whether the norm is Ritschl's category of evangelical *Lebensfuehrung*, or the *sola scriptura/sola fide* norm ascribed to the Reformation, the function is the same: to permit the theologian to be selective and at the same time faithful to the entire Christian witness.

It is precisely at this point that the theologian faces a dilemma. His norm must necessarily be an abstraction functioning as the "essence of Christianity," but if it is true that the primary datum of Christian faith is an occasion of life that has been penetrated by divine grace and that Christian faith is a phenomenon of the sensibilities, then no single "essence" can qualify as norm. Abstraction or essence and the primary datum of Christian faith are diametrically opposed to each other. The Christian message speaks of a redemptive reality that is free to penetrate all of the manifold possibilities of life. This freedom includes the possibility of assuming forms that are just as unique as each instance of life is unique. An essence cannot deal with the concrete uniquenesses of existence, because the characteristic of an essence is to focus abstractly upon that which various instances have in common at the expense of the unique. God's grace, however, has no investment in the abstractions that human thought utilizes to analyze reality; that grace has only the purpose of so penetrating human existence and other forms of life that in each occasion of that life, genuine reconstruction can be effected. No matter how accurately an essence may describe the shape that grace has taken in its reconstructive work, that essence remains subordinate to the reality itself of the redemption that is incarnate within human existence. Even when the essence does present a valid interpretation of the primary datum of Christian faith, its product is a partial one that cannot exhaust the manifold of redeemed life. There is perhaps no single point that Ritschl himself so utterly failed to grasp as this one. This failure, more than anything else, underlies the sort of methodological blunder that was outlined in Chapter 3.

The conclusion is that no abstraction can qualify as norm for Christian theology. There is no single "essence" or meaning of Christianity, and the theologian or Churchman dare not pretend there is. The only adequate norm is a configuration of human life which knows itself to be transfigured by God's redemptive work and which can never be identified wholly with any interpretation of it. *The only entity that can be a norm for reflection upon the primary fact of Christian faith is itself the actuality of life that has been redeemed.* The appropriate criterion for judging discourse about redeemed life is another instance of that life itself. The theologian is therefore constantly wrestling with the dilemma of how he can structure his norm which is inescapably abstract so as to preserve in every moment of his work the prior authority of the reality of redemption in human existence.

In the practical circumstances of his work, the theologian's reflection upon this dilemma yields two conclusions: The first is that the instances of redeemed life which serve as the primary datum of faith and theology and also as prior authority for his work are most naturally and most abundantly available to the theologian *in the past,* specifically, the past occurrences of human existence that confesses its redemption at God's hands, in Christ. If contemporary redeemed life is nevertheless available to the theologian, it is chiefly in the form of documents and reports—all of which share the qualities of being in the past. Very little of this vital material comes to the theologian at first hand. The past is, for all practical purposes, the locus of the datum which undergirds the theologian's work. Secondly, it follows that if Christian theology is to proceed upon the basis of its primary datum in a reasonable and scholarly manner, then it demands a mode of knowing which operates on the basis of these past occurrences, *a historical mode of knowing*.

A HISTORICAL MODE OF KNOWING AND
VERIFYING TRUTH FOR THEOLOGY

If it is true that the primary datum of faith which serves both as substance and norm of theological work is to be found in history, then we cannot avoid the conclusion that *history somehow serves the Christian theologian as a principle of knowledge and a rubric of truth*. In the context of this discussion, the term "history" refers to the past as it impinges upon conscious awareness in the present, and as it is efficacious within that present awareness. When this understanding of the term "history" is brought into conjunction with Christian theology, it must be taken to refer to the concrete, empirically given, historical witness of the Christian community (conceived both as a corporate entity and as a communion of individuals) as this witness is efficacious in any present moment.

In order to understand this conception of history as the principle of knowledge and rubric of truth for Christian theology, an excursus is necessary to clarify the nature of religious experience and knowledge.

We are presupposing the following general structure of experience: The common deliverance of our immediate awareness is that the self is confronted by some sort of a not-self (or not-selves), which stands over against the individual but yet in some sort of relationship to him.[17] As the individual progresses in ordering the data of awareness, he is conscious that, in some situations, the not-self places an extraordinary demand upon him; this is the

17 This general structure of experience is a common feature of the modern philosophical tradition. It is basically the structure described by Immanuel Kant in the first pages of his first Critique—*Immanuel Kant's Critique of Pure Reason*, Norman Kemp Smith, trans. (London: Macmillan, 1958), pp. 41 ff. More specifically, however, I am indebted here to the structure that is presented by Miss Dorothy Emmet in her *The Nature of Metaphysical Thinking* (London: Macmillan, 1957).

demand that the self submit to the not-self as the ordering principle of the self's existence. Experience in such circumstances is religious experience; and the not-self who places this absolute demand upon the individual is God. This dimension of experience certainly makes its impression upon all of the individual's life, but the heart of religious experience lies in this situation of becoming aware of an ordering principle of existence, and committing oneself to it.

This picture of human existence is, of course, quite common. It is a picture of man faced with the decision to commit himself to a God. The category of "leap of faith" or "existential decision" is not out of place here as a description of the individual's situation when confronted by the decision for commitment. It must not be assumed, however, that the tones of agony and trauma in which existentialist philosophers normally paint their pictures of the leap of faith are universal human phenomena. These tones are suggestive of what the human situation of ultimate commitment may be, but no more than that can be predicated of them. Least of all can they be elevated to some sort of a normative status wherein they determine what religious experience ought to be like. Men may actualize their commitment to an ordering principle of existence in several ways.

As significant as this situation of decision before a God may be, it certainly is not all that one can point to in the religious experience. It is one of the foci about which religious experience is oriented; but there is another, and it is equally important. It is not enough that the self simply becomes aware of an ultimate Other that demands submission. In addition, *knowledge* of that Other is necessary so that man can understand the wider implications of its demand for his total life and for all of reality as he knows it; knowledge is necessary, furthermore, if man is to communicate with others concerning this Other and its demand. The individual does not stand forever teetering upon the brink of decision, dominated by the trauma of submission to an awe-full Other. He is aware not simply of an Other who demands decision and commitment; he is also aware of an Other who enables this commitment, this submission to the Other as the ordering principle of existence. In this situation, the individual celebrates the presence of a grace that has enabled what otherwise would have been impossible for him, namely his submission to God and the dependence upon him as the ordering principle of life. This celebration of grace's presence is significant because it furnishes the knowledge which in turn is the *guidance* and *certainty* that the individual or the community needs as they strive to understand precisely what constitutes commitment in any particular moment, and what constitutes *right* commitment (the question of truth) in relation to the wider reaches of their understanding of the world and other persons. The situation in which the individual receives the grace to submit bestows upon him at the same time the knowledge which includes the guidance and certainty that he seeks.

The picture of religious experience that we are considering here has two foci: the challenge to submit to an ultimate Other and the confession of the presence of grace which that Other has already engendered in his existence under the forms of power to submit and the knowledge which brings guidance and certainty. The situation described by the first of the two foci points to the awareness of God which the individual knows as an imperative in his life; the second of the foci describes the knowledge and acquaintance that the individual gains of God as a liberating indicative for his life. Both aspects are inescapable in the religious experience; the first aspect impresses upon man that there is a God who demands something of man, the second tells him who his God really is and what God's presence means. Each of these dimensions is necessary for the fulfillment of the other. The transition from no commitment to full commitment is a decisive moment in the Christian faith; it is not always recognized that the transition from vague ignorance to a knowledge of God is just as decisive. Kierkegaard's man who is called upon to cast himself into 70,000 fathoms of water may be our paradigm of the first trauma; the story of Moses' call in the desert may be paradigmatic of the second—a man who acknowledged his meeting with a God, but who was reluctant to acknowledge this God and therefore hesitated in obeying what God commanded (Exodus 3:13-16) until he could *know* who the God was.

What we have discussed here as the general structure of religious experience stands as a rough phenomenological description of what we spoke of earlier as the primary datum of Christian faith and theology, specifically, human life that has been penetrated decisively and reconstructed by divine grace—the unshakable core of the Christian faith. It is important to recognize that this primary datum carries within it the thrust towards both commitment and knowledge (including guidance and certainty as aspects of *knowing* God), corresponding to the two foci within the religious experience. It is generally acknowledged that knowledge of God (in the Christian view) must include commitment, but it is not always equally clear that commitment must include knowledge, and this knowledge emerges from the indicative of reconstructed life. Unless the individual or community knows its God, commitment is an empty, often romantic, ideal (for instance, the example of Moses). Without hard consideration of who our God is, commitment is an idealized notion that stands quite in opposition to the fullness of Christian faith.

When the individual or community, caught up within the structure of religious experience that I have just sketched, begins to ask questions of knowledge, certainty, and guidance (all with an eye towards the commitment that makes his life), the inescapable question of norms and authorities enters in. We have suggested that, when the issue is one of life, nothing else but an occasion of life itself can ultimately serve as norm. When the issue under consideration is redemption or grace incarnate within existence, then nothing else but an instance or instances of grace-in-existence can be normative.[18] At this point, history enters as an instrument in acquiring knowledge and certainty with relation to God, *inasmuch (as we have observed above) as these instances of grace-in-existence reside, overwhelmingly, in the past.* This search for knowledge within the process of commitment to the ultimate Other clarifies the interrelation of history and existence. On the one hand, as we have described religious experience, it is in the context of existence that history (as part of the quest for knowledge) presses in upon man, and it is in the service of existential clarity that history becomes a matter of concern. But on the other hand, existence contains within itself the inevitable drive beyond itself into history (inasmuch as the quest for knowledge leads to history). Therefore, Christian theology, if it is faithful to the primary datum of faith, finds that the processes of human existence push it inescapably towards the Christian past and a historical mode of knowledge, with a historical norm.

One would think that this inescapable movement from existence into history would be self-evident. If it is true that existentialism is concerned about the reality of the individual concrete life and that it desires particularly to defend concrete life from violation by mass society and technology, then it should follow that nothing less than the untrammeled and inviolate datum of human existence itself could serve as guide into the ways of existence and as criterion for judging the authenticity of existence. Existentialism has, however, tended to permit itself to be tyrannized by the phenomenological method that is otherwise so helpful in resisting the threats of objectification and violation by outside forces. By a careful phenomenological analysis, men like Martin Heidegger, Rudolph Bultmann, and Friedrich Gogarten have erected an ab-

---

18 It must be noted that this type of a norm is not anthropocentric. It is theocentric, inasmuch as it speaks always of *God's presence* within human existence. Human existence is the *locus* of the norm. This means that existence is inescapable for the theologian, but it does *not* mean that his work is anthropocentric or subjective.

stract picture of existence which serves them both as guide and criterion of authentic existence. This threatens, however, to short-circuit the drive for knowledge and self-certainty that every living person exhibits in his existence. If this drive is given its freedom to course where it will, it does not find knowledge and certainty in abstractions derived from phenomenological investigations. Rather it finds its quest satisfied in concourse with other living persons and in testimonies they give about what is true and authentic in life. Concourse with living persons is concourse with history, because the documents, institutions, and actions, and other monuments of history bring us testimony that expands the severely limited scope of our own personal acquaintance. When the life we are concerned with is life transfigured by the God of the Old Testament–New Testament tradition, then the history which clarifies that life is the history of the Christian community.

Professor Carl Michalson has given considerable thought to the inevitability of history as a factor in Christian knowledge and truth, and his contributions to theological methodology, as a result, are extremely provocative. As he outlines his position in *The Rationality of Faith*,[19] however, it becomes evident that his use of the term "history" is deceptive. History for Michalson seems almost synonymous with the phenomenological analysis of the self-consciousness that men like Maurice Merleau-Ponty have undertaken. As a consequence, history becomes, under Michalson's pen, a matter of the self-consciousness, a term that could be rendered as "time" with very little loss of meaning. In the paragraphs above, I have meant to say that instances of redeemed existence, in their objective reality outside my self-consciousness, in all of their integrity and strangeness, serve as the principle of knowledge and criterion of truth when I search for understanding into just what redeemed existence is. History is not synonymous with time or the self-consciousness. History is the moving repository of events and monuments that emerge from those events. Although it is in my self-consciousness that the desire for knowledge about existence arises, it is from the objectivities of existence outside my self-consciousness that I find instruction and guidance, as well as the criteria for making judgments of truth. As a consequence of his preoccupation with the self-consciousness, Michalson can give little place in his methodology to historical events as such, as the general historian would deal with them. Rather, Michalson must work with "meanings" of events as they impinge upon the self-consciousness. This is particularly true of his account of the resurrection of Jesus. In this discussion, he does not speak

[19] Carl Michalson, *The Rationality of Faith: An Historical Critique of the Theological Reason* (New York: Charles Scribner's Sons, 1963).

of the resurrection in terms of a historical event, but rather as "the event in which it is revealed through Jesus of Nazareth who God really is and in which that revelation brings to life the new people of God, the church."[20] The inappropriateness of the term *history* in this connection can be seen clearly if we were to discuss the American Revolution *solely* as the event in which it was revealed, what it means to be an American and in which the American nation was brought to life. The statement is certainly not untrue, but it is not the description of the American Revolution as a historical event but rather a discussion of its impact. As such, it is a phenomenological description of an American's appreciation and appropriation of the Revolution. Whether this is "history" is a matter of debate. "History" includes the impact of events, but not in isolation from those events as objective happenings. The paragraphs immediately above (on pages 126–129) employ a phenomenological analysis, but with the explicit awareness that this analysis is incomplete unless amplified by history.

History enters Christian theology as the witness of the Christian community. This witness is constituted of the material that emerges from the life of the Christian community in all of its historical continuity and contemporary breadth. Whatever emerges as a monument or distillate or vestige from man's life with God in the Christian tradition (historical and contemporary piety, worship, canonical writings, dogma, theology, and actions, including specifically ethical actions as well as internal and external institutional relationships) can be counted as part of the witness. The witness is constituted, then, by many specific responses (which, taken together, form one massive response or confession) which have been engendered within human existence (whether negatively or positively, indirectly or directly) by God's encounter with the Christian community. This notion of "monument, distillate, or vestige" furnishes important methodological considerations. Every historical material from the Christian tradition—whether document, artifact, art object, ethical consequence, or whatever—is approached as if it were a sign telling where persons have been in their living encounter with the Other which has called them to commitment and confession. Moreover, these signs are read with respect to what they can disclose, first of all, about that Other. The Christian, like the general historian, wants to reconstruct the events out of which the monuments have come; he is not concerned solely with "meanings," but he reconstructs so as to learn from the events about God's presence within the structures of life. Many other things can and must be said about the vestiges of Christian existence that constitute this historical witness; and, furthermore,

[20] *Ibid.*, p. 52. See the entire discussion, pp. 48–55.

this witness can be approached from many different perspectives and scrutinized by differing methodologies. The most important judgment for the Christian concerning the witness, however, and the one that is therefore indispensable, which our hermeneutical stance demands is this: These vestiges have emerged from events in the life of a community whose existence (both as a corporate entity and as a collection of individuals) has somehow been transfigured by God's grace, and at the same time thereby challenged to ultimate commitment and vivified by the confession of reconstructive power in its midst. These events, as the vestiges themselves, are said to be continuous and parts of an ordered whole by virtue of the action of God to which they testify.

This historical witness, then, is in fact a historical continuum, model, or system; that is to say, it is constituted by the issue of historical events which (singly and as a constellation) are interpreted in such a way as to make fundamental statements concerning the nature of the Other who has been encountered and concerning the nature and destiny of the human existence that has been transfigured by the encounter. The Other is said to be in some way the doer or progenitor of the events that comprise the historical witness.[21]

There are two important observations that need to be made about this historical witness as a continuum of events that originate in God. The first is the recognition that the events which constitute the continuum are empirically available. These events must be available to all men, for all to observe their structure and meaning. The events in the historical witness are not created by the Christian community. Along with this empirical availability goes the recognition that the claim of these events to be God's action is also empirically available to all. Although the events in the historical witness are susceptible of several interpretations by the various disciplines of study, their claim to be associated with God's dealings with men must also be acknowledged as evident to all. Recognizing these events and their claim, therefore, is not distinctively the work of the Christian community, nor is it distinctively the activity of faith. The distinctive work of the Christian community and its faith is the *peculiar use* that the community makes of these events and their claim. It is only the Christian community which asserts that of all the possible inter-

21 The precise description of the relation between God and the events in the historical witness is a very subtle problem. Miss Emmet speaks persuasively of the relation as one of "systematic concomitant variation" (*op. cit.*, pp. 62–63). Pannenberg speaks of it in less precise terms as "indirect" in *Offenbarung als Geschichte*, pp. 16–20 (see *supra*, p. 101, note 30). Ritschl dealt with this problem in terms of Lotze's epistemology, whereas Baur employed the Hegelian dialectic in his approach.

pretations of these events the most important (indeed, the key to their most fundamental meaning) is their place within the continuity of God's dealing with men. Only this community employs these events to make basic assertions about the nature of God and the destiny of man. The work of faith does not lie in the mere acquaintance with these events and their claim; it lies in doing with them what only the Christian community does.[22]

The upshot of all this is that *the Christian community uses the historical continuum that constitutes its witness as a principle of knowledge and rubric of truth.* The community claims that this organically continuous history—in its totality—constitutes a history of the presence of God, that it is thus the revelation of God's will and intention for men. This historical continuum is therefore a model or system which gives the Christian community its picture of God and his will for man. It is because this historical model furnishes the authoritative picture of God for Christians that we can say that it is their principle of knowledge and rubric of truth. By means of this historical continuum, the Christian community seeks to render its past (and that of each of its individual members) intelligible, to clarify and guide present commitment, and to sustain and direct future hope. Reason functions within this historical system by bringing the present religious experience of the community and its members into relationship with the other events in the system. This work of reason provides the knowledge and truth that the Christian community strives for, the clear continuity between its present moments and the continuum of God's action in prior generations of the community's life. This is the knowledge that is petitioned in the ancient prayer at the canonical hour of Prime, as Christians have traditionally prayed it before going to their daily work:

To the beginning of this day you have brought us, O Lord God Almighty. Preserve us now by Your power so that throughout this whole day we may not fall into any sin; *rather, that all our words, thoughts, and acts become part of Your holy, providential plan. . . .*[23]

Reason functioning in this model observes the continually unfolding present and places it within the historical continuity of the community's witness. It achieves thereby the peculiar type of knowledge of which it is capable, and which the Christian theologian seeks. Thus, each moment of commitment and confession

---

[22] Pannenberg undergirds this sort of argument by reference to Luther's notion of the "external clarity" of Scripture. See his *"Heilsgeschehen und Geschichte," Kerygma und Dogma*, 5:277–278, October 1959.

[23] See William G. Heidt, O. S. B., ed., *A Short Breviary for Religious and the Laity*, 3rd ed. (Collegeville, Minn.: Liturgical Press, 1962), p. 199. Italics added.

is related to God's faithfulness, to his continuity-establishing action
in history. Professor Pannenberg has elaborated upon this point
in a manner that is most appropriate to the argument. He writes:

Only the source of the contingent character of historical events, because of its interior unity with itself, can also be the source of the
relatedness of those events without compromising their nature as
contingent. The unity of the events is not, however, constituted by
some transcendent point of origin. The events are, moreover, not
only contingent in respect to each other, but they also stand together
with each other. This relatedness that inheres in each event has its
basis in the transcendent unity of God, which manifests itself as his
faithfulness. If, however, the interrelation of the data of history is
grounded in the faithfulness of a free God, we must not look for
continuity which persists in history from the past into the future—
somewhat in the form of "development." Rather, the events, which
are themselves contingent, are linked together, as it were, from the
present backwards; they are referred backwards to that which has
already happened. By means of such a backward-linking the continuity is always being established anew. It is in this way that the
faithfulness of God expresses itself. Only in this manner, as a back-
ward-reaching incorporation of the contingently new into that which
has already happened—and, conversely, never as a forward-reaching
guiding and effecting—can the basic unity of history be conceived
without forfeiting its contingency. We come to this same conclusion
when we consider that the continuity of the events of history is first
surveyed from the present backwards.[24]

It follows, then, from this line of reasoning that *the norm by
which the Christian theologian attains his knowledge and certainty consists of the totality of the events in the Christian historical witness as they appear in any present moment.*

THE FUNCTIONING OF HISTORICAL REASON

The proposal we have just made concerning history as a principle of knowledge within the Christian community may be
rendered more intelligible if at least brief attention is turned
to the functioning of historical reason, as it is presupposed in the
foregoing discussion. The earlier discussion presupposed a theory
that knowing and verifying are basically a process of *ordering*
the actual data of awareness which one encounters. Essentially,
this process of ordering consists of demonstrating a relationship
between a center or focus from which one operates and the data
of experience with which one must effect some sort of a modus

[24] *"Heilsgeschehen und Geschichte,"* p. 285. Translation by this writer.

vivendi at the several moments of his life. The ordering process is implemented by erecting a system or model or continuum that can effectively include both the center from which one operates and the data of awareness that one seeks to relate to that center. The system or model enables the knower to demonstrate the relationship he seeks. This demonstration need not be exclusively an intellectual one; it may prove to be so irresistible at the level of sensibilities that little conceptual support is necessary. When a clear relationship has been established, we can say that meaning has been attained; order has been achieved; a system has been erected and implemented. Knowing within this framework is systematizing; the distinctive work of reason is system-building.[25]

Most of the models or systems that we use in ordering the data of our awareness are not of ultimate significance. Many are only temporary, as those erected in the natural and physical sciences. Some few, however, are erected to explain the significance of all of reality, and the persons involved stake their very existence and its meaning on the model. The basic models that theology deals with are of this last type, models whose significance is of an ultimate, rather than a penultimate, nature.

This description of knowing, specifically in theology, is a description of how reason works. When we speak of reason knowing reality through models that are of ultimate, rather than penultimate, significance, we are referring to reason in what Whitehead calls its "speculative," and Tillich its "ontological" nature, in which it does actually seek union with the reality outside itself, as contrasted with the mechanical or "technical" reasoning that achieves order of a more operational nature. Revelation is not the violation of reason within this scheme, but rather it is the rare situation in which reason's ordering (remembering that this ordering is not exclusively an intellectualistic one, but one that includes all dimensions of man's being) succeeds in finding the meaning of the deepest realities of existence.

As corollary to this insight that knowing is system-building, the placing of the data of awareness into meaningful contexts or models, is the acknowledgment that there are differing types of systems which deal with differing types of questions within the quest for knowledge, and which thus give different types of answers to those questions. As a rule of thumb, it is helpful to recognize that systems ask different sorts of questions and that

25 For discussions of this function of reason, see A. N. Whitehead, *The Function of Reason* (Boston: Beacon Press, 1958), Chap. 3; Dorothy Emmet, *The Nature of Metaphysical Thinking* (London: Macmillan, 1957), Chaps. 4–7, 9; Henry Margenau, *The Nature of Physical Reality* (New York: McGraw-Hill, 1950). Margenau is particularly instructive in his theory of how the mind theorizes. (See also his *Ethics and Science*.)

they are oriented upon differing centers. In its operation, each system or model is self-contained and self-authenticating. These characteristics of systems of knowing—that each is restricted to the types of questions it can ask, and that each system is self-authenticating—remind us that sophistication as to the limited character of any system of knowing must accompany the use of the system itself.

Any manner of ordering is possible and legitimate; proceeding from any center or focus, relationship can be established with encountered reality so as to order it. Not all systems of order are equally adequate, however, nor are all legitimate in Christian theology. The adequacy of any system depends upon the seriousness of that which forms its center or focus and upon the clarity and firmness of the relationship which has been established between this center and the reality which the knowing self has encountered. Some students of the subject have suggested that there are only two basic systems of ordering reality, the ontological (sometimes called the logical or cosmic) and the historical (sometimes called the psychological).[26] Our investment in any such categorization need not be great. For our purposes here it is enough to insist that several types of systems are possible, and that one of these is a historical system or mode of knowing.[27]

If, however, for purposes of clarification, one were to draw a comparison between ontological and historical systems of knowing, he might do so in the following terms. An ontological system (a system of being) will seek to know the data of awareness in terms of their quality or status of being. And although, as in any other system, its knowledge takes as referent or focus the basis of those data, this basis must be conceived of as being, in its most general categories, being-itself, or some other equivalent. Such a system will ask questions of the type, "How are the data of my experience related to being-itself?" The possibility of cognition, as well as its content, is dependent upon recognition of this relationship and its character. Knowledge in such a system is the awareness of the unity of being and the place within that unity which is held by the knowing self and the data of its perceptual

26 See Thorlief Boman, *Hebrew Thought Compared with Greek* (Philadelphia: Westminster, 1960), Chap. 5; Dorothy Emmet's discussion of models in *op. cit.*, Chaps. 4, 7. Carl Michalson, *op. cit.*, Chap. 1; Alan Richardson, *History Sacred and Profane* (Philadelphia: Westminster, 1964), pp. 81 ff.

27 There may be several forms of historical systems for knowing. For example, Hegel, Marx, and J. C. K. von Hoffmann may be presenting different modes of knowing, each of which is "historical" in some sense. If this is so, then the question arises as to which is most adequate. The course of this book's argumentation clarifies what the present writer considers the canons of such adequacy to be, and what sort of system is most fully consonant with these canons.

experience in relation to being-itself as the focus of the system. A historical system will seek to know the data of the awareness in terms of their continuity as historical events. Its knowledge, too, will take as referent the basis of these data; but it will designate this basis with a term such as "Progenitor" or "Doer" of the events. By such a term the system means to designate the continuity-establishing-Something which one is aware of in the event. This Continuity-Establisher or Progenitor becomes the focus or center of this system. This system of knowing will ask questions of the type, "Wherein lies the continuity of the events in which I am and have been aware of an Other who calls me to ultimate commitment?" Knowledge (order) in this system is the awareness of a historical unity (or continuity) and the place that is held within that unity by the knowing self and the data of its experience in relation to the Establisher of that continuity.

This comparison is only illustrative. It is certainly impossible to argue for any ultimate separation of the various systems for knowing; a historical system, for example, certainly presupposes a theory of being. The contention is, however, that there are several systems of knowing available to man, and that the Christian faith demands a historical mode or system of knowing on the grounds that were set forth earlier in this chapter, namely, that it takes its origin in the actualities of reconstructed human existence.

However one may conceive of a historical system of knowing, three considerations are decisive for understanding the present train of thinking. The historical mode of knowing is concerned to put particular emphasis upon the continuity between events within any particular continuum (in our case, the continuum of the Christian communal witness), upon the interrelations of these events in the continuum as a whole (as one integral entity), and upon the spontaneity, contingency, and novelty which belong to the historical events under discussion. At several points, the argument of this chapter has dealt or will deal with these three considerations. It should be clear now, however, that the inadequacies of abstraction as a basis for theological methodology that were noted earlier are thrown into sharp focus by these considerations within a historical mode of knowing. Abstractions, including historical "analogies," tend to substitute structural *congruence* or *identity* for historical *continuity*.[28] A historical mode of knowing

28 It is at this point that one would have to question the work of H. Richard Niebuhr in *The Meaning of Revelation* (see footnote 27), when he speaks of "patterns" for understanding history (for example, pp. 86 f., 109 ff.). Richard R. Niebuhr's position seems even more unsatisfactory when he speaks of Christ's resurrection as an "analogy" for interpreting history, particularly when he identifies this analogy rather simplistically with justification by

looks for continuities and discontinuities rather than for congruence of forms. Or again, the abstraction isolates events from their position within the whole of the continuum and judges them according to the non-historical lineaments of form. A historical mode of knowing assigns meaning to an event by discovering its interrelations with the totality of the continuum in which it takes its place. Finally, abstraction denies spontaneity, novelty, and contingency, because its form defies these. It is for this reason that abstraction is peculiarly misleading when applied to the study of human existence. A genuinely historical mode of knowing recognizes that its system of knowing must have built into it an inherent ability to allow for the spontaneity, novelty, and contingency that belong to the integrity of the data encountered within the awareness.

When the theologian carries on his work within the historical system of knowing, as it has been outlined here, he finds that a peculiar dimension of his life's commitment is illumined. This illumination attends the recognition that a historical mode of knowing entails a specific commitment to a certain continuity between his own belief, life, and work, and the belief, life, and work that is represented in the Christian communal witness, the historical model by which he gains theological knowledge. This commitment to continuity is often little recognized for the decisive factor that it really is in Christian life and theology. My comments above, in a reference to Professor Michalson's thought, indicate that current discussions of history sometimes restrict themselves to a dialectic within the self-consciousness that is unable to deal with the objective events which must be included in any conception of history. When history is considered only in terms of the processes of the self-consciousness, the objective continuity of history is also depreciated, inasmuch as the individual's "stream of consciousness" supplants any continuity events might possess more objectively. Even so lucid a discussion as Professor Gordon Kaufman's discussion of man speaks of the importance of history chiefly in terms of its presence and continuing influence within the processes of consciousness—as a personal decision, for example, is past, and yet constitutively efficacious in the present.[29] Our intention in this discussion of history as an epistemological model gives more emphasis to the objective continuity which events may have outside the consciousness of the knower (though indeed, it is the knower's interpretive imagination that makes possible his

faith—*Resurrection and Historical Reason* (New York: Scribner, 1957), pp. 149–155.

[29] Gordon Kaufman, "The *Imago Dei* as Man's Historicity," *The Journal of Religion*, 36:157–168, 1956.

understanding of the continuity). If our conception of historical reason is valid, we must say that man, as a historical being who seeks to know historically, has built into him a desire to place himself within one historical continuity or another, and it is from this inherent desire that the past derives its tremendous efficacy. This is the significance of the prayer from the office of Prime; Christians, as historical thinkers, are uneasy until they have placed themselves (or find themselves placed) within the continuity of the communal witness-model.

This commitment to continuity is comprised by four elements: First, it includes the conviction that the Other, or not-self, to which the individual Christian responds in his engagement with reality (and which is the source of the data he knows in his awareness) is the same Other which the historical community and its individuals have encountered and which that community asserts to be the focus upon which its system of knowing is oriented.

Second, it includes the assertion that the ordering principle which the individual perceives in his transaction with reality (and to which he submits) is the same principle as that which the community and its individuals accepted, successively, in history.

Third, it includes the assertion that the historical responses which comprise the community's witness bear the same correlation to the Other which engendered them as the individual's own response.[30]

Fourth, it includes the affirmation that the efficacy of the community's model has extended to and embraced the individual Christian's very own existence. In a sense, the individual is "bringing the community's history up-to-date" in his response, by affirming that he, too, holds a place in that history by virtue of his encounter with the Other and his submission to it. In his commitment, he accepts the past of the community as his own. He accepts its model or system. The system of knowing which is constituted by the community's witness exists for clarifying the present. By accepting the historical witness, the individual affirms that it makes his present intelligible; he places himself and his present experience within a "total picture of significant action" (H. R. Niebuhr). He affirms a principle of unity which indicates to him where he is, where he has come from, and where he is going. And where he has been is where the community has been. That is, the context of events and their source which makes his existence meaningful is the context of the community's model.

We have called this attitude toward continuity a "commitment to continuity" in order to emphasize that it is not simply an intellectual recognition of continuity, but rather what H. Richard

---

[30] See *supra*, pp. 126–129.

Niebuhr terms "a moral event."[31] It corresponds to the second of the two foci within religious experience, as described above. Accepting this continuity and therefore also the community's model is part and parcel of the "existential" commitment that constitutes what Christian belief calls "faith." As Pannenberg has pointed out, the obverse side of this commitment to continuity is faith in God's faithfulness, which is indispensable to the Christian faith. Acceptance of the community's model of knowledge and certainty rescues the believer from bondage to the imperative, the continual uncertainity and incompleteness that attend the existentialist notion of encounter. Such uncertainty and incompleteness, as the category of encounter expresses, do not represent the whole truth of the Christian's awareness of God. The knowledge or order which the community's witness affords does broaden the partial truth that the "encounter" terminology expresses, so as to bring into clearer focus the consciousness of the indicative that is included in the Christian awareness, the indicative which speaks of the restoration that God works now, together with the continuity of restorative work that God has performed in the past.

A HISTORICAL NORM FOR THEOLOGICAL WORK

In an earlier section of this chapter, we noted a major methodological dilemma that confronts the theologian. On the one hand he must incorporate into his work at every point the dynamic stuff of the actualities of redeemed human life that constitute the Christian faith; but on the other hand the intellectual processes that comprise much of his activity entail an abstracting from the materials of the faith that threatens to dissolve the dynamics of life. In this section we must take a step, on the basis of the preceding discussion, towards resolving this methodological dilemma. In the final analysis, it is impossible to escape the processes of abstracting, but it is possible to reshape abstractions on the basis of the considerations we have mentioned.

Abstraction enters most pertinently into the theologian's work when he considers the *norm* for his thinking. A norm serves the function of buttressing the theologian's certainty about his work. It is that to which he takes recourse as a means of gaining the consideration of his audience, and that which gives him the confidence that he is not seriously in error. A norm also serves a selective function. The norm inescapably serves to limit the theologian's vision, telling him what is important in the materials that come under his glance, and by implication discarding the remainder

31 H. Richard Niebuhr, *The Meaning of Revelation* (New York: Macmillan, 1941), pp. 81–90.

as unimportant. The norm determines what meaning the theologian will find in the mass of data that come his way. Much as the theologian would like to, there is no way to escape the need for certainty and the propensity for selectivity. What the theologian can do, however, is to acknowledge the dangers of abstraction and seek to broaden his vision in the face of the frightening closure that his norm threatens. In the light of the present discussion, we might say that the theologian must recognize that the most appropriate norm for his work is *the total continuum of Christian history, as this continuum is focused in any one present moment on any single concern and as this continuum is observable in the responses of the Christian community, responses that have been incarnate in human existence.*

This norm carries with it several important implications. In the first place, the norm is both cumulative and concrete. The term *cumulative* reminds the theologian that he is beholden to the totality of human commitment and confession that God's presence has engendered. This means that the theologian can never stop with one person or epoch of Christian history as if it were so forceful a statement of Christian faith that nothing else could matter. To rest content with one man's or one epoch's statement is to abstract that peculiar configuration of redeemed human existence as preeminent over all others. This was Ritschl's blunder. We should understand also by the term "cumulative" that the succeeding instances of Christian commitment and confession are not simply tacked on to each other, as if their totality were the equivalent of an arithmetic sum of all Christian experience. Rather, the interplay between confessions and commitments, within one era and across epochs, leaves its impact on each confession. The commitment and confession associated with Martin Luther, for example, is not an isolated entity that rises above the ages, but it is to be interpreted in the light of changing Protestant and Roman Catholic responses to Luther and interpretations of him. Any consideration of Luther today, as normative for theology, would therefore have to consider more than the man and his statements in the sixteenth century. In order to understand who Luther was and what he has to say to us today, the whole spectrum of response to him since the 1500s must be taken into account, in a critical fashion.

The *concrete* character of the norm is a continual restraint in the face of the temptation to subvert the cumulative aspect of the norm by application of arithmetic concepts of the totality or by any other abstracting operations. It is not the theologian's idealization of a particular configuration of historical Christian existence that deserves authoritative status, but rather the concrete shape of that existence and its concrete impact upon other instances of Christian existence.

It is not an easy thing for the contemporary American mind to accept a norm for thinking that is as comprehensive as the one suggested here nor one which embraces within itself the concrete fullness of history as a normative prerequisite for present thinking. There is no need to elaborate here how American thought has on the one hand conceived of our culture as a totally new enterprise blazing new paths in the wilderness, and on the other so fully dedicated itself to the technological enterprise that it has flattened the dimensions of time into one endless present. There are certain contemporary modes of thought and activity, however, that are awakening our sensibilities to the possibility that the flattening of the time-dimension is actually contradictory of what we know about reality itself, as a result of our empirical studies of life.

The first of these modes of thought emerges from contemporary biological evolutionary theory.[32] This theory paints for us a picture of life which is comprised of organisms poised in the attempt to cope adequately with an environing world. Evolutionary theorists understand that coping adequately with the environment is to establish the sort of modus vivendi with environment that will enable life to maintain itself. These theorists suggest that the life which is thus maintained is at every point the product of the inter-action between the total environment which the organism has confronted and the total resources which the organism possesses within itself. It is not the case that an organism brings to its world certain established traits which it then uses to subdue the environment. Rather, the organism enters its negotiations with the world in possession of a bundle of inherited potentialities (what the biologists call a genotype) which assume their shape (termed phenotype, by evolutionary theorists) and take on certain traits only as those negotiations stimulate development in certain directions rather than in others (natural selection). We call attention to the fact that everything which the organism possesses and everything which it brings with it into the world is caught up into its life-activity of effecting a modus vivendi with the environment. Every organism, from man on down, brings a past with it into the present, and it is efficacious at every moment. Nor is this past restricted to the individual's past, but on the contrary includes the past of the race and even all of life.[33]

The burgeoning new field of cybernetics is a second mode of

32 For an authoritative discussion, see Theodosius Dobzhansky, *Mankind Evolving* (New Haven: Yale, 1962).

33 See Loren Eiseley, *The Immense Journey* (New York: Vintage Books, Random House, 1946).

contemporary thought that is pertinent to our consideration of theological thinking.[34] Cybernetics, which might be described technically as the science of information and control, is the discipline that has observed how decisions are made in complex systems, whether these systems be living organisms or machines or other concatenations of atoms. The conclusions of the cyberneticists indicate that decisions are made by bringing materials from the past history of the system to bear upon present problems, whether those materials from the past are programed into a computer or whether they constitute the heritage of sensibility and adaptation emerging from a lifetime of successful adjustment within a living organism to the environing world. The system seeks to regulate or control present activity in the light of the past it possesses, inasmuch as this past contains within it a description of the system's purpose, as well as information which gives instruction as to how that purpose can best be actualized. "Control" and "information" have therefore assumed a very important place in cybernetics, inasmuch as they designate the chief functioning of the system as that of controlling activity so as to implement a purpose; and this controlling is dependent upon the effective handling of information from the system's past (however that may be defined) and present activity. The shape of this functioning is designated by the term "feedback," which refers to the circulating of information into the control centers of the system concerning the conditions within the system and the efficiency of its attempts to perform the action that is intended. Feedback enables the system to control itself on the basis of its actual performance in relation to the tasks it intends to perform. Feedback activates a thermostat to control heat in a room, even as it helps a golfer to improve his swing or a person to reach a forkful of food to his mouth.

The point that we wish to derive here from the study of cybernetics is that the system functions with the totality of its "memory bank" or past at its disposal to guide present decisions. In every decision the total relevant past is synthesized or recapitulated anew in a relevant expression of purpose. The provocative question that awaits the reflection of those men who can synthesize great bodies of knowledge is whether this image of thought which cybernetics furnishes is not a fundamental principle of all of life. The work

[34] For helpful discussions of cybernetics, see W. Ross Ashby, *An Introduction to Cybernetics* (New York: Wiley, 1963). Also the following by Norbert Wiener: *The Human Use of Human Beings,* 2nd ed. (Garden City: Doubleday Anchor Books, 1954); *Cybernetics or Control and Communication in the Animal and the Machine,* 2nd ed. (New York: M. I. T. and Wiley, 1961). Also D. A. Bell, *Intelligent Machines: An Introduction to Cybernetics* (New York: Blaisdell, 1962).

of such thinkers as S. C. Alexander and Alfred North Whitehead would seem to indicate that it is.[35] The insights of these metaphysicians, however, is not often able to get a hearing in our time, principally because our American ethos is by nature ill-disposed toward metaphysical speculation. The biological and cybernetic materials that I have just referred to suggest that our current enthusiasm for the present and for the future to the exclusion of a consideration of the role that our total past plays in our behavior rests on a misunderstanding of the laws of life—even as those laws are understood by the empirical studies which our age cherishes so much.

Only a full-length study could document and elaborate the implications of what we have discussed in the previous three paragraphs. The relevance of these scientific materials for the methodology of theological thinking is enormous, however. The first and most obvious implication of these materials for our study is that theological thinking takes place within a community, the Church, whose life is continuous with the underlying principles of all life, and which therefore, in consonance with the images of evolutionary theory and cybernetics, is engaged in establishing a modus vivendi with its environing world, a purpose that can be sustained only on the basis of the Church's total ecumenical resources—past and present. Writers in sociology and social theory have made it clear that evolutionary theory is applicable to groups inasmuch as man's evolution unfolds within his socially formed culture, rather than solely within the arena of his genetic composition.[36] James M. Gustafson has been a leading expositor of the opinion that the Church is a community whose laws of being are continuous with man's cultural and social life generally. In his book, *Treasure in Earthen Vessels*,[37] he includes in a chapter entitled, "The Church: a Community of Memory and Understanding," provocative analyses that are related to the insights we have gathered from biology and cybernetics. In this chapter, he asserts the irrevocable relationship between the past and the present in the Church's activity of maintaining its identity, and then goes on to demonstrate that:

Differentiation between the Christian community and, e.g., the nation cannot be made according to the nature of the processes by which the communities continue to exist. The difference lies in what meanings

[35] See Alfred N. Whitehead, *Process and Reality: An Essay in Cosmology* (New York: Harper & Row, 1960), esp. Chap. III, Part II, pp. 127–168. S. C. Alexander, *Space, Time, and Deity*, 2 vols. (London: Macmillan, 1920), see especially Alexander's concept of Space-Time, Vol. I, 61–84.

[36] See Dobzhansky, *op. cit.*, pp. 7–10, 17–23, *passim*. Also Kurt Mayer's comments in his *Class and Society* (New York: Random House, 1955), p. 3.

[37] James M. Gustafson, *Treasure in Earthen Vessels* (New York: Harper & Row, 1961).

are remembered, understood, relived, and newly expressed. The same processes serve different meanings and values.[38]

If evolutionary theory (with its sociological extension) and cybernetic theory are applicable as clarifications of the Church's functioning as a community, then it is not surprising that they also clarify the methodology of theological thinking, inasmuch as theology is a function of the organism of the Church.[39] The proposals contained in this chapter constitute a call for Christian theology to acknowledge, in a very practical way, its position within a community of life. Such a realistic acknowledgment must drive theology back into fuller participation in and recapitulation of the distinctive activity and heritage of the community in which it exists, and such participation and recapitulation will bring with it fuller conformity with the fundamentals of life that evolutionary theory and cybernetics have uncovered. The specific proposals contained within our program, particularly the emphasis upon history and participation (see below, pages 148 ff.), have been advanced under the assumption that theology is in fact caught up in such a vital relationship with a community whose activity conforms with the fundamental laws of life; and the program must thus be interpreted in this light. It may very well be that the theological methodology —including the norm we have described above, which characterizes our program—is simply an articulation of how theological thinking must proceed if evolutionary and cybernetic theory are indeed reliable in their conception of the underlying laws of life. Ritschl himself did not devote enough attention to the relationship between his *Lebensfuehrung* concept and the laws of life.[40] His normative use of a category rooted in *life* certainly opens up the question, however, of how such laws are related to the theological enterprise. Our concern for the concrete and cumulative impact of redeemed life upon the norm of theological thinking is one way of taking into account the basic character of the life which theology and its community share with all of reality. Although it cannot be documented here, this is of a piece with the perennial concern of the Church that its life and theology be Catholic, that they articulate an identifiable Christian expression in the present which includes within itself the substance of the Christian past and the fullness of the contemporary *Oikumene*. This may account for the insistence by Chris-

[38] *Ibid.*, p. 85.

[39] See my "The Church's Liturgy and Theological Renewal," in Herbert Lindemann, ed., *Renewal in the Church* (St. Louis: Concordia, 1966).

[40] Ritschl's association with the philosopher and scientist, Hermann Lotze, did open such vistas to him, however. See Lotze's *Microcosmus: An Essay Concerning Man and His Relation to the World*, 2 vols. (New York: Scribner and Welford, 1885).

tians that their theology rely upon the Fathers and the Brethren, inasmuch as this insistence, together with the awareness of catholicity, is a way of asserting that the Church (specifically, its theological thinking) is a total organism or system which is always engaged in articulating a contemporary expression of its distinctive being within an environing world, on the basis of the full resources, past and present, which it recapitulates in every moment of its being.

A theological methodology, therefore, which seeks to escape the concrete and cumulative impact of redeemed life—through some sort of abstraction or reduction—may be undertaking an enterprise that flies in the face of the fundamental character of life even as it deviates from the perennial Christian concern for catholicity. Our program adheres to the normative role of the total continuum of God's acts in history in an attempt to rescue theology from a subversion and blotting out of the heritage which is essential if theology is to retain a genuinely Christian character. It is this objectively conceived continuum of history that must amplify the current tendency to identify history, as Professor Michalson does, with the image of time within the self-consciousness. The researches of the biologists and the cyberneticists make it indelibly clear that the concern for the continuum of objective history is rooted in the nature of life itself; this concern cannot be brushed aside by phenomenology as an illicit "positivism" which violates the self-consciousness. Rather, the objective continuum augments the phenomenological analysis, revealing the proper placement of that analysis and providing it a sure basis in reality itself.

A second implication of our statement of the norm for theology is its essential theocentricity. The locus of the theologian's material is in human existence. The pressures and characteristics of human existence account for much of his methodology. In the final analysis, however, the theologian approaches the confessional vestiges left by reconstructed human existence in order to learn of the God who was active in that existence. If the theologian keeps this in mind, he need not fear the dangers of anthropocentrism. The continuum of the events of Christian existence, it must be kept in mind, functions as a system of knowing. A system of knowing does not draw attention to itself, but on the contrary exists to furnish knowledge of the Other or not-self that has encountered man in the awareness of data that confront him in his experience. This role as a system of knowledge is an incontrovertible testimony to the theocentricity of the scheme we are proposing here. This theocentricity is not apparent, however, when the material of the Christian communal witness is subjected to scrutiny by attempts that utilize another system of knowledge. From the point of view of another system or model, the Christian communal witness may indeed appear to be a history of human religious experience, or the history of a religious community as it attempts to adjust to alien environments. Such judgments are quite legitimate in terms of the systems of knowing from which they originate. Whatever their cogency, these judgments must not blind us to the integrity that the witness holds on its own as a system of knowing in its own right.

The very fact that the Christian faith does most appropriately utilize a historical system of knowing, in the form of the continuum of its own witness, indicates that (in the mind of the Christian community, at least) knowledge of God is not available to us except through the total continuum of historical events in the communal witness. If this is so, then although each event of the witness does indeed testify of a genuine knowledge of God, no single event or confession can claim a totalitarianism of knowledge. Such a claim would appear absurd in the face of the actuality of other confessions. More important, however, if God has reserved himself the right to act spontaneously in genuinely new configurations in the past, he certainly reserves the right to do so in the future. As long as there is no other access to knowledge of God except within the witness-system, we have no other recourse but to rely upon the system and its continual unfolding. The upshot of such considerations as these is that theology is tied to specific problems that arise in concrete situations. The norm of theological work can be stated in advance of these concrete situations only in formal terms. Any material formulation of a norm must grow out of the concrete situation in which the theologian is bringing his energies to bear upon a specific problem. Theology is not a high-flying discipline that can always predict what it will have to say in all circumstances. A theologian can articulate the substantive norm that he is applying in the situation at hand, even as the historian can report the norms that have been applied in a substantive way in past situations within the Church's life, but no theologian or historian can predict in advance what material norm he will bring to bear in his work. This is the third implication of the norm that we are proposing for theological methodology: *The norm is continually changing.*

At this point in our resolution of the methodological dilemma described under the second heading in this chapter, we are attempting to allow for the integrity and normative character of human existence by insisting that the theologian consider it authoritative in its entire range of manifestations; at the same time, we seek to mitigate the compromising effects of abstraction by denying that any abstract formulation of a theological norm can be of more than formal significance for the theologian. The statement of the norm as described above is, therefore, not a description of the "essence" of

Christianity, but rather a designation of the locus within which the theologian will find the kinds of materials that are normative for his work in any given concrete situation. On the one hand this program broadens immeasurably the scope of the theologian's methodology by bringing into range the entire history of concrete Christian experience as in some way normative. On the other hand the discussion urges restraint in the pretensions that systematic theology can realistically entertain. Realistically considered, the comprehensive formulations of theology and the syntheses which those formulations necessitate are bound rather strictly to the precise conditions in which they are conceived and to the specific problems which they are designed to resolve.

One is impressed even more by the severe limitations of theological formulations when he considers the difficulties which attend the theologian's appropriation of the materials designated by the norm and their application in his work. There is the imponderable mass of material constituting the continuum of events within the Christian witness that defies mastery by any single individual theologian. In addition, as we have already mentioned, there is the question of what principle of selectivity can possibly be faithful to all of the material that comprises the witness. Finally, there is the question, basic to much of our discussion, of how the theologian can appropriate materials, which, by virtue of their incarnation within human life, defy all abstracting selectivity. Our program forces the theologian to abandon any deception that would encourage him to meet these problems merely by sharpening his abstractions more finely. This line of argumentation acknowledges freely, with regret, that a methodology for systematic theology, which seeks to capture the normative Christian faith in abstract forms, is structurally incapable of succeeding, for the reasons we have discussed in this chapter.

The alternative for apprehending the normative material of the Christian witness is not necessarily more likely to succeed in being faithful to the entire continuum of revelation, but it is more realistic and more appropriate to the type of material that theology deals with. The alternative to which we refer is the recognition that the theologian apprehends the normative materials of the continuum of revelation in the Christian witness by *participating* critically as fully as possible in that continuum, at the same time balancing this participation with full involvement in the cultural situation in which he finds himself.

Full participation in the continuum of the Christian communal witness refers to nothing else but *complete openness to the monuments of that witness at all levels of human sensitivity, with a keen awareness for what the sense of that witness is in the particular situation to which the theologian is directing his energies.* This emphasis puts the methodology of the systematic theologian precisely and realistically in the difficult and ambiguous circumstances of life where it belongs. The emphasis on full *participation* acknowledges that if the primary datum with which the theologian works is a datum of full-orbed life—in confession and commitment—then the most appropriate mode of apprehending that datum must itself engage the full-orbed life of the theologian. This is not to be construed as a statement of piety nor a plea for *theologia regenitorum.* Rather, the emphasis on participation in the continuum of the historical witness is a reasoned conclusion that when one is dealing with the kind of datum that confronts the theologian, the *scientifically* most appropriate means of access to that datum is full psychosomatic participation in the continuum in which that datum appears. The data which concern the theologian include highly discursive formulations provided by his colleagues and the theological tradition; but they also include confessional vestiges that represent forms of piety, worship, ethical action, institutional manipulation.

It is utterly unreasonable (even unscientific) to suppose that anything less than full-orbed participation in the realities to which these data refer can work satisfactorily in theology. There is a sense in which the theologian thinks his way into the continuum of the community's witness; indeed, most theological education (and unfortunately much of our worship) centers on this phase of participation; the theologian in this phase of his work analyzes theological texts (generally treatises and dogmata that are highly discursive in nature). It needs to be recognized, however, that there is a sense in which the theologian "worships his way" into the continuum, in that he purposely opens his worship life, both private and corporate, to incursions from a wide number of traditions. The theologian also gains access to the communal witness by his actions —his personal ethical actions, his life as a teacher of pastors and teachers, and his participation in institutions which macerate him even as they provide the resources for his work. The theologian's sensitivity to the painting, music, and literature of the witness is also a factor in his work. Let it be said for the last time that this full-orbed participation is not dictated chiefly by piety (although that is a factor) nor by the desire to appear sophisticated in the world, but rather by *scientific* considerations that follow from our analysis of the primary datum of the theologian's work.

In addition to its *scientific* appropriateness, the emphasis upon full participation as the means of access to the data of the theologian's work calls attention to the fact that the *sense* of the Christian communal witness in any given situation is a synthesis or recapitulation that has been worked out within and is resident within the sphere of the human life of the theologian. This in turn clarifies both the manner in which the sense of the Christian witness is brought to bear upon a problem and also the limitations of any single recapitulation of the witness. In that the sense of the historical witness is recapitulated in the life of the theologian we see the genuinely cybernetic character of Christian historical thinking. The comparative prominence or importance of the various factors within the witness is determined by actions and interactions that take place between the parts of the witness within the life activity of the theologian and his community. The importance of any single strand in the witness cannot be measured by any arithmetic reckoning of its longevity; rather, its importance emerges out of its interrelations with the rest of the witness as well as out of its usefulness for the specific problems at hand. The cybernetic character of this process is captured by T. S. Eliot, when he speaks of the historical sense in his essay on tradition:

The historical sense compels a man to write not merely with his own generation in his bones, but with a feeling that the whole of the literature of Europe from Homer and within it the whole of the literature of his country has a simultaneous order. This historical sense is a sense of the timeless as well as of the temporal and of the timeless and the temporal together.[41]

Even as this point of view enhances our appreciation of how each individual synthesis in theological work recapitulates the historical witness, it also chastens our expectations of the comprehensiveness of the synthesis. Tied as the theologian's synthesis is, to a concrete situation, his own person, and human life in its manifold dimensions, it is somewhat pretensious to expect, for example, that there can be formulated a single correct theological resolution for each problem that confronts theology. It may well cause us nervousness and bend our egos to admit it, but it seems likely that for every problem that arises there are *several* correct theological responses; the total number of appropriate responses may indeed be limited, but it is unrealistic, on the basis of the methodology that we have been considering, to expect but a *single* correct response.

Finally, the emphasis upon full participation in this context reminds us that cultural relevance is built-in as a part of the theologian's work. All of his work aims at a theological result which focuses the sense of the Christian communal witness upon a specific problem that has arisen within a set of concrete circumstances in the world in which the theologian lives. The picture of the cyber-

[41] T. S. Eliot, "Tradition and the Individual Talent," in *Selected Essays*, 3rd ed. (London: Faber and Faber, 1951), p. 14.

netic function is illuminating here, with its emphasis upon the fact that the aim of the living organism is to organize a response that is positively relevant to the environmental situation which faces the organism at the moment. (Similar insights may be concluded from the discussion above of evolutionary theory.) In each present moment, all of the organism's past and all of its contemporary awareness is recapitulated, eventuating in one temporal and spatial expression that is supremely relevant, in one way or another, to the environmental conditions in which the organism exists. Here it is clear that the process of abstraction may be of as little relevance in charting the cultural career of the Christian faith as it is in determining the sense of the Christian witness. Just as conceptualities may betray the material of the Church's interior meaning, so they may betray the dynamics of the movement within the cultural situation. The theologian does not attain cultural relevance simply by applying philosophical, sociological, or psychological conceptualities to the world about him, but rather by submitting himself to the demands of the concrete situation in which he lives and by speaking clearly to that situation.

Participation as an integral part of theological methodology gives the theologian a fresh attitude toward his work. It reawakens him to the fact that his work consists neither in the perpetuation of a theological conceptuality once attained nor in the transfer of traditional Christian meanings into some stereotyped "secular" ideology. Participation does call the theologian to a double sense of involvement, as an individual who lives in each moment under the burden of a Christian heritage that includes the total communal witness and also under the demand of a concrete worldly situation in which problems have arisen that need his theological attention.[42] Perhaps the clearest example of what this participation means for theological methodology was presented in this writer's hearing by the contemporary poet and critic Randall Jarrell. When asked how the reader could distinguish good poetry from bad, he replied somewhat as follows:

I cannot give you a simple answer to that question. All I can say is that you must begin to read all of the poetry you can lay your hands

---

[42] As our images from history, biology, and cybernetics mean to indicate, the lived heritage to which the theologian is (even scientifically) beholden, when balanced with the theologian's present concerns within the worldly situation in which he finds himself, will compel him to produce work that is genuinely new and relevant, even as it is of a piece with the tradition in whose historical continuity he stands. Participating as he does within the continuum of tradition, the theologian is free to respond in a relevant way to the world in which he lives. Participation in the world assures that the theologian's work will be as much a part of the world he faces as of the tradition that he bears within himself.

on. Read the poetry that others tell you is good; read the poetry that appeals to you for one reason or another. You must fill yourself to the brim with poetry. Then, everytime you pick up a poem, you must decide for yourself, on the basis of all the poetry you have become acquainted with, whether it is good or bad.[43]

This is not just a naive, pious, or simplistic view of how one discriminates good poetry from bad. Rather, it is a deceptively simple way of stating a very profound understanding of how the human organism operates in certain areas to gain knowledge and to make discriminating judgments about what it learns. In our opinion, Jarrell's statement can serve as a valid description of the basis of theological methodology, as well as a starting-point for a theological program that can open new avenues for theological work. We have attempted in this chapter to raise this assertion of the poet to the level of disciplined, scholarly theological discourse. It seems to us, when judged by the canon of appropriateness to the primary datum of the Christian faith, as well as the canons of simplicity, elegance, and honesty, to be the most satisfactory theory of the disciplined thinking that the theologian employs.

The broad range of discussion that has marked this present chapter lies right at the heart of theological thought, pressing as it does to the questions of how a theologian thinks and how he goes about his task. This discussion has moved far away from Ritschl, both in terminology and in the substance of its reflection. Nevertheless Ritschl stood in his methodology on the boundary of the areas we have just surveyed. He had a vision which if followed up, leads to the most sophisticated appreciation of life and history as the foundations of theological thought. The discussion of this chapter should make us more sensitive to his creativity and to the sureness of his instincts, even as it makes us more painfully aware of enormity of his failure, as outlined in Chapter 3. In his concern for *Lebensfuehrung*, in his argument against *Schulmaessigkeit* in theology, and in his diligent grappling with the history of the Christian tradition, he ranks as a pioneer, a Maker of Modern Theology. With this contemporary consideration of what life and history mean to theology behind us, however, the assertion of Chapter 3 stands out even more decisively: Ritschl's vision may stimulate us to fruitful work, but his own achievement is almost irretrievably marred by his inability to implement the respect for life and history which his instincts thrust upon him.

[43] These comments are recalled from a private conversation.

5

The Current Retreat
from the Vitalities of History

THE THEOLOGICAL METHODOLOGY sketched in the last chapter is admittedly fragmentary. In the sketch, however, we did consider certain essential building-blocks upon which that methodology presumes to build. The first of these blocks is the conviction that Christian faith has preeminently to do with *life*, and that a category of life, somehow reconstructed by God, is the only category that does justice to the central focus of Christianity. Proceeding very strictly from this category, we asserted the necessity of a *historical mode of thinking* in theology; and by a historical mode we refer to a manner of thinking which orders the data of present awareness by means of models that are constituted by the events, empirically given, which make up the history of the Christian community, conceived both in its historical breadth and its contemporary range. This led us to assert that the most appropriate means of access to the materials of Christian theology is that of participation, wherein the total humanity of the theologian is brought within the total sensibilities of the datum that vivifies and constitutes the faith of the Christian community.

The line of thinking we observed in the previous chapter does not appear explicitly in methodological practice among the major Protestant systematic theologians now working. However, at least two recent important statements have called for reappraisal in theological work in a fashion that may point to the sort of methodology under consideration in this book. The first of these is Professor Paul Lehmann's *Ethics in a Christian Context*. Professor Lehmann roots ethical action and decision in the Christian's relationships within a community whose life is structured by God's messianic activity. For example, in one particularly provocative

section of his book, Lehmann discusses the possibility of finding
an ethical norm that can bridge the gap between logical norm and
concrete action. He finds this norm in the "dynamics of the Christian *koinonia*," which he has already defined as the community
which centers in Christ, the *ecclesiola in ecclesia*, in which God's
messianic work in this world is distinctively luminous. The particularly provocative character of Lehmann's thought lies in his
assertions that such a context for ethics implies the primacy of
the concrete human life (or lives) and the efficacy of "translogical"
verification of ethical truth over abstraction.[1] The character of
ethical knowledge is translogical precisely because the primary
center for Lehmann lies within the dynamic "wholeness and fullness" of humanity itself. Verification is found not in conformity
to proposition, but in *"indicative* congruence" with God's action
in the world. By this one would assume that Lehmann is calling
attention to the fact that verification in the Christian context is
not lacking nor is it disorderly or alogical, but it is an order that
differs from traditional logic in that it is an order appropriate to
life. In his willingness to allow the context of this community's
life to shape Christian ethics at a fundamental level, Lehmann
reveals a methodological concern for the integrity of human existence within theological thought that may very well be parallel to
the concern that animates our own program, and which is not
removed from the concern for life that initiated Ritschl's efforts.

Professor Krister Stendahl has spoken with equal force in his
article on "Biblical Theology" in *The Interpreter's Dictionary of the
Bible*. In a sharp criticism of current modes of theologizing, Stendahl puts his finger on contemporary theology's inability to balance
adequately the realities of the biblical record and the exigencies
of the present age. He suggests that the proper way of proceeding
is to pursue a "systematic theology where the bridge between the
centuries of biblical events and our own time was found in the
actual history of the church as still ongoing sacred history of God's
people."[2] This emphasis on the Christian community as the category of continuity in Christian history and theology reveals a
concern for both life and history, rather than abstractions about
life, as the center of the theological focus. Stendahl himself says:
"Such a theology would conceive of the Christian existence as a
life by the fruits of God's acts in Jesus Christ, rather than as a
faith according to concepts deduced from the teaching of the
prophets, Jesus, and Paul regarding God's acts."[3] A fuller explana-

[1] Paul Lehmann, *Ethics in a Christian Context* (New York: Harper & Row,
1963), pp. 238–250, esp. 248 f. See also Chaps. 2 and 3.
[2] Krister Stendahl, in *The Interpreter's Dictionary of the Bible* (New York:
Abingdon, 1962), Vol. I, p. 428.
[3] *Ibid.*

tion of what such a program might entail for systematic theological methodology does not lie within the scope of Stendahl's purpose in his article. It is not altogether unreasonable, however, to assume that a concern for the Christian life rather than deductions about that life and for the ongoing history of God's people rather than for abstract leaps across the centuries from Bible to present day would lead Stendahl towards some of the considerations that we mentioned in the previous chapter.

That few theologians grapple today with the issues raised in Chapter 4 (and this fact seems to be corroborated by the sort of protest that underlies the comments of Lehmann and Stendahl) gives a clue to understanding some of the problems that face contemporary Protestant theology. In the context of our study of Ritschl, together with the program that has been stimulated by reflection on his work, we should have to conclude that the most prominent strands of Protestant theology today come dangerously close to reiterating the methodological blunder that marred his work. As far removed as we are from Ritschl—thanks chiefly to the so-called "neo-orthodox" theology that emerged between the two world wars—we seem to have retained the perversities of his methodology, even as we have forgotten the important concerns that animated his work.[4] If it is true that Ritschl's blunder still stands as the blunder of our generation of theologians as well, then we can learn much from Ritschl's fate, and the reflection that his fate provokes may be able to stand as a corrective to our present course.

It is to this end that we take up the work of Gerhard Ebeling, James M. Robinson, and the school of "biblical theology" in this chapter. The achievement of these schools of thought is to be played off against both Ritschl and the programmatic suggestions of Chapter 4, as a means of throwing still more light on the issues of life and history that have occupied the center of our attention throughout this study. The polemic which this process necessarily entails must not be considered as an end in itself. It is a polemic whose only purpose is to clarify the issues raised by Ritschl and dealt with in our own programmatic suggestions, with the hope of contributing to the ongoing enterprise of Christian theology. This chapter, therefore, as the preceding one, utilizes contemporary concerns to amplify the framework in which Ritschl is to

[4] This statement is not intended as a *genetic* theory of the presence of this blunder in contemporary theology. This study cannot probe the origin of the blunder. Rather, we intend to say that attention to Ritschl, in light of the critique of Chap. 3, reminds us that, whatever its origin, this methodological blunder is with us today, and its consequences may well be as unfortunate for us as they were for Ritschl.

be evaluated, deepening our appreciation of his sensitivities even as it sharpens our insight into his limitations.

THE THEOLOGY OF GERHARD EBELING

Gerhard Ebeling stands at the center of one dominant force in theology. He is hailed as a leader on one of theology's "new frontiers," as being for our generation what Barth and Bultmann were for an earlier time, and as the "most important German theologian to have established himself since World War II." It appears rather obvious that any theological program that hopes to make its way in Protestant circles today must relate itself to Ebeling's thought. It may be helpful for clarifying the issues of our own theological program to point to the areas in which this program stands in sharp disagreement with Ebeling. And, as we shall also see, Ebeling's work is instructive in the attempt to understand the continuing presence of Ritschl's methodological blunder.

Ebeling's systematic theological achievement to date is constituted by his application, with devastating effect, of a specialized category of existentialist philosophy to an interpretation of the biblical and historical materials of the Christian faith. Riding at the crest of a European wave of theological thought that has thoroughly absorbed existentialist thinking, Ebeling's work may be considered to be the ultimate refinement of its type. Despite the claims and counterclaims concerning the Heideggerian provenance of his thought,[5] the basic structure of Ebeling's system is familiar as an expression of the dialectic of the linguistic character of existence as that was articulated by a group of theologians and philosophers who spoke in terms of "I and Thou" and related categories.[6] This way of thinking posited that human existence

[5] See the unpublished paper by Robert W. Funk, "Language Event in the Theology of Ernst Fuchs and Gerhard Ebeling: An Interpretive Essay," esp. footnote 3, pp. 32–33.

[6] It would be somewhat misleading to speak of an "I-Thou school," inasmuch as the men who employ I-Thou categories have not banded together formally, or even informally, as such. Nevertheless, the dialectic of the linguistic which they employ is certainly of one piece. The following works must be included in the group of thinkers we are referring to: Karl Barth, *Kirchliche Dogmatik,* III/2, *"Die Grundform der Menschlichkeit"* (Zuerich: Evangelischer Verlag A. G. Zollikon, 1948). Emil Brunner, *Truth as Encounter* (Philadelphia: Westminster, 1964). Martin Buber, *I and Thou* (New York: Scribner, 1942). Ferdinand Ebner, *Das Wort und die geistigen Realitaeten* (Pustet, 1921). Herbert Farmer, *The Servant of the Word* (New York: Scribner, 1942). See also the works of Friedrich Gogarten, especially *Ich Glaube an den Dreieinigen Gott* (Jena: E. Diederichs, 1926), and *Glaube und Wirklichkeit* (Jena: E. Diederichs, 1928). Martin Heidegger, *Being and Time,* par. 27, "Everyday Being-one's-Self and the 'they'" (New York: Harper & Row, 1962). Karl Heim, *Glaube und Denken,* 1st ed. (Berlin: Furche-Verlag, 1931).

is constituted in its authentic sense by an encounter between an I and a Thou. This encounter centers in the "word." By "word," this group symbolized the total impact made upon the I by the uninhibited and spontaneous presence of the Thou. Spoken and written words are crucial for this total impact of the Thou, but the symbolic use of the "word," implies the total Thou. The dialectic proceeds by asserting that the "word" is thus the bearer of the encounter which makes existence authentically human; by means of the "word," the I responds in a manner appropriate to the Thou, and thus "linguisticality" furnishes a framework for I-Thou relationships. From this point it is a simple step to the assertion that the ultimate Thou is Christ, who confronts us in the ultimate Word, calling forth man's ultimate response of faith. The German language lends itself particularly to the development of this dialectic, inasmuch as one can say that he is confronted with the *Wort* (word) of the Thou which calls for his *Antwort* (answer, word over against another), and thus the consummation of the I-Thou relationship is one of *Verantwortlichkeit* (responsibility, response-ability).

Ebeling has made this dialectic of the linguistic central to his interpretation of the Christian faith. The linguistic event (*Sprachereignis*) is constitutive of human existence and of all of reality; it focuses in the phenomenon of conscience, in which man is aware of the demands of the Thou. At its ultimate level, where the Word is Christ, so Ebeling's dialectic goes, salvation itself is actualized within the shape of the "word-event," including the responsive self-giving which that event engenders. The relationship that eventuates thus between God and man is faith. Furthermore, the "word-event" is identical with what Ebeling means by history. Christianity must take history seriously, must acknowledge the historicality of human existence; that is, Christianity must acknowledge the decisiveness of the "linguisticality" of revelation and its impact upon human existence.

We can ill afford to overlook the power of this presentation of the Christian faith. No amount of criticism here or elsewhere can gainsay the freshness with which this presentation has opened up the richness of faith. Ebeling's dialectic speaks of the newness and unexpectedness with which God comes in his Word; it describes the personal force which God's Word possseses, as well as the personal and uninhibited manner in which one must respond to the Word of God. These characteristics lend weight to Ebeling's claim that he is pointing towards the revivifying of preaching. In an age like ours, when men have been desperately concerned to recover the meaning of being a person as well as to probe the discontinuity and bewilderment of the time which makes personhood problematic—in such an age, the theological program of Gerhard Ebeling, centering as it does in the encounter between persons, has promise of very great apologetic power. It has promise of restoring Christian faith to a significant place in the human enterprise. From a technical theological point of view, it cannot be gainsaid that Ebeling has redirected our attention to the problems of interpreting Scripture, reminding us that disciplined exposition dare not rest content with a clarification of the archeological, linguistic, or historical circumstances in which the Scriptural texts are imbedded, but that exegesis must also extend the efficacy of the Word of God, with the result that the efficacious presence of the Word is not separate from the exegetical task but rather its only legitimate goal, and thus an integral part of "exegesis."

The question arises, however, the power of Ebeling's work notwithstanding, whether its theological investments have not been made so decisively and so exclusively, whether the commitment to one abstract philosophical category has not been undertaken so narrowly, that the end result is a somewhat desiccated and much too partisan interpretation of Christian faith to be convincing. The ease, for example, with which Ebeling compresses every aspect of the Christian faith into his dialectic of linguisticality is achieved only at the expense of casting aside a full-orbed presentation of what is and has been authentically Christian. The question, therefore, is whether Ebeling does not reiterate, methodologically, the blunder we noted as Ritschl's in Chapter 3. The I-Thou category of linguisticality must be recognized for what it is: a phenomenological description of the self-awareness of the individual when he encounters a personal Other. The dialectic of the linguistic describes the shattering effect that breaks in upon the awareness when a personal Other makes the claim of its integrity upon one's own integrity. It describes the closure and "thingification" that threatens if the Other is shunted aside with no respect of its integrity. Ebeling's work shares all the power of this description. By its very nature, however, this phenomenological description can only be a description of the individual awareness in encounter, and cannot bear the weight of an ontological description that would illumine the structure of God's presence in his creation and the effects of this presence. In this respect, Ebeling's central category shares the limitations of a psychological description that cannot step outside the individual's own self-awareness. Furthermore, this phenomenological description is by its very nature individual. A structure of thought that is by nature the description of self-awareness (even if that self-awareness is of the God-man encounter) and purely individualistic cannot serve to gather up the entire scope of Christian faith and theology as

Ebeling wants it to. Two examples will suffice to clarify this criticism.

(*1*) Ebeling's presentation of Christology is cut to the measure of the individual's self-awareness within the encounter with God. In his essay, "The Question of the Historical Jesus," Ebeling puts this in a typical way:

> The point of the Easter story is, that Jesus as the witness to faith became the ground of faith and that those who thus believe are witnesses to faith as witnesses to Jesus. It can hardly be denied that the point of the appearances of the Risen Lord, which form the heart of the Easter tradition, is the *rise of faith in Jesus*. Nobody was granted an appearance who did not thereby become a believer, and likewise nobody who did not already know Jesus before and thus in some measure recognize him.[7]

That this is no isolated reference is shown by Ebeling's insistence in his essay on Christology that "the task of Christology, then, is to give an account of the statement, 'I believe in Jesus'. . . . the question of who Jesus is and the question of what faith means cannot be answered apart from each other, but only in conjunction with each other."[8] And, "the task of Christology is in fact no other than to bring to expression what came to expression in Jesus himself."[9] (And what came to expression was the encounter and self-giving to the ultimate Thou that is designated by the "word-event" of the I-Thou school.) What Ebeling has done here is to take a necessarily abstract description of the phenomena of the self-awareness in the God-man encounter (as perceived by the I-Thou existentialists) and then to say that this constellation of phenomena in the awareness is the goal, the purpose, and the total task of the work of God in Christ. Jesus and faith are inseparable, descriptively; but, is personal faith *the* goal of the resurrection?

As we have indicated, the phenomenological description is not without its validity and cogency. It is, however, quite another thing, and of questionable validity, to assert that this description, bound as it is to the individual self-awareness as conceived abstractly by one very specific philosophical point of view, is large enough to encompass the redemptive act in Jesus Christ.[10] Nor is the phenomenological analysis of faith large enough to do justice

---

[7] Gerhard Ebeling, *Word and Faith* (Philadelphia: Fortress Press, 1963), p. 301.

[8] *Ibid.*, p. 202.

[9] *Ibid.*, p. 304.

[10] See *ibid.*, p. 409, where Ebeling explicitly identifies "word-event" and "salvation-event." See also the entire argument of his *The Nature of Faith* (Philadelphia: Fortress Press, 1961), esp. Chaps. 4 and 5, where Christology is very nearly telescoped into complete identity with the act of faith.

to the historical event of the resurrection.[11] There is no question that Ebeling intends to emphasize the historical resurrection; he asserts the necessity for accepting a "physiological conception of the resurrection."[12] The question is whether his methodology does not neutralize or even nullify the reality that is at stake in the resurrection—as well as in the rest of Christology and Christian belief—because it is so peculiarly wedded to faith's phenomenology. Another way to put the point is to say that Ebeling collapses all of Christology into soteriology. with the anthropocentric reductionism that inevitably results, regardless of his own broader intentions.[13]

The program that we are suggesting, together with the lessons learned from Ritschl's blunder, furnishes the basis upon which to criticize Ebeling's too exclusive investment in I-Thou existentialism. On the basis of the starting-point from which we asserted that the primary datum of Christian faith is reconstructed life— in all of its dynamic, with its full integrity—we must reject at the outset equating any abstract conceptualization of the self-awareness with the redemptive act in Christ, or from designating the purpose of God's redemptive work with that conceptualization. Here, Ebeling reveals the same methodological temptation that marred Ritschl's work. Again, the historical mode of knowing we set forth in Chapter 4, reminds us that both in the New Testament and in later Christian history, the Christian understanding of Christ has reached out far beyond the confines of the self-awareness of the believer. Christology has cosmic and social dimensions—to mention only the two most prominent features that Ebeling overlooks—which simply cannot fit into the phenomenological description that existentialism gives us.

(2) Along with the compression of Christology into I-Thou categories, Ebeling's most astounding assertion is perhaps his virtual identification of Reformation Christianity with the critical historical method.[14] In his programmatic essay on Protestantism and critical historical method, Ebeling weaves together concerns for Protestantism's positive relationship to primitive Christianity, the Reformation, and the contemporary cultural situation. For his purposes, these three concerns converge in an emphasis on self-criticism and historism. Self-criticism, because the concern for

[11] See, for example, the current research on the resurrection in Hans Grass, *Ostergeschehen und Osterberichte* (Goettingen: Vandenhoeck und Ruprecht, 1964), pp. 233–249; and Wolfhart Pannenberg, *Grundzuege der Christologie* (Guetersloh: Gerd Mohn, 1964), pp. 15–23, 32–44.

[12] *The Nature of Faith*, p. 68.

[13] See the discussion of such a collapse in Pannenberg's *Christologie*, pp. 32–44.

[14] See "The Significance of the Critical Historical Method for Church and Theology in Protestantism," in *Word and Faith*, pp. 17–61.

truth which shatters every shibboleth is of a piece with the Reformation faith as expressed in the *sola gratia* and contemporary science; historism, because the heart of the primitive Christian and Reformation understanding of revelation is that it exists within the relativities of history, even as it is constituted by the personal encounter that marks the ever-changing historical continuum, and even as contemporary cultural sensitivities have also focused upon the relativism of all reality.

It is clear how the existentialist (and now universally western cultural) assertion of the *Geschichtlichkeit* of all existence underlies Ebeling's analysis here,[15] which combines the categories of historism, criticism, and revelation as encounter. The crisis of Protestant theology, preaching, and church order today hinges on the Protestant willingness to "take up into its own approach," "to take seriously," "the whole outlook of the critical historical method."[16] Ebeling does not simply assert that the Protestant church must utilize critical historical method; he draws a natural and decisive relationship between the Gospel of Reformation Christianity and the critical historical method. He writes:

Indeed, I venture to assert that the Protestantism of the nineteenth century, by deciding in principle for the critical historical method, maintained and confirmed over against Roman Catholicism in a different situation the decision of the Reformers in the sixteenth century. That of course is not to say that wherever in the history of modern Protestant theology the motto of the critical historical method has been most loudly proclaimed and most radically applied, there men have also really been nearest to the Reformation in every respect. But what it certainly does mean is, that wherever they made way for the critical historical method and, however grievous their errors, took it seriously as their task, there if certainly often in a very paradoxical way, they were really asserting the fundamental principle of the Reformers in the intellectual situation of the modern age.[17]

As he goes about his work of uncovering "definite essential inner connections" between Reformation Christianity and the "critical historical method of modern times," Ebeling seizes upon the Reformers' *sola fide*:

The *sola fide* of the Reformation doctrine of justification both contains a rejection of any existing ways of ensuring present actualization, whether ontological, sacramental or hierarchical, and also positively in-

[15] For a discussion of further implications of this concept, see Gerhard Bauer, *"Geschichtlichkeit": Wege und Irrwege eines Begriffs* (Berlin: de Gruyter, 1963).
[16] *Word and Faith*, pp. 59–60.
[17] *Ibid.*, p. 55.

cludes an understanding of actualization in the sense of genuinely historic, personal encounter. If this encounter with the historic revelation takes place solely in hearing the Word, then the shattering of all historical assurances that supposedly render the decision of faith superfluous is completely in line with the struggle against the saving significance of good works or against understanding the working of the sacraments in the sense of the *opus operatum*.[18]

From this argument Ebeling moves easily to the assertion that this critical function, which is the "reverse side of the certainty of salvation *sola fide*" is embodied in critical historical method.[19] Negatively, then, the continually critical element of the critical historical method is of a piece with the Reformation faith, whereas positively the *Geschichtlichkeit* of existence which emerges from the use of that method properly defines the Reformation understanding of revelation.

Cogent as this juxtaposition of critical historical methodology and the Reformation may be, Ebeling's comparisons possess nevertheless the air of incongruousness that makes the whole appear to be something of a tour de force rather than an adequate interpretation of Reformation faith. The incongruousness attends his attempt to fit the reality of faith (in this case, Reformation faith) into the form dictated by an abstract methodology. The structures of protest and encounter simply are not broad enough or basic enough to exhaust the reality of the Reformation expression of Christian faith.[20] Life lived under the *sola gratia* of the Reformation faith presupposes the presence of God in an ongoing fashion and the continuity of his faithfulness in history in such a way that simply eludes description by the existentialist categories of protest and encounter. These two factors of protest and encounter cannot illumine broadly enough the reality of life lived in community under the confidence that divine grace alone sustains life. Protest and encounter are tortured categories that grow out of a certain anxiety over against form and the instability of historical movement. Life lived in the certainty of God's grace emerges from confidence, not anxiety. Here Ritschl's insights into the nature of Reformation Christianity are safer than Ebeling's. Ritschl recog-

[18] *Ibid.*, p. 56. See also the essay "Sola Scriptura und das Problem der Tradition," where Ebeling equates *sola scriptura* and the dialectic of the linguistic, in K. E. Skydsgaard and Lukas Vischer, eds., *Schrift und Tradition* (Zurich: EVZ Verlag, 1963), pp. 95–127.

[19] *Word and Faith*, pp. 57 f.

[20] See Jaroslav Pelikan, *Obedient Rebels: Catholic Substance and Protestant Principle in Luther's Reformation* (New York: Harper & Row, 1964) and Paul Tillich, "Der Protestantismus als kritisches und gestaltendes Prinzip," in *Der Protestantismus als Kritik und Gestaltung*, "Gesammelte Werke," VII (Stuttgart: Evangelisches Verlagswerk, 1962), pp. 29–53.

nized that the thrust of the Reformers had to be described in terms of life, and he was sensitive to the inappropriateness of abstract theories which threatened to displace the confident life that is signified by the *sola fide* and the *sola gratia*. It is therefore not incorrect for Ebeling to insist on a relationship between Reformation faith and the critical historical method; rather, it is inappropriate to make what Ebeling makes out of this relationship, and to assert it so strenuously, as if the critical historical method, an abstract methodology for the study of historical phenomena, could become a kind of intellectual surrogate for life lived in God's grace.

If a specifically Christian judgment finds the dialectic of the linguistic too narrowly abstract to interpret the Christian faith, a generally humanistic judgment finds it too narrow to do justice to the fullness of human existence. This is crucial for Ebeling's work, inasmuch as it presents a certain anthropology as the foundation upon which Christology and theology are to be erected. His anthropology is based upon the "word-event" as constitutive for man:

If the word is the thing which shows what the speaker is, then we should have to say: the precise *purpose which the word is meant to serve is, that man shows himself as man*. For that is his destiny. And for that reason word is absolutely necessary to man as man. For his destiny is to exist as response. He is asked what he has to say. He is not destined to have nothing to say and to have to remain dumb. His existence is, rightly understood, a word-event which has its origin in the Word of God and, in response to that Word, makes openings by a right and salutary use of words. Therein man is the image of God.[21]

This is not the same thing as the statement that man is distinctively a user of language, inasmuch as the "word-event" is a highly stylized philosophical category.

Even though the "word-event" is central in Ebeling's work, it is shrouded in ambiguity. The ambiguity lies primarily in the meaning attached to "word," and the human processes which it sets in motion to appropriate its meaning. In his book, *The Nature of Faith*, Ebeling suggests that "word," is more than a single word and that its basic nature is found in speaking. He suggests that "communication" is the best synonym for "word," provided that this includes "the power of words" to "touch and change our very life."[22] He adds, "We do not get at the nature of words by asking what they contain, but by asking what they effect, what they set going,

21 *Ibid.*, p. 327.
22 *The Nature of Faith*, p. 186.

what future they disclose."[23] These comments are in accord with
the I-Thou school, in its tendency to use "word" to symbolize the
impact of the I upon the Thou. The ambiguity arises, however, in
that Ebeling does not operate in a wholly consistent manner with
this category of "word." One would expect on the one hand that
Ebeling would attend to all communication that works in a personal
manner to "touch and change our very life," and on the other that
he would give heed to the impact of the "word-event" upon the whole
man involved. But these expectations are disappointed. The tone of
Ebeling's presentation definitely exalts the "natural, oral word
taking place between man and man" as the primary form of human
and divine communication.[24] Furthermore, the impact of this
"word" upon man is narrowly conceived in terms of the intellectual
processes by means of which man renders the "word" intelligible
and then acts upon it (although Ebeling is silent on the means
by which this transition between intellectual apprehension and
action is negotiated).

We say that Ebeling's usage here is ambiguous because his actual
operation with the categories of "word" and "word-event" are so
narrowly oral and intellectualistic as to fail to do justice to the
matters of existence that he obviously wants to deal with. In the
first place, the communication that touches and changes the very
lives of men is obviously never as exclusively oral as Ebeling indicates. He reveals this confusion, for example, when he writes
that Lutheran Orthodoxy erred because it did not bear in mind
"that to the essence of the Word belongs its oral character."[25] The
communication of significant meanings that change lives is through
a great number of associations and learned contents which make
their contact with the individual through what he hears (which is
not exclusively spoken words), reads, feels, and imagines. In a
symbolic sense all of these associations and learned contents can
be designated as the "word." But there is more than oral communication involved. Even if a specific oral word "taking place between
man and man" is decisive, that word will not communicate unless
the encounter utilizes associations and contents that arose prior
to and alongside the oral communication.

Significant communication necessarily involves the whole being
of the men involved, and yet Ebeling insists on exalting the intellectual processes of appropriation when he speaks of the impact of
the "word." This is strange, because the whole scheme of Ebeling's
dialectic of the "word" means to emphasize that communication
has an effect upon existence. This intellectualizing comes out most

23 *Ibid.*, p. 187.
24 *Word and Faith*, p. 325.
25 *Ibid.*, footnote 1, pp. 312–313.

clearly, perhaps, in a passage in which Ebeling discusses the various ways in which revelation is actualized in human existence. He rejects what he calls "imitative and contemplative historizing" as the means of actualizing revelation. These terms refer to actualization "by imitative reconstruction of an exceptional situation, by assimilation of the present to the past" through representation in mime, repetition, and so on.[26] In the same analysis, Ebeling rejects sacramental actualization and actualization through participation in the community or institution of the Church as a spiritual entity.[27] In contrast to these forms, Ebeling invokes actualization through the "word" and faith, through the "word-event" in which Christ is actualized in encounter and in which man responds to him; this actualization of Christ takes place apparently through Scriptural exposition in the preached sermon.[28]

Two things need to be asserted strongly in criticism of this position. First, to speak of the impact of the revelation of God upon man in terms of spoken word and existential response is to make a totalitarian claim for the existentialist dialectic as the only proper exposition of how man receives and responds to revelation. Second, to emphasize the oral communication and the existentialist response is to strip man of much of his basic human equipment when he enters into significant communication. There is more to man than the existentialist dialectic pictures. There are the continuities of existence and history, the peaceful transitions between stages in life's way, which do not exclude, but which recast, the existentialist emphasis. Furthermore, despite Ebeling's polemic against imitative and contemplative historizing and sacramental participation, man does receive truth by means of imaginative participation in the world outside himself, by means of dramatic and mythic representation, and by means of cultic participation in the ways of his society. To assert otherwise is patently to dehumanize man in favor of an abortive oral-intellectual scheme; and, furthermore, it is so patently ill advised to fly in the face of the researches of contemporary psychology, social-psychology, and sociology that documentation is hardly necessary.[29] Professor Amos Wilder has called attention very sharply to this failure of Ebeling to do justice

26 *Ibid.*, pp. 32–33.
27 *Ibid.*, pp. 34–35.
28 *Ibid.*, pp. 35–36.
29 See the point of view, for example, of such works as Erving Goffman, *The Presentation of Self in Everyday Life* (Garden City: Doubleday Anchor Books, 1959); Peter L. Berger, *Invitation to Sociology: A Humanistic Perspective* (Garden City: Doubleday Anchor Books, 1963); Karl Menninger, *The Vital Balance: The Life Process in Mental Health and Illness* (New York: Viking, 1963); Theodosius Dobzhansky, *Mankind Evolving* (New Haven: Yale, 1962); Maurice Merleau-Ponty, *The Primacy of Perception* (Evanston: Northwestern Univ. Press, 1964), pp. 5 ff.

to man as fully human[30] in his contribution to the German-American discussion in *The New Hermeneutic,* when he writes that Ebeling and Fuchs give us:

a kind of existentialist skeleton of human nature, a kind of X-ray photograph, and a fleshless mathematics of the divine-human trans-action. . . . man is not man as we know him, but a kind of generalized *anthropos.*[31]

Man is a totality of perceptions and responses that permeate and utilize his entire psychosomatic being. One of the most serious weaknesses of the existentialist theology of our day in general, and of Ebeling's constructions in particular, is that they deny, at least in the actual operations of their thinking, this full-orbed humanity of man. Theology must redress this dehumanizing tendency by insisting that the materials of theology and faith are appropriated and passed on in the context of participation by the whole man, with the result that his total being shares in both knowing and proclaiming the faith that is incarnate in his life.

In summary, our argument with the work that Gerhard Ebeling has thus far presented to us, is the conflict between the claim of too narrow a commitment to an abstract philosophical category, with a resultant dessication both of Christology and anthropology, and the claim for a broader investment, rooted in life itself as the realm in which grace is incarnate, which does more justice to the integrity both of the God who gives life and the man who receives it. And in asserting this claim, we speak out of the analysis which exposed Ritschl's ironic inability to do justice to the *life* he was so concerned to exalt. At this point, it may be helpful to correlate this criticism with that of the American contributors in the dialogue contained in *The New Hermeneutic.* As Professor John Cobb summarizes:

All three American contributors see in existentialist theology a tendency to treat existentialist categories themselves unhistorically and thereby to separate faith too much from its concrete involvement in culture.[32]

Professors Cobb, Dillenberger, and Wilder, all seem to rest uneasy with Ebeling's (and Fuchs') tendency to use his categories ab-

[30] One cannot but note the irony that a philosophical position which, like existentialism (and particularly its I-Thou expression), has worked so energetically to repossess a full perspective on man, and which speaks so often of "authentic humanity," falls under criticism from several quarters for failing to do justice to man!

[31] Amos Wilder, in *The New Hermeneutic,* James M. Robinson and John B. Cobb, Jr., eds. (New York: Harper & Row, 1964), Chap. 6, esp. pp. 202–208. This quotation is from p. 205.

[32] John Cobb, in *ibid.,* p. 220.

stractly, in a manner that estranges his categories from "concrete involvement." Dillenberger speaks of this as "a circumscribed scope," "reduction," and "abstraction"; Wilder, as "generalization" and "abstraction." From this basic insight, the Americans suggest that German theological thought has estranged itself from the concrete historical cultural realities, apart from which the theological construct assumes an air of unreality. The Americans reject theological categories that are abstracted from history and culture. The criticism I have leveled at Ebeling proceeds from a similar insight into the reductionist and abstractionist tendencies in his thought. However, from this insight I have gone on to suggest that Ebeling's thought has estranged itself from the primary datum of authentic Christian faith and from the authentic human life which figures in that faith. It may be that we are witnessing an "emerging consensus" (among American critics, at least) concerning the structural inadequacies of the theological effort that is designated as "the new hermeneutic." From this central structural inadequacy, the criticisms go out in several directions to pinpoint a significant estrangement between the abstract conceptuality of the linguistic character of "word" and "faith" and the concrete realities which constitute both "word" and "faith." The criticisms suggest that, in certain important areas of theological methodology, Ebeling has not progressed beyond late nineteenth-century abstractionist thinking.

JAMES M. ROBINSON AND THE NEW QUEST OF THE HISTORICAL JESUS

Along with Gerhard Ebeling, the work of James M. Robinson has certainly proved to be one of the most spectacular streams of theological thinking today, particularly in the United States. When we speak of Robinson, we speak of the entire movement in New Testament studies that has given rise to the phrase, "the new quest of the historical Jesus." This so-called new quest is not altogether irrelevant to our discussion of Ebeling's work, because both he and the new quest assert emphatically that a certain hermeneutical task devolves upon theology which consists largely in carrying through the existential dialectic that is embodied in Ebeling's concept of "word-event."[33]

The importance of the new quest is clear from Robinson's own statements of its purpose.[34] This purpose is the exercise of a certain

[33] The common outlook of the men can be understood when one reads Robinson's works on the new quest in conjunction with the symposium he edited on Ebeling's thought. Cf. James M. Robinson and John B. Cobb, Jr., eds. *The New Hermeneutic.*

[34] Robinson's program is spelled out in his *Kerygma und historischer Jesus* (Zuerich: Zwingli-Verlag, 1960). In English, one must read his *A New Quest*

type of critical function upon the Christian kerygma. This criticism amounts to a comparison of the Church's preaching about Christ with Jesus' own understanding of existence as that understanding is revealed in the literary units which critical New Testament scholarship ascertains are authentic. This critical function enables the scholar to determine whether the Church's preaching is continuous with Jesus himself. The critical category of Jesus' own understanding of existence is fashioned by utilizing the researches of New Testament scholars insofar as they have determined both what the authentic literary units are and what message is embodied in them. Later preaching is then judged, not on the basis of whether it preserves an authentic logion, but rather according to whether it transmits Jesus' understanding of existence. Robinson summarizes the thrust of the new quest as follows:

It is concerned neither to replace the kerygma with the preaching of the historical Jesus nor to demonstrate the truth of the kerygma historically. Rather, it is to test critically, on the basis of the material itself (sachkritisch), in every single instance, the legitimacy of referring that kerygma back to Jesus. This task can only be discharged when we extract the content of the historical Jesus' understanding of existence and compare it with the understanding of existence that is implied in the kerygma.[35]

It is clear what Robinson intends: the erection of a criterion of Christian faith that is constituted by a concept of existence. The understanding of existence which he distills from the authentic historical Jesus is a formal structure marked by an "eschatological polarity." That is to say, "the message of Jesus consists basically in a pronouncement to the present in view of the imminent eschatological future."[36] Robinson insists that this works itself out in the Jewish apocalyptic doctrine of the two aeons, so that the one member of the eschatological polarity speaks of the evil aeon, whereas the second speaks of the aeon to come. This is not to be construed as a temporal distinction between the two aeons, but rather as a material antithesis between the two aeons, which resolves into a dialectic of the evil versus the good, the evil being characteristic of the present, the good of the imminent future, as for example in the beatitude: "Blessed are you poor, for yours is the kingdom of

---

of the Historical Jesus (London: SCM Press, 1959) together with "The Formal Structure of Jesus' Message," in Current Issues in New Testament Interpretation ed. by William Klassen and Graydon F. Snyder (New York: Harper & Row, 1962).

35 Kerygma und historischer Jesus, p. 182.
36 "The Formal Structure of Jesus' Message," in Klassen and Snyder, p. 97.

heaven."[37] This dialectic of the two aeons, with the diminishing of the temporal element so that the message is one of God's imminent "breaking" upon the present becomes the "material characteristic" of the formal structure as Robinson describes:

> The eschatological message of Jesus, which is rooted *religionsgeschichtlich* in Jewish apocalypticism's doctrine of two aeons, and the polarity of which leads to a two-member structure in many sayings of Jesus, was directed so consistently to the present that an existential dialectic became visible. It gave expression to Jesus' understanding of the present and thus became the content of Jesus' understanding of existence. For this eschatologically qualified present, this coming of God, is the context, the source, the constitutive ingredient of believing existence. Jesus' action consists in the actualization of this existence. His message consists in bringing the understanding of existence to expression.[38]

This category—a present that is eschatologically qualified by the imminent future in which God is coming—becomes the norm by which one determines the authentic message of Jesus, and which determines the "theological legitimacy" of the Church's preaching.

The preserving and transmitting of this understanding of existence is not by doctrine alone; rather, there must be an appropriation of Jesus' understanding of existence:

> For only when and if the act in which Jesus' existence consists happens in the Christian's life, as he commits himself to Jesus' understanding of existence in his act of faith—only then can one say theologically the person is actually united with Christ and a participant in his new life. For here resides the "mystical union" with Christ which is neither mystical or mythological, existential reality. . . . the critical question (in judging the Church's preaching) is whether, in each transformation of the sayings of Jesus and in each subsequent development of Christological conceptualizations, Jesus' understanding of existence and, hence, that which constitutes his person, has been faithfully proclaimed and believed.[39]

With this augmentation of his program, Robinson brings breadth to the scope of his program: he has presented a task for contemporary theology as it seeks to understand Jesus, as it transmits Jesus' message in its own work and in preaching, and as it judges whether its preaching has properly been appropriated.

One is a bit dismayed when he surveys the breadth of Robinson's suggestion because despite its sophistication and breathtakingly

[37] *Ibid.*, p. 102.
[38] *Ibid.*, p. 104.
[39] *Ibid.*, pp. 105–106.

massive scholarly apparatus, its results are quite commonplace to theologians who have been influenced by recent European trends: The Christian faith is a fulfillment of the existentialist dialectic in which authentic existence breaks in as a challenge for man's ultimate decision. Here is where Robinson's basic agreement with Ebeling's work appears. Ebeling emphasizes that the encounter with authentic existence is structured as a "word-event"; Robinson emphasizes that the authentic existence stands as a future entity which is even now breaking in upon man and calling for his commitment to it as a factor which qualifies the present; the existentialist dialectic underlies both, even constitutes both. One is dismayed to note that the new quest, at least insofar as it implies more than a technical scientific study of the New Testament literature, is yet one more instance of contemporary Protestant theology making an almost ultimate investment in the power of an abstract conceptuality to serve as norm for the faith. And the new quest expresses its abstract conceptuality as bloodlessly as any abstraction; we are told merely that this abstraction entails a "commitment" that is more than mysticism and myth in its ability to relate us to Christ. The criticism that we have leveled at all abstractions that function normatively in this manner must obtain here: that the integrity of human life, in which the faith is incarnate, is sacrificed, with no real gain, to the ruthless formality of the abstract existentialist conceptualization.

There is yet another reservation concerning the normative interpretation of the faith which the new quest offers. The new quest replaces the ineradicable indicative of Christian faith, in whose light Christians affirm that their life has already been reconstructed in and through Christ, with an imperative that moves reconstruction always into the future, however imminent that future might be. The import of this subtle transformation from the central Christian affirmation of an indicative to the imperative deserves much attention.[40] Robinson underlines the imperative character of his proposal in a discussion of Easter as the proclamation of Jesus as Cosmocrator.[41] After acknowledging that "Christian existence is not possible without Easter" because "the kerygma's proclamation of Jesus as Cosmocrator brings ontologically to expression what happened ontically in Jesus," Robinson goes on, enigmatically turning his back on "what happened ontically in Jesus," to say that in order to be "theologically legitimate" Christian preaching cannot simply proclaim Christ as Cosmocrator, but must instead demonstrate the unity of that proclamation with the pre-Easter Christ by proclaiming "also materially, Jesus' understanding

40 See Hefner, *The Scope of Grace*, pp. 190 ff.
41 Klassen and Snyder, pp. 105 f.

of existence," because only in one's commitment to this understanding of existence can one be said to be united with Christ. Now it is not altogether clear just what Robinson intends here, but it results in a vitiating of the "ontical happening" in Jesus, revealing that Robinson's program seems incapable of acknowledging that the first fact of Christian faith is the joyous affirmation of reconstructed life through Christ. It seems rather to insist that the alleged existential stance of the historical Jesus with its dialectic of incompleteness is enshrined as normative for all Christians. No matter how sophisticated or technically impressive, such a program must be seriously questioned on the grounds that it is structurally incapable of attending to the authentic Christian datum. The ground of this structural incapability is also clear: the new quest is not rooted in the primary datum of Christian faith, but rather in an abstract conceptuality which is distilled on the basis of the pre-resurrection existence of Jesus of Nazareth—a conceptuality which, centered as it is in *decision*, attends only to the unfinished character of the Christian hope. Robinson's suggestion invests itself in this abstract existentialist conceptuality so heavily that the Christian affirmations, as we illustrated them above, for example, in the proclamation of Covenant, Incarnation, and Easter-Pentecost presence of Christ in the Spirit are not taken into consideration in any substantial way. As a result, even as the pre-resurrection Jesus of Nazareth is not the full subject of Christian faith, so the normative picture of Christ which the new quest gives us is but a truncated version of what Christians have found to be the vivifying presence of God in their midst.

If it is true that the normative category which Robinson suggests for our consideration is structurally incapable of describing the primary datum of Christian faith, it is even more evident that his category does not permit itself to be shaped by that datum. To be shaped by the primary facts of Christian faith, the categories of the new quest would have to attend to the history of the Christian community, whereas the category of Jesus' understanding of existence simply catapults from twentieth-century existentialist philosophy over the intervening years to the textual vestiges of the pre-Easter Jesus of Nazareth. The very simplicity with which the new quest brings this off, and the lack of methodological self-criticism which accompanies this indifference towards Christian history, raise questions as to the validity of its enterprise. It reminds one very much of the former attempts to distill an "essence" of Christianity which would serve as formal norm for all interpretations of the materials of Christian faith. By shunting aside, at a methodological level, the shaping power of Christian history, the categories of the new quest have deprived themselves of important safeguards against narrow subjectivism and cultural conditionedness in their interpretations of Christianity. If, as it now appears, existentialist philosophy is itself very closely identified with a certain epoch in Western culture (specifically Western European cultural history at that), then this indifference towards safeguards is very serious indeed.

The validity of the "new quest of the historical Jesus" lies in its use of historical method in exegesis in a manner that utilizes the best of contemporary historical methodology. The new quest stands as a welcome counterbalance to exegetical methods that threatened to dissolve the empirical historical elements contained in the New Testament materials.[42] If what we have observed here is correct, however, the new quest must modify its claims to be a reliable "second avenue of access" to Jesus,[43] alongside the *kerygma,* inasmuch as its encounter with Jesus is so patently bound by the abstractions of our age. The new quest has achieved its power and cogency, utilizing these abstractions at the expense of the richness of the original historical materials, thereby executing a leap out of history, because its method so subordinates history to existentialist categories. Even as Ritschl violated the materials of Christian faith by imposing his Kantianism, so Robinson does by his Existentialism.

The consequences of Robinson's program, as well as Ebeling's, become even clearer when we put the question of knowledge to their systems of thought. How does one locate and designate the datum of existence which constitutes the threshhold, beyond which one finds the imminent eschatological reality of God, or beyond which one steps into the encounter which consummates the "word-event?" How does one *know* or recognize the circumstances which accompany the *genuine* "dialectic of existence" (to use Robinson's term) or the *genuine* "word-event" which eventuates in "response-able" (*verantwortlich*) existence (to use Ebeling's phrase)? There are two levels upon which the answer to this question of knowledge is to be given: the level of utmost generality—the *formal* level, and the level of the concrete—the *material.* At the formal level, it is very clear that the two men introduce normative categories *from outside* the Christian faith in order to answer the question of certainty in knowledge. In both cases the categories seem to come from twentieth-century existentialist philosophy.

This is clear in Robinson's thinking by his consistent method of discarding the historically Christian materials as in any sense normative as an interpretive key, but instead using them solely as

42 See the rather positive Roman Catholic assessment in Avery Dulles, S.J., "Jesus as the Christ," *Thought* (154) 39:359–379, 1964.
43 *A New Quest of the Historical Jesus,* p. 85.

texts to be interpreted by an existentialist key. In his essay, "The Formal Structure of Jesus' Message," for example, Robinson strips away, one by one, the elements in the Christian materials that could be normative for interpretation. The eschatological form itself, comprised of the Jewish apocalyptic doctrine of the two aeons is discarded because it is not "itself the new or essential element" in Jesus' message.[44] The *ipsissima verba,* the mere presence in itself of an authentic logion of Jesus, cannot be the normative factor, because the presence of authentic logia does not necessarily imply a proper existential stance.[45] Nor, finally, does the affirmation of the present efficacy of what happened ontically (that is, we should say, objectively) in Jesus serve any normative function, because this necessarily post-Easter assertion of what happened in Jesus must always be linked with the pre-Easter existential understanding of Jesus.[46] Thus, all the characteristics indigenous to the Christian material itself are pared away as being inadequate to serve as normative interpretive keys—the eschatological structural form of Jesus' message, the authentic *ipsissima verba,* the affirmation of what really happened ontically in Jesus' life and death. What remains as normative is that which Christian faith shares with twentieth-century existentialist philosophy, namely Jesus' understanding of existence, which implies commitment in the face of existentialist challenge to decision which is posed by the imminent eschatological entity. An incomplete existence, fraught with the decision to accept an imminent reality which challenges it and promises to transform its life—that is the familiar existentialist pose, and it is the new quest's normative category for interpreting all of the materials of Christian faith.

At the formal level, the suggestions of Gerhard Ebeling are not strikingly different. This is to be seen from two of his most important essays, "Word of God and Hermeneutics" and "Jesus and Faith." In the first essay, he asserts very strongly that the task of theology is synonymous with "hermeneutics," that is, with the interpretation of the Word of God, including the proclamation of that Word in a form that makes it available to faith, with faith assuming a significant position (which is elaborated in the second essay) as the goal of theology and proclamation and as the condition in which man achieves union with God, the consummation towards which Christian faith tends. (This central position of faith is also emphasized in his *The Nature of Faith.*) All of the key terms in this train of thought are defined in the terms of the I-Thou dialectic of the linguistic.

44 Klassen and Snyder, p. 98.
45 *Ibid.,* p. 105.
46 *Ibid.*

Ebeling defines Word of God as an event that tends towards proclamation, a "word-event that leads from the text of holy scripture to the proclamation."[47] And although at one point Ebeling defines this proclamation in very broad terms,[48] it is later associated very precisely with language,[49] and then still more precisely with the "natural, oral word taking place between man and man."[50] In spite of the great ambiguity in his specific statements, Ebeling's view of the Word does hang together consistently within the I-Thou conceptuality. The career of the Word brings man into encounter and response which completes the "word-event," and theology aids the entire dialectic by interpreting, or "bringing to expression" what the Word entails. In this sense, theology is hermeneutics, in the grand design that Ebeling has set forth in what has been described as "the new hermeneutic."

Towards the end of the first essay, Ebeling describes man's stance within the "word-event" in terms that give a premonition of the existentialist dialectic of decision over against an entity that will give him authentic existence, but which is not yet actual:

This opens up a deeper insight into the nature of the word-event. As communication word is promise. It is most purely promise when *it refers to something that is not present but absent*—and that, too, in such a way that in the promise the absent thing so to speak presents itself; that is, when in word the speaker pledges and imparts himself to the other and opens a future to him by awakening faith within him.[51]

This existentialist I-Thou stance is carried out to its full implications in the essay, "Jesus and Faith." Here faith is defined as an abandoning of oneself (*Sich-selbst-Verlassen*), within an encounter between men, in which the Thou speaks and the I responds.[52] This Thou, of course, is God, encountering man through his Word.

Ebeling sets before the reader a dazzling scholarly apparatus. He expounds his theological position within the context of a tremendous amount of biblical and later historical material. But the fact remains that the essence of Christian faith, that which illumines with certainty the concrete path that man must take towards the fulfillment of his faith, is the familiar existentialist dialectic, particularly as this is interpreted by the I-Thou thinkers. Such massive scholarship in the service of reductionism reminds us of no one so much as Albrecht Ritschl and his student Adolf von

---

47 *Word and Faith,* pp. 313–314.
48 *Ibid.,* p. 311.
49 *Ibid.,* p. 318.
50 *Ibid.,* p. 325.
51 *Ibid.,* p. 327. Italics added.
52 See, for example, *Ibid.,* pp. 208, 213, 240, 243.

Harnack.[53] Man caught up in an encounter with the divine Thou in a "word-event," which leaves man poised in decision towards the future in commitment to an imminent promise—that is the norm which provides knowledge; Gerhard Ebeling applies it to all the materials that come beneath his gaze in his attempt to expound authentic Christian faith.

An analysis of the thought of Robinson and Ebeling, then, must conclude that when they deal with the problem of certain knowledge in Christian faith, they expound a position within the context of Christian materials, but that the interpretive key which serves as norm for knowing that material has its origin outside that material in twentieth-century existentialist categories—at least at a formal level. When we turn to the material level, the arena of concrete knowledge, we find that Ebeling and Robinson really have not considered the epistemological problems. The existentialist categories that serve at a formal level are devoid of specificity and historical content. As it has been put classically, the existentialist dialectic tells man that he must exist authentically, that he must know despair, confront the challenge of authentic existence in an encounter (with that Thou, or its equivalent) which bids him make the transition away from his inauthenticity through the decision which faces forward in the leap of faith. But the existentialist dialectic does not presume to tell man where this leap will transpire, where it will take man concretely, or what form it will take. When these uncertainties are transferred *in toto* to Christian theology, an unnecessary vagueness is introduced which is untrue to the Christian understanding. The Christian, it is true, is committed to a life of venture, but he does know where to go for certainty in his knowledge, and he does know something of the locus of his career and its destiny. To tell man, as Robinson and Ebeling in effect do, that Christ is found in commitment to the promise of the imminent eschaton that is challenging him to decision is not enough, because man is confronted with many challenges to his decision, not all of which are to be designated as the Christ. Protestant theologians today tend to court as many ambiguities as possible, content to respond to questioners that "justification by faith" means that ambiguities must be accepted as part of life (as Ebeling does, when he equates the Reformation *sola fide* with self-criticism and historism). One might prefer to argue that justification by faith has not so much to do with the ambiguities of life (which, in fact, man is constantly trying to clarify), as it does with the confidence that man has in God to guide him through the pitfalls that he knows perfectly well lie ahead of him. And the reason that the Christian has this

53 See Wayne Glick, "Adolph Harnack as Historian and Theologian" (unpublished Ph.D. dissertation, University of Chicago, 1957).

confidence is because he knows full well where assurance and guidance are to be found to sustain him in difficulties of any sort, namely, in the presence of Christ within the community of love, in the assurance of absolution, in commitment to the hope of God's people. By referring men to the formalities of the existentialist conceptuality, Robinson and Ebeling provide very meager material for the solution of the epistemological problems attending the search for knowledge of the circumstances of existence that yield authenticity. What materials they do provide are conspicuously removed from any peculiarly Christian focus.

Now it is certainly not our intention to call into question the power and the truth-claims of existentialist philosophy. The insights which this point of view has furnished the human quest for truth need no elaboration here. One does, however, hold certain reservations about a theological methodology that must so patently go outside the distinctively Christian perspective to furnish what meager resources it does for resolving the question of certain knowledge of God. This methodology falls into the same pattern that Ritschl's did, namely, it imposes one particular cultural form of sensibility upon the whole of Christian faith, thus obligating every Christian seeker to invest his energies in that cultural form, in this case the existentialist dialectic, if he would gain knowledge and certainty in a formal manner. In addition, one must conclude that the existentialist methodology in theology is incapable of taking into account the specifically Christian material in the datum of faith and that it is blind to the realities of history. The existentialist theologians do not interpret Christ in terms of Christian history, but in terms of philosophical categories. These weaknesses render this methodology quite inadequate as the formulation for Christian theological methodology.

The program that we have espoused stands sharply opposed to this methodology. The historical mode of knowing that we delineated in the previous chapter asserts that the Christian does not go outside the Christian perspective for gaining knowledge, but that on the contrary Christian faith presupposes its own universe of discourse, and hence its own distinctive method of ordering the data of experience. This historical mode of knowing points the knower to the communal witness of the community that believes its life to have been reconstructed by the power in Jesus Christ. This historical model represents a specific solution to the problems of certain knowledge that attend Christian faith. It is every bit as formal and abstract as the existentialist categories of knowledge that we have been criticizing, but it does point the knower to the concrete locus in which the only possible Christian certainty of knowledge is available. It is formal, but it does permit itself to be shaped by the concrete historical materials. This epistemological suggestion places Christian knowledge where it belongs in the life that emerges from total participation in the reality designated by the Christian communal witness. On the basis of this model, knowledge is obtained of the redemptive configuration of existence and of the Christ who works such redemption in and through participation in the reality that the communal witness points to, and certainty in this knowledge is attained when one's existence is said to be continuous with that witness. Many problems yet remain for the knower; the precise shape of redeemed existence is left open, according to the circumstances of life; but the locus within which knowledge and certainty of the redemptive reality are to be found is precisely designated. The same must be said of the norm for interpretation of the Christian materials that is derived from this historical mode of knowing: the difficulties in establishing the norm are tremendous, but the precise locus of the norm is clear—in the historical and contemporary breadth of the communal witness, as it is efficacious in the present through participation.

"BIBLICAL" THEOLOGY

The constructive thrust of our program may become clearer by looking briefly at the contrast it presents to another theological trend which has been dominant in Protestant theological circles. This trend is the so-called "biblical theology," by which we refer to that school of thought which tends to equate biblical interpretation, in the form of an almost naive—although systematic—repetition of the biblical motifs, with the task of systematic theology. This school of thought has come in for vigorous criticism of late,[54] but it nevertheless persists as the methodology that is regnant in much of Protestant theological education and in the Protestant ecumenical movement.

Although a number of very cogent arguments have been raised against "biblical"[55] theology's conviction that systematic theology is nothing else but the systematic statement of the motifs of thought that occur in the Bible, we are interested in only two of these arguments from the point of view of the methodology we are putting forth. The first of these is that "biblical" theology tends, in the final

[54] See, for example, Roger Hazelton, *New Accents in Contemporary Theology* (New York: Harper & Row, 1960), Chap. 3, for a representative criticism. Also Krister Stendahl, see note 55.

[55] The quotation marks are used throughout this section to remind the reader that "biblical" theology as we are criticizing it is to be distinguished from the descriptive study of biblical theology as, for example, Krister Stendahl has discussed it in his article cited above, in *The Interpreter's Dictionary of the Bible*.

analysis, to be sectarian, in that it permits the theologian and his particular group to substantiate their own cherished points of view in the biblical text itself and to dignify them with biblical authority. Theoretically, this should be impossible, inasmuch as the biblical text stands as an objective factor which minimizes the possibility that individual and group prejudices should be read into it. In practice, however, "biblical" theology has been pressed into service by widely divergent groups to justify their own positions. The reason for this malleability of the biblical materials is clear: The diversity and scope of the biblical texts makes the Bible vulnerable to partisan interpretation; the Bible tends to echo the theological position that is read into it by the interpreter. This should not surprise us, in light of the fact that in many of the major disputes over doctrine and practice in Christian history both sides have relied on extensive biblical interpretation. The Gnostics quoted Scripture as well as Irenaeus and Tertullian; the Arians as well as Athanasius; the Pelagians as well as Augustine; the Reformers as well as the Counter-Reformation. The vulnerability of the biblical materials to partisan interpretation emerged clearly in our analysis of Gerhard Ebeling and James M. Robinson. Both men bring to the interpretation of Scripture an adequate scholarly apparatus, combined with a due scientific regard for the objectivity of the text. But neither of them escapes reading out of the Bible the very existentialist theology that they read into it. The past generation has seen the erection of vast systematic theological edifices, termed "biblical."[56] These theological achievements are now being recognized for what they are: systematic attempts which, despite their invocation of biblical authority, cannot escape the partisan predilections of their progenitors. As a consequence of Scripture's vulnerability, the quesiton arises how the Bible is to be interpreted so as to reduce as far as possible the danger of sectarianism.

A second charge against "biblical" theology is that it tends to reduce the living faith of the biblical literature into systematic intellectual concepts that are deduced from the great messages of the Bible. Thus, one is presented with the "biblical universe of meaning," or the "chief motifs of biblical thought," such as the "prophetic" motifs, "Pauline" motifs, and so on. The result, ironically, is a system or systems of thought that are abstracted from the life of the community in which the Bible took shape. In other words, even "biblical" theology reveals the same blunder that marked Ritschl's work. The clearest and most revealing testimony to this is that "biblical" theology has caught on so successfully in a mid-twentieth-century American Protestantism whose life and piety is quite decidedly opposed to the sort of doctrinal, liturgical, and

56 See note 54 above.

political development that marked the community out of which the Bible emerged. With very little embarrassment, this American Protestantism can abstract biblical concepts from the life of the biblical community, holding to the former, while remaining indifferent to the latter. That this radical reduction and abstraction is possible indicates that "biblical" theology has no real regard for the concrete realities of Christian history, whether biblical or post-biblical. A thoroughgoing concern for the realities of Christian history would inhibit the simplistic reading of twentieth-century positions in the biblical texts on several grounds: a concern for Christian history would reveal to the interpreter how many of his predecessors had fallen victim to the same temptation of confusing contemporary partisanship with Scripture; such a concern would bring forcibly to the expositor's attention how many other legitimate interpretations are claiming equality with his own; finally, concern for history would call seriously into question the tendency to collapse all barriers between the present and the first century. "Biblical" theology in this sense may well typify a sophisticated version of what one observer has referred to as Protestantism's indifference towards any past except "the day of the infant church." "Biblical" theology enshrines this indifference to the past in the very structure and methodology of Protestant systematic theological thought.

Not only does this reduction and abstraction indicate an indifference towards history, but it represents an indifference towards the full humanity of the man who is concerned with Christian faith. This indifference towards the humanity of Christian man is expressed by the "biblical" theology's tendency (as we just noted) to perpetrate a reductionism by which the vitalities of Christian faith are identified with a set of abstract deductions based upon the biblical literature; these abstract deductions are thus elevated in a highly intellectualized form over all other aspects of Christian faith, whether in the biblical period or in present circumstances. So, for example, the biblical *understanding* of Christ is considered to be more authentic and more efficacious than the cultic, church-political, or later dogmatic enactments of his presence. This biblical "understanding" is generally interpreted to mean the summary or systematization of the biblical motifs with very strong emphasis on fidelity to the language and thought-forms of the biblical texts themselves. The result is a theology composed of apodictic statements, characterized by one observer as: "flat assertions, take-it-or-leave-it propositions, emphatic repetitions."[57]

The programmatic response which we have given to the thought of Ebeling and Robinson has set the pattern of our response to the problems posed by the dominant "biblical" theology today. On the

57 Hazelton, p. 69.

one hand the "biblical" theology encounters the problem of avoiding
the natural tendencies towards sectarian partisanship, and on the
other hand of giving proper attention to the full human dimension
that is necessarily involved in Christian faith, by virtue of faith's
locus within life. One of the peculiar characteristics of the "biblical"
theology is that it has no greater safeguard against partisanship
inherent in its structure than the biblical texts themselves have
against the vulnerability to partisan interpretation. At one level, the
"biblical" theological methodology is objective, namely, when it employs scientific historical and literary methods for the exegesis of
Scripture upon which its abstractions are based. At the next level
of its work, however, that of theological interpretation and systematization of biblical motifs, objectivity is difficult to attain. Here
"biblical" theology encounters the same difficulty that besets Ebeling
and Robinson, who employ the scientific method of exegesis with
admirable objectivity, only to find that objectivity at the level of
scholarly study of texts is no safeguard against an almost crassly
simplistic and partisan use of philosophical and theological categories as interpretive keys for those meticulously expounded texts.
Objectivity at the level beyond scientific literary and historical
analysis is indispensable for theological methodology; such objectivity is to be found by taking recourse to the historical and contemporary breadth of the Christian community, as the community
which grounds its life in the events that are witnessed in Scripture.
Openness to the traditions of interpretation and the present options
for interpretation within this community is at the same time the
most reliable and the most Christian safeguard against unfortunate
partisanship, inasmuch as the community's experience provides
the sophistication that the theologian needs to preserve balance in
his vision.

It would be self-deception to pretend that partisanship is avoid-
able in theological work, however. The danger is that partisanship
will become so enamored of its own cause that it loses its authentic
Christianness. The problem that faces Ebeling and Robinson is
that a simplistic and arbitrary acceptance of existentialist categories
threatens the authentically Christian referent in their theological
work. "Biblical" theology is threatened with a canonization of one
strand of biblical thought to the exclusion of the rest, or with the
beatification of the metaphysical substructure of Hebrew thought-
forms to the exclusion of any other pattern of thought.[58] Recourse

[58] This beatification of a Hebrew metaphysics is the danger that besets
works like Thorlief Boman's *Hebrew and Greek Thought Compared* (Philadelphia: Westminster, 1960) and G. Ernest Wright's *God Who Acts* (Naperville,
Ill.: Allenson, 1952). The analysis of Boman and Wright may be quite correct
(although see James Barr's critique in *The Semantics of Biblical Language*
(London: Oxford, 1961) and *Biblical Words for Time* (Naperville, Ill.: A. R.

to the community's common history safeguards against an exaggerated emphasis on any single strand of the interpretation of the faith, while at the same time opening one to the possibility that several types of underlying thought-forms have been available as carriers of faith. Therefore, a partisanship that emerges from a serious and responsible grappling with the historical and contemporary breadth of the community and which issues in a recapitulation of that breadth can assert much more plausibly that it has retained a genuinely Christian character.

Another of the most serious (and often recurrring) criticisms of "biblical" theology is its frequent assumption that there is a single unified "theology," or set of deduced motifs, within the Bible. This criticism is embarrassing for biblical theology, because its abstractionist methodology has difficulty reflecting the diversity of confessions within the Bible. On the other hand, as H. H. Rowley has argued, biblical theology represents a sound instinct in its insistence that the biblical literature emerged from one common enterprise, namely, God's dealing with his people.[59] Our methodology seeks to take seriously the diversity of confession without forfeiting this sound insight of the biblical theologians into the Bible's unity.

Finally, following up closely the pattern of our response to the work of Ebeling and Robinson, we call attention to the fact that a methodology that attends to the full life of the historical and contemporary community of faith does by necessity attend to the full human dimensions of participation in faith. A methodology which attends to the fullness of this communal witness cannot consistently emphasize the abstract intellectualization of faith as the "biblical" theology does. If systematized biblical thought-forms cannot claim to represent the normative factor in the biblical communities themselves, even less can these "biblical systems of thought" claim normative status for present theological efforts. Theological work today must demur against any totalitarian claim by "biblical *thought*," because it insists that New Testament cultic, ethical, and church-political dimensions offer resources for theology just as surely as biblical thought-forms. Only so can theology acknowledge that it is doing its work within the fullness of the created world, in which both the theologian and his audience insist upon their full humanity.

Allenson, 1962). However, the question still remains: Despite the fact that the biblical witness seems to presuppose a certain metaphysic, are we justified in condemning other metaphysical structures or denying their power as thought forms within which men may approach and appropriate the Christian faith? This is a question which Boman and Wright, unfortunately, show no disposition to deal with.

59 H. H. Rowley, *The Unity of the Bible* (New York: Living Age Books, 1957), Chap. 1.

CONCLUSIONS

As we look back upon the various phases of this study, it is obvious that we have used Albrecht Ritschl as an access to an important problem for theological methodology, the problem of history and its relation to the life in which it is embedded. At no point has Ritschl been an end in himself for our study. At the same time, it is equally obvious that we have used a problem as a means of getting at Albrecht Ritschl, as a key for unlocking his own dominant concern, the profound insights he has to give into the ways of theological thinking, and also as a touchstone for judging the serious flaws in his methodology and illumining their unfortunate consequences. The judgment made at the outset, that the problem and the man are inextricably related, has proven to be the very foundation of our own methodology for assessing Ritschl.

The consequence is an impressionistic study, but one which, we hope, can nevertheless contribute to a reassessment of Ritschl, as well as a redirection of theological methodology. The panorama against which we have judged Ritschl is a large one: the scope of his own writings, programmatic reflections upon his work, and the playing out of his own unresolved problems in three important contemporary theological schools. Against this panorama, it should be clear why we concluded in Chapter 3 that Ritschl deserves our full admiration for his sure instincts into the importance of life and history for theology, even as we share dismay over his failure to implement his own best insights by violating decisively the life and history he was dedicated to. If the programmatic comments of Chapter 4 have any merit at all, then our admiration for Ritschl will be increased, as we observe how fruitful a reconsideration of life and history can be for contemporary theology. Similarly, if our assessment of Ebeling, Robinson, and "biblical" theology is correct, our dismay is deepened, because we appreciate anew just how perverse an abstractionist overpowering of life and history can be for theology. And all of these reflections, recapitulated into a whole furnish us with the best perspective from which to know Albrecht Ritschl, his work and his concerns, and from which we can push on, informed by Ritschl's history, to new fields of theological construction.

AN EPILOGUE TO THE CHURCHES

Concerned as it is with the refinements of theological methodology, it might seem out of place to refer this programmatic essay to the practical life of the Protestant churches. On the other hand, it would be short-sighted and even undesirable to present a program for theological methodology that cannot take its place within the fabric of the total life of the community of God's people.

At the end of the preceding chapter, we indicated that theology stands under a double responsibility—to preserve the Christianness of its statements while at the same time speaking relevantly to the situations in which it finds itself. Theology must, therefore, recapitulate its essential Christian character in every present moment so as to be genuinely alive, Christianly speaking, within the circumstances which its environment sets before it. This double responsibility or rhythm characterizes the total Christian life, in all its dimensions from the most refined speculation of the philosophical theologians to the most mundane life of the ecclesiastical bureaucracy and the most poignant life of the individual spirit in its pilgrimage towards fulfillment in Christ. Although this essay has riveted its attention almost exclusively upon one aspect of this double rhythm, the full life of recapitulating Christian substance and bodying forth relevant expression must always be kept in mind.[60] The programmatic comments that we have made can contribute to the churches' attaining the fullness of both aspects of this double rhythm.

Almost without exception, the analysts of American Protestantism have called attention to the loss of Christian identity that has characerized the churches' rapprochement to American culture.[61] The critics have charged that the perversions which have weakened the churches have their root in the failure to be fully Christian. The point is well taken, but, strangely, the vast amount of literature and effort that focuses on the churches' life in today's world seems much more oriented towards the demands of relevance than towards the resources and imperatives of Christian identity.[62] This failure to be fully Christian, coupled with the continuing superordination of relevance to Christian substance, is all the more ironic when one remembers that the American Protestant churches have considered themselves particularly bound to the Bible. This is but another testimony to the vulnerability of the Bible and its inability to interpret itself in an objective manner.

Inasmuch as the American Protestant loss of Christian identity

[60] See a fuller discussion in Hefner, *The Scope of Grace*, p. 208.

[61] Martin Marty, *The New Shape of American Religion* (New York: Harper & Row, 1958); Gibson Winter, *The Surburban Captivity of the Churches* (New York: Macmillan, 1962); Peter L. Berger, *The Noise of Solemn Assemblies* (Garden City: Doubleday, 1961).

[62] See the telling criticism that Daniel J. O'Hanlon, S. J., makes of Protestantism's neglect of Christian identity in favor of "relevance," in William J. Wolf, ed., *The Protestant Churches and Reform Today* (New York: Seabury Press, 1964), pp. 143–150.

has gone hand in hand with a disregard for Christian history (except for that of a certain aspect of the "infant" Church), one cannot help but suggest that a concern for the history of the Church's life and belief would serve as a positive counterbalance to present trends within the churches. On the one hand, renewed attention to the history of the understanding and interpretation of Scripture could offset the subjectivism that often reigns now. On the other hand, an earnest concern for the faith of the Fathers—including the study within the congregations of what the Church has been in the various crucial epochs of its history, as well as patient consideration of what has animated and guided Christians in their worship, their church administration, and their ethical action—can provide a rudder by which the churches can steer their course in our day. A study of what the ministry has been, for example, both in its glorious moments and in its degradations, when coupled with a commitment to recapitulate the essential substance of that ministry, should clarify much of the present ambiguity concerning the authority and forms of the ministry in the churches. Similar studies of the Mass, the Church's private devotional life, and its preaching, when accompanied by the commitment to realize their substance in present circumstances, should furnish the equilibrium that can counter the anxiety and confusion that marks Protestant efforts.

On another front, the concern for the primary datum of concrete redeemed life in God can provide resources for the churches in their proclamation to generations for whom life seems to be meaningless or whose historical existence takes place in the "age after Christendom."[63] It is precisely the "imperative-centered"[64] proclamation, so much at home in nineteenth-century American Protestantism, whose calls to decision and challenges to commitment seem irrelevant to the age after Christendom and hollow for men and women whose inability to find meaning makes every variety of challenge seem unnecessarily quaint. The very logic of the predicament which confronts American society, in its increasing tendency towards a technological society (with all that implies regarding automation, the leeching of depth out of existence, and vulgarization of culture),[65] militates against a preaching which is centered in the imperative, since the interior resources that provide the depth in which the imperative can be taken seriously are largely desiccated. A culture that is marked by alienation at all

[63] Martin Marty, "The Age After Christendom," *Dialog* (4) 1:14–17, 1962.
[64] Hefner, *The Scope of Grace*, pp. 188–195, discusses the imperative-addiction in Christian proclamation at some length.
[65] See Bernard Meland's theory and definition of secularization, in his *The Realities of Faith* (New York: Oxford, 1962).

levels and by desiccation does not find its health in renewed calls to decision so much as in the affirmation, wherever it may be found, of life in its fullness. For this reason, one must question whether the repeated calls for an increasingly abrasive proclamation of the infinite qualitative difference between man and God or an evangel that emphasizes the shattering effects of the inbreaking eschaton are not abortive, even self-defeating for the churches. Rather, the churches must regain confidence in the datum of redemption that has tabernacled in their midst in Jesus Christ, so that they can affirm the life that our culture lacks. True relevance today will be found in the traditional Christian affirmation that what seemed shallow and hollow in existence has been filled with the depth of life. The so-called "age after Christendom" suffers from a cynicism that makes all calls to commitment implausible; only the vigorous affirmation of a reconstructed life can counter cynicism. This redeemed life can make a cogent witness to itself only in a community of Christians who are animated and vivified by the life of God in Christ—in their personal associations with one another, in their ethical actions, and in their cultic experience. The sheer testimony of joy that resides in this community will, in the long run, be the most relevant strategy that the churches can employ. And it is this joy, as the primary datum of Christian faith in life, alone, that can give our strategies substance.

Bibliography

A. RITSCHL'S WORKS, A SELECTED LIST

Books

1. *Die christliche Lehre von der Rechtfertigung und Versoehnung*
   Vol. 1, *Die Geschichte der Lehre*. Bonn: Adolph Marcus, 1870, with revised edition in 1882.
   Vol. 2, *Der biblische Stoff der Lehre*. Bonn: Adolph Marcus, 1874, with revised editions in 1874, 1882, 1889.
   Vol. 3, *Die positive Entwicklung der Lehre*. Bonn: Adolph Marcus, 1874, revised editions in 1883, 1888.
   Vol. 1 is translated under the title, *A Critical History of the Christian Doctrine of Justification and Reconciliation*. Tr. John S. Black. Edinburgh: Edmonton and Douglas, 1872.
   Vol. 3 is translated under the title, *The Christian Doctrine of Justification and Reconciliation*. Tr. H. R. Mackintosh and A. B. Macaulay. Edinburgh: T. and T. Clark, 1900. Republished in 1966 by Reference Book Publishers, Inc., Clifton, New Jersey.
2. *Die christliche Vollkommenheit and Unterricht in der christlichen Religion*. Critical edition in one volume, ed. Cajus Fabricius. Leipzig: J. C. Hinrich'sche Buchhandlung, 1924.
   Unterricht is translated under the title, *Instruction in the Christian Religion*, by Alice Mead Swing, in A. T. Swing, *The Theology of Albrecht Ritschl*. London and Bombay: Longmans, Green, and Co., 1901.
3. *Die Entstehung der altkatholischen Kirche: Eine kirchen- und dogmengeschichtliche Monographie*. Bonn: Adolph Marcus, 1850; rev. 1857.
4. *Fides Implicita: Eine Untersuchung ueber Koehlerglauben, Wissen und Glauben, Glauben und Kirche*. Bonn: Adolph Marcus, 1890.
5. *Geschichte des Pietismus*. 3 vols. Bonn: Adolph Marcus, 1880-86.
6. *Schleiermachers Reden ueber die Religion und ihre Nachwirkungen auf die evangelische Kirche Deutschlands*. Bonn: Adolph Marcus, 1874.

7. *Theologie und Metaphysik: Zur Verstaendigung und Abwehr.* Bonn: Adolph Marcus, 1881; rev. 1887.

Articles

1. "Die Entstehung der lutherischen Kirche," *Gesammelte Aufsaetze.* Freiburg i.B. and Leipzig: J. C. B. Mohr, 1893.
2. "Geschichtliche Studien zur christlichen Lehre von Gott," *Jahrbuecher fuer Deutsche Theologie.* Gotha: Rudolf Besser. V (1860) 4.
3. "Ein Nachtrag zur Entstehung der lutherischen Kirche," *Gesammelte Aufsaetze.* Freiburg i.B. and Leipzig: J. C. B. Mohr, 1893.
4. "Ueber geschichtliche Methode in der Erforschung des Urchristentums," *Jahrbuecher fuer Deutsche Theologie* VI (1861).
5. "Ueber das Gewissen," *Gesammelte Aufsaetze.* Neue Folge, Freiburg i.B. and Leipzig: J. C. B. Mohr, 1896.
6. "Ueber die beiden Principien des Protestantismus," *Gesammelte Aufsaetze.* Freiburg i.B. and Leipzig: J. C. B. Mohr, 1893.
7. "Ueber die Methode der aelteren Dogmengeschichte," *Gesammelte Aufsaetze.* Freiburg i.B. and Leipzig: J. C. B. Mohr, 1893.

See also Otto Ritschl. *Albrecht Ritschls Leben.* 2 vols. Freiburg i.B.: J. C. B. Mohr, 1892, 1896.

B. SECONDARY SOURCES

(See the bibliography in Høk's work. The bibliography that follows does not duplicate Høk's, except for certain works in English and certain extremely important works.)

Akers, Samuel. *Some British Reactions to Ritschlianism.* Yale Studies in Religion, No. 8. Scottdale, Pa.: Mennonite Press, 1934.
Barth, Karl. *Protestant Thought from Rousseau to Ritschl.* New York: Harper & Row, 1959.
Deegan, Dan. "Albrecht Ritschl As Critical Empiricist," *Journal of Religion,* 44:149-60, April, 1964.
Deegan, Dan. "Albrecht Ritschl on the Historical Jesus," *The Scottish Journal of Theology,* 15:133-50, June, 1962.
Deegan, Dan. "The Ritschlian School, The Essence of Christianity and Karl Barth," *The Scottish Journal of Theology,* 16:390-414, December, 1963.
Fabricius, Cajus. *Die Entwicklung in Albrecht Ritschls Theologie von 1874 bis 1889.* Tuebingen: J. C. B. Mohr, 1909.
Guthrie, George P. "Kant and Ritschl: A Study in the Relation Between Philosophy and Theology." Unpublished Ph.D. dissertation, University of Chicago, 1962.
Haenchen, Ernst. "Albrecht Ritschl als Systematiker," *Gott und Mensch.* Tuebingen: J. C. B. Mohr, 1965.

Harnack, Adolph. "Ritschl und seine Schule," *Reden und Aufsaetze.* Gieszen: Alfred Toepelmann, 1906.

Hefner, Philip. "Albrecht Ritschl and His Current Critics," *The Lutheran Quarterly,* 13:103-112, May, 1961.

Hefner, Philip. "Baur Versus Ritschl on Early Christianity," *Church History,* 31:259-278, September, 1962.

Hefner, Philip. "Catholicity and Liberal Theology," *Una Sancta* 20:51-58, 1963.

Hefner, Philip. "The Role of Church History in the Theology of Albrecht Ritschl," *Church History,* 33:338-355, September, 1964.

Herrmann, Wilhelm. "Albrecht Ritschl, seine Groesse und seine Schranke," *Festgabe von Fachgenossen und Freunden, A. von Harnack, zum siebzigsten Geburtstag dargebracht.* Tuebingen: J. C. B. Mohr, 1921.

Herrmann, Wilhelm. *Der evangelische Glaube und die Theologie Albrecht Ritschls.* 2nd ed. Marburg: N. G. Elwert'sche Verlagsbuchhandlung, 1896.

Herrmann, Wilhelm. "Faith as Ritschl Defined It," *Faith and Morals.* New York: G. P. Putnam's Sons.

Høk, Gøsta. *Die elliptische Theologie Albrecht Ritschls: Nach Ursprung und innerem Zusammenhang.* Uppsala Universitets Arsskrift, 1942:3.

Jersild, Paul. "Judgment of God in Albrecht Ritschl and Karl Barth," *The Lutheran Quarterly,* 14:328-346, November, 1962.

Jersild, Paul. "Natural Theology and the Doctrine of God in Albrecht Ritschl and Karl Barth," *The Lutheran Quarterly,* 14:239-257, August, 1962.

Jundt, André. Le role de la métaphysique et de l'histoire dans la dogmatique protestante moderne. Essai sur les principes de l'école de Ritschl. Montbéliard: Société anonyme d'imprimerie Montbéliardaise, 1920.

Koch, A. *Irrgaenge und Wahrheitsmomente der Theologie Ritschl's.* Oldenburg i.Gr.: Verlag von Eschen und Fasting, 1897.

Koenig, Emil. "The Use of the Bible in Ritschl's Theology." Unpublished Ph.D. dissertation, University of Chicago, 1953.

Lamm, Karl. *Christi, Person und Werk mit Bezug auf die Christologie Ritschl's und dessen Schule.* Frankfurt a.M.: Heyder and Zimmer, 1896.

Lehmann, Paul. *Forgiveness: Decisive Issue in Protestant Thought.* New York: Harper & Brothers, 1940.

Luthardt, Chr. E. "Zur Beurtheilung der Ritschl'schen Theologie," *Zeitschrift fuer kirchliche Wissenschaft und kirchliches Leben,* 2:617-658, 1881.

Mackintosh, Hugh Ross. "The Theology of Moral Values: Albrecht

Ritschl," Types of Modern Theology. New York: Charles Scribner's Sons, n.d.

Mackintosh, Robert. Albrecht Ritschl and His School. London: Chapman and Hall, Ltd., 1915.

Mead, Charles M. Ritschl's Place in the History of Doctrine. Hartford: Hartford Seminary Press, 1895.

Mozley, John K. Ritschlianism. London: James Nisbet and Co., 1909.

Orr, James. The Ritschlianism Theology and the Evangelical Faith. London: Hodder and Stoughton, 1897.

Pfleiderer, Otto. Die Ritschl'sche Theologie kritisch beleuchtet. Braunschweig: C. A. Schwetschke und Sohn, 1891.

Ryan, Michael. "The Function of the Discipline of History in the Theological Interpretation of Albrecht Ritschl," unpublished Ph.D. dissertation, Drew University, 1966.

Staehlin, Leonhard. Kant, Lotze, and Ritschl. Edinburgh: T. and T. Clark, 1889.

Swing, Albert T. The Theology of Albrecht Ritschl. London and Bombay: Longmans, Green, and Co., 1901.

Walcott, Gregory D. The Kantian and Lutheran Elements in Ritschl's Conception of God. New York, 1904.

Walther, Christian. "Der Reich-Gottes-Begriff in der Theologie Richard Rothes und Albrecht Ritschls," Kerygma und Dogma, 2:115-138, 1956.

Wobbermin, Georg. Schleiermacher und Ritschl in ihrer Bedeutung fuer die heutige theologische Lage und Aufgabe. Tuebingen: J. C. B. Mohr, 1927.

Woelber, Hans. Dogma und Ethos, Christentum und Humanismus von Ritschl bis Troeltsch. Goettingen: Vandenhoeck und Ruprecht, 1950.

Wrzecionko, Paul. Die philosophischen Wurzeln der Theologie Albrecht Ritschls. Berlin: Toepelmann, 1964.

Index of Names

Format by Morris Karol
Set in Linotype Primer
Composed, printed and bound by The Haddon Craftsmen, Inc.
HARPER & ROW, PUBLISHERS, INCORPORATED